Brief Contents

A Pocket Style Manual

NINTH EDITION

with Exercises

Diana Hacker

Nancy Sommers
Harvard University

bedford/st.martin's
Macmillan Learning

Boston | New York

Vice President: Leasa Burton
Program Director, English: Stacey Purviance
Senior Executive Editor: Michelle M. Clark
Director of Content Development: Jane Knetzger
Executive Development Manager: Maura Shea
Associate Editor: Melissa Rostek
Assistant Editor: Aislyn Fredsall
Director of Media Editorial: Adam Whitehurst
Senior Media Editor: Barbara Flanagan
Marketing Manager: Vivian Garcia
Director, Content Management Enhancement: Tracey Kuehn
Senior Managing Editor: Michael Granger
Senior Manager of Publishing Services: Andrea Cava
Senior Content Project Manager: Kendra LeFleur
Senior Workflow Project Manager: Jennifer Wetzel
Production Supervisor: Brianna Lester
Director of Design, Content Management: Diana Blume
Interior Design: Claire Seng-Niemoeller
Cover Design: William Boardman
Director, Rights and Permissions: Hilary Newman
Text Permissions Researcher: Udayakumar Kannadasan,
    Lumina Datamatics, Inc.
Photo Permissions Editor: Angie Boehler
Director of Digital Production: Keri deManigold
Media Project Manager: Allison Hart
Project Management: Lumina Datamatics, Inc.
Project Manager: Valerie Bradenburg, Misbah Ansari,
    Lumina Datamatics, Inc.
Editorial Services: Lumina Datamatics, Inc.
Copyeditor: Lifland et al., Bookmakers
Indexer: Lumina Datamatics, Inc.
Composition: Lumina Datamatics, Inc.
Printing and Binding: RR Donnelly

Library of Congress Control Number:
2020933307 (Standard Edition)
2020933311 (Exercise Edition)

ISBN 978-1-319-16954-1 (Standard Edition)
ISBN 978-1-319-50327-7 (Exercise Edition, MLA Update)

Printed in China.
1 2 3 4 5 6   25 24 23 22

Acknowledgments

Acknowledgments and copyrights appear on the same page as the text and art selections they cover; these acknowledgments and copyrights constitute an extension of the copyright page.

For information, write: Bedford/St. Martin's, 75 Arlington Street, Boston, MA 02116

Clarity

1   Tighten wordy sentences.

Long sentences are not necessarily wordy, nor are short sentences always concise. A sentence is wordy if it can be tightened without loss of meaning.

1a   Redundancies

Redundancies such as *cooperate together, yellow in color,* and *basic essentials* are a common source of wordiness. There is no need to say the same thing twice.

▶ Daniel ~~is employed~~ at a private rehabilitation
   works
   center ~~working~~ as a physical therapist.

Modifiers are redundant when their meanings are suggested by other words in the sentence.

▶ Sylvia ~~very hurriedly~~ scribbled her name and
   phone number on the back of a greasy napkin.

1b   Empty or inflated phrases

An empty word or phrase can be cut with little or no loss of meaning. Common examples of empty phrases are word groups that weaken a writer's authority by apologizing or hedging: *in my opinion, I think that, it seems that,* etc.

▶ ~~In my opinion,~~ their current immigration policy is
   T
   misguided.

An inflated phrase can be reduced to a word or two.

▶ Funds are limited ~~at this point in time.~~
   now.

INFLATED	CONCISE
along the lines of	like
because of the fact that	because
due to the fact that	because
for the purpose of	for
in order to	to
in spite of the fact that	although, though
in the event that	if

1c Needlessly complex structures

Simplifying sentences and using stronger verbs can help make writing more direct. Look for opportunities to strengthen the verb.

▶   Researchers ~~were involved in studying~~ the effect

         studied

of classical music on unborn babies.

▶   The financial analyst claimed that she could not

~~make an~~ estimate ~~of~~ the company's future profits.

2   Prefer active verbs.

Choose an active verb whenever possible. Active verbs express meaning more vigorously than forms of the verb *be* or verbs in the passive voice. Forms of *be* (*be, am, is, are, was, were, being, been*) lack vigor because they convey no action. Passive verbs lack strength because their subjects receive the action instead of doing it.

BE VERB   A surge of power *was* responsible for the destruction of the pumps.

PASSIVE   The pumps *were destroyed* by a surge of power.

ACTIVE   A surge of power *destroyed* the pumps.

2a When to replace *be* verbs

Not every *be* verb needs replacing. The forms of *be* (*be, am, is, are, was, were, being, been*) work well when you want to link a subject to a noun that clearly renames it or to an adjective that describes it: *Orchard House was the home of Louisa May Alcott. The harvest will be bountiful after the summer rains.*

If using a *be* verb makes a sentence needlessly wordy, consider replacing it. Often a phrase following the verb contains a noun or an adjective (such as *violation* or *resistant*) that suggests a more vigorous, active verb (*violate, resisted*).

▶   Burying nuclear waste in Antarctica would ~~be in~~

                                      violate

~~violation of~~ an international treaty.

▶ When Rosa Parks ~~was resistant to~~ *resisted* giving up her
   ^
   seat on the bus, she became a civil rights hero.

NOTE: When used as helping verbs with present participles to express ongoing action, *be* verbs are fine: *She was swimming when the whistle blew.* (See 11b.)

2b When to replace passive verbs

In the active voice, the subject of the sentence performs the action; in the passive, the subject receives the action. The active voice is usually more effective because it is clearer and more direct.

ACTIVE   The committee *reached* a decision.

PASSIVE   A decision *was reached* by the committee.

In passive sentences, the actor (in this case, *committee*) frequently does not appear: *A decision was reached.*

In most cases, you will want to emphasize the actor, so you should use the active voice. To replace a passive verb with an active one, make the actor the subject of the sentence.

▶ *Investigators*
   ~~Samples were~~ collected daily from the stagnant *samples*
   ^   ^
   pond.

▶ *The settlers stripped the land of timber before realizing*
   ~~The land was stripped of timber before the settlers~~
   ^
   ~~realized~~ the consequences of their actions.

The passive voice is appropriate in some disciplines and writing situations. In much scientific writing, for example, the passive voice properly emphasizes an experiment or a process, not a person. In the following sentence, the writer intends to focus on the tobacco plants, not on the people spraying them: *Just before the harvest, the tobacco plants are sprayed with a chemical to prevent the growth of suckers.*

3 Balance parallel ideas.

If two or more ideas are parallel, they should be expressed in parallel grammatical form. Single words should be balanced with single words, phrases with phrases, clauses with clauses.

A kiss can be a comma, a question mark, or an
exclamation point. — Mistinguett

This novel is not to be tossed lightly aside, but to
be hurled with great force. — Dorothy Parker

3a Items in a series

Balance all items in a series by presenting them in parallel grammatical form.

▶ Cross-training involves a variety of exercises, such
as running, swimming, and *~~lifting~~* weights.

▶ Children who study music also learn confidence,
discipline, and *creativity.* ~~they are creative.~~

▶ Racing to work, Sam drove down the middle of
the road, ran one red light, and *ignored* two stop signs.

3b Paired ideas

When pairing ideas, underscore their connection by expressing them in similar grammatical form. Paired ideas are usually connected in one of three ways: (1) with a coordinating conjunction—*and, but, or, nor, for, so,* or *yet;* (2) with a correlative conjunction—*either . . . or, neither . . . nor, not only . . . but also,* or *whether . . . or;* or (3) with a word introducing a comparison, usually *than* or *as.*

▶ Many states are reducing property taxes for home
owners and *extending* ~~extend~~ financial aid in the form of tax
credits to renters.

The coordinating conjunction *and* connects two *-ing* verb forms: *reducing . . . extending.*

▶ **Thomas Edison was not only a prolific inventor**

but also ~~was~~ **a successful entrepreneur.**

The correlative conjunction *not only . . . but also* connects two noun phrases: *a prolific inventor* and *a successful entrepreneur.*

▶ **It is easier to speak in abstractions than** ^{to ground}~~grounding~~

one's thoughts in reality.

The comparative term *than* links two infinitive phrases: *to speak . . . to ground.*

NOTE: Repeat function words such as prepositions (*by, to*) and subordinating conjunctions (*that, because*) to make parallel ideas easier to grasp.

▶ **Our study revealed that left-handed students were**

more likely to have trouble with classroom desks
and ^{that}**rearranging desks for exam periods was**

useful.

4 Add needed words.

Sometimes writers leave out words intentionally, without affecting meaning. But often the result is a confusing or an ungrammatical sentence. Readers need to see at a glance how the parts of a sentence are connected.

4a Words in compound structures

In compound structures, words are often omitted for economy: *Tom is a man who means what he says and [who] says what he means.* Such omissions are acceptable as long as the omitted words are common to both parts of the compound structure.

If omitting a word from a sentence would make the sentence ungrammatical because the word is not common to both parts of the compound structure, the word must be left in.

▶ Advertisers target customers whom they identify
who
through demographic research or have purchased
^
their product in the past.

The word *who* must be included because *whom . . . have
purchased* is not grammatically correct.

accepted
▶ Mayor Davidson never has and never will accept
^
a bribe.

Has . . . accept is not grammatically correct.

4b The word *that*

Add the word *that* if there is any danger of misreading
without it.

▶ In his obedience experiments, psychologist
that
Stanley Milgram discovered ordinary people were
^
willing to inflict physical pain on strangers.

Milgram didn't discover people; he discovered that
people were willing to inflict pain on strangers.

4c Words in comparisons

Comparisons should be made between items that are
alike. To compare unlike items is illogical and distracting.

▶ The forests of North America are much more
those of
extensive than Europe.
^

Comparisons should be complete so that readers
will understand what is being compared.

INCOMPLETE   Depression is more common in adolescent
girls.

COMPLETE   Depression is more common in adolescent
girls than in adolescent boys.

Also, comparisons should leave no ambiguity about
meaning. In the sentence on the next page, two inter-
pretations are possible.

AMBIGUOUS	Kai helped me more than my roommate.
CLEAR	Kai helped me more than *he helped* my roommate.
CLEAR	Kai helped me more than my roommate *did*.

5   Eliminate distracting shifts.

5a   Shifts in point of view

The point of view of a piece of writing is the perspective from which it is written: first person (*I* or *we*), second person (*you*), or third person (*he, she, it, one,* or *they*). The *I* (or *we*) point of view, which emphasizes the writer, is a good choice for writing based primarily on personal experience. The *you* point of view, which emphasizes the reader, works well for giving advice or explaining how to do something. The third-person point of view, which emphasizes the subject, is appropriate in most academic and professional writing.

Once you settle on an appropriate point of view, stick with it. Shifting points of view within a piece of writing confuses readers. (See also 12a.)

▶   Our class practiced rescuing a victim trapped in a wrecked car. ~~You~~ **We** were graded on ~~your~~ **our** speed and skill in freeing the victim.

▶   ~~Travelers~~ **You** need a signed passport for trips abroad. You should also fill out the emergency information page in the passport.

5b   Shifts in tense

Consistent verb tenses clearly establish the time of the actions being described. When a passage begins in one tense and then shifts without warning and for no reason to another, readers are distracted and confused.

▶   Our candidate lost in the debate. Just as we gave up hope, she ~~soars~~ **soared** ahead in the polls.

Writers often shift verb tenses when writing about literature. The literary convention is to describe fictional events consistently in the present tense. (See p. 27.)

6   Untangle mixed constructions.

A mixed construction contains sentence parts that do not sensibly fit together. The mismatch may be a matter of grammar or of logic.

6a Mixed grammatical structure

You should not begin a sentence with one grammatical plan and then switch without warning to another. Rethinking the purpose of the sentence can help you revise.

▶ ~~For~~ M̂ost drivers who have a blood alcohol level of

.05 percent increase their risk of causing an accident.

> The prepositional phrase beginning with *For* cannot serve as the subject of the verb *increase*. The revision makes *drivers* the subject.

▶ Although Luxembourg is a small nation, ~~but~~ it has

a rich cultural history.

> The coordinating conjunction *but* cannot link a subordinate clause (*Although . . .*) with an independent clause (*it has a rich . . .*).

6b Illogical connections

A sentence's subject and verb should make sense together.

▶ Under the revised plan, first-generation college

          financial-aid benefits for

students/ ~~who now receive financial-aid benefits,~~

will increase.

> The benefits, not the students, will increase.

> Tiffany
> The court decided that ~~Tiffany's welfare~~ would be
> ^
> safer living with her grandparents.

Tiffany, not her welfare, would be safer.

6c *Is when, is where,* and *reason . . . is because* constructions

In formal English, readers sometimes object to *is when*, *is where*, and *reason . . . is because* constructions on grammatical or logical grounds.

> a disorder suffered by people who
> Anorexia nervosa is ~~where people~~ diet to the point
> ^
> of starvation.

Where refers to places. Anorexia nervosa is a disorder, not a place.

> T
> ~~The reason~~ /the experiment failed ~~is~~ because
> ^
> conditions in the lab were not sterile.

7 Repair misplaced and dangling modifiers.

Modifiers should point clearly to the words they modify. As a rule, related words should be kept together.

7a Misplaced words

Limiting modifiers such as *only*, *even*, *almost*, *nearly*, and *just* should appear in front of a verb only if they modify the verb. If they limit the meaning of some other word in the sentence, they should be placed in front of that word.

> Research shows that students ~~only~~ learn new
> only
> vocabulary words when they are encouraged to read.
> ^

Only limits the meaning of the *when* clause.

▶ If you ~~just~~ interview chemistry majors, your
picture of students' opinions on the new policies
will be incomplete.

just ^

The adverb *just* limits the meaning of *chemistry majors*,
not *interview*.

When the limiting modifier *not* is misplaced, the sentence usually suggests a meaning the writer did not intend.

▶ In the United States in 1860, all black southerners
were ~~not~~ slaves.

not ^

The original sentence means that no black southerners were slaves. The revision makes the writer's real meaning clear.

7b Misplaced phrases and clauses

Although phrases and clauses can appear at some distance from the words they modify, make sure your meaning is clear. When phrases or clauses are oddly placed, absurd misreadings can result.

▶ ~~There~~ are many pictures of comedians who have
performed at Gavin's. ~~on the walls.~~

On the walls ^

The comedians weren't performing on the walls; the pictures were on the walls.

▶ The robber was described as a six-foot-tall man
with a mustache. ~~weighing 170 pounds.~~

170-pound, ^

The robber, not the mustache, weighed 170 pounds.

7c Dangling modifiers

A dangling modifier fails to refer logically to any word in the sentence. Dangling modifiers are usually introductory word groups (such as verbal phrases) that suggest but do not name an actor. When a sentence opens with such a modifier, readers expect the subject of the next clause to name the actor. If it doesn't, the modifier dangles.

DANGLING   Upon entering the doctor's office, a skeleton
caught my attention.

This sentence suggests—absurdly—that the skeleton entered the doctor's office.

To repair a dangling modifier, you can revise the sentence in one of two ways:

1. Name the actor in the subject of the sentence.
2. Name the actor in the modifier.

▶ Upon entering the doctor's office, a skeleton ~~caught my attention.~~ *I noticed*

▶ ~~Upon entering~~ *As I entered* the doctor's office, a skeleton caught my attention.

You cannot repair a dangling modifier simply by moving it: *A skeleton caught my attention upon entering the doctor's office.* The sentence still suggests that the skeleton entered the doctor's office.

▶ Wanting to create checks and balances on power, *the framers of* the Constitution divided the government into three branches.

   The framers (not the Constitution itself) wanted to create checks and balances.

▶ After completing seminary training, ~~women's~~ *women were often denied* access to the priesthood. ~~was often denied.~~

   The women (not their access to the priesthood) completed the training. The writer has revised the sentence by making *women* (not *women's access*) the subject.

7d Split infinitives

An infinitive consists of *to* plus a verb: *to think, to dance.* When a modifier appears between *to* and the verb, the infinitive is said to be "split": *to slowly drive.* If a split infinitive is awkward, move the modifier to another position in the sentence.

▶ Cardiologists encourage their patients to ~~more carefully~~ watch their cholesterol levels/ *more carefully.*

Attempts to avoid split infinitives sometimes result in awkward sentences. When alternative phrasing sounds unnatural, most experts allow—and even encourage—splitting the infinitive. *We decided to actually enforce the law* is a natural construction in English. *We decided actually to enforce the law* is not.

8 Provide sentence variety.

Sentence variety can help keep readers interested in your writing. If most of your sentences are the same length or begin the same way, try combining them or varying sentence starters.

8a Combining choppy sentences

If a series of short sentences sounds choppy, consider combining sentences. Look for opportunities to tuck some of your ideas into subordinate clauses. A subordinate clause, which contains a subject and a verb, begins with a word such as *although, because, if, unless, which,* or *who.* (See p. 326.)

▶ We keep our use of insecticides to a minimum/
    because we
    ~~We~~ are concerned about the environment.

Also look for opportunities to tuck some of your ideas into phrases, word groups that lack a subject and a verb. You will usually see more than one way to combine choppy sentences; the method you choose should depend on the details you want to emphasize.

▶ The Chesapeake and Ohio Canal, ~~is~~ a 184-mile

waterway constructed in the 1800s/. ~~It~~ was a

major source of transportation for goods during

the Civil War.

This revision emphasizes the significance of the canal during the Civil War. The first sentence, about the age of the canal, has been made into a phrase modifying *Chesapeake and Ohio Canal.*

▶   *Used as a major source of transportation for goods during the Civil War, the*
~~The~~ Chesapeake and Ohio Canal is a 184-mile waterway constructed in the 1800s. ~~It was a major source of transportation for goods during the Civil War.~~

This revision emphasizes the age of the canal. The second sentence, about the canal's use for transportation of goods, has become a participial phrase modifying *Chesapeake and Ohio Canal*.

When short sentences contain ideas of equal importance, it is often effective to combine them with *and*, *but*, or *or*.

▶   Shore houses were flooded up to the first floor*/,* *and*

Brant's Lighthouse was swallowed by the sea.

8b Varying sentence openings

Most sentences in English begin with the subject, move to the verb, and continue to an object, with modifiers tucked in along the way or put at the end. For the most part, such sentences are fine. Put too many of them in a row, however, and they become monotonous.

Words, phrases, or clauses modifying the verb can often be inserted ahead of the subject.

▶   *Eventually a*
~~A~~ few drops of sap ~~eventually~~ began to trickle into the pail.

▶   *Just as the sun was coming up, a*
~~A~~ pair of black ducks flew over the pond. ~~just as the sun was coming up.~~

Adjectives and participial phrases (beginning with verb forms such as *driving* or *exhausted*) can frequently be moved to the start of a sentence without loss of clarity.

▶   *D*
~~The committee,~~ ~~d~~iscouraged by the researchers' *the committee*
apparent lack of progress, nearly withdrew funding for the prizewinning experiments.

NOTE: In a sentence that begins with an adjective or a participial phrase, the subject of the sentence must name the person or thing being described. If it doesn't, the phrase dangles. (See 7c.)

9 Find an appropriate voice.

An appropriate voice is one that suits your subject, engages your audience, and conforms to the conventions of the genre in which you are writing, such as lab reports, informal essays, research papers, business memos, and so on.

In academic and professional writing, certain language is generally considered inappropriate: jargon, clichés, slang, and sexist or biased language.

9a Jargon

Jargon is specialized language used among members of a trade, discipline, or professional group. Use jargon only when readers will be familiar with it or when plain English will not properly convey your meaning.

JARGON   We outsourced the work to an outfit in Ohio because we didn't have the bandwidth to tackle it in-house.

REVISED   We hired a company in Ohio because we had too few employees to do the work.

Sentences filled with jargon are hard to read and often wordy.

▶ The CEO should ~~dialogue~~ talk with investors about ~~partnering~~ working with clients to buy land in ~~economically deprived zones.~~ poor neighborhoods.

9b Clichés

The pioneer who first announced that he had "slept like a log" no doubt amused his companions with a fresh and unlikely comparison. Today, however, that comparison is a cliché, a saying that can no longer add emphasis or surprise. The next page lists a few common sayings. To see just how predictable clichés are, put your hand over the right-hand column and then finish the phrases given on the left.

beat around	the bush
busy as	a bee, a beaver
cool as	a cucumber
light as	a feather, air
white as	a sheet, a ghost
avoid clichés like	the plague

The solution for clichés is simple: Delete them.

► When I received a full scholarship from my
second-choice school, I ~~found myself between a~~ *felt pressured to settle for*
~~second-best.~~ *second-best.*
~~rock and a hard place.~~

9c Slang

Slang is an informal and sometimes private vocabulary
that expresses the solidarity of a group such as teenagers, rap musicians, or sports fans. Although slang has
a certain vitality, it is a code that not everyone understands. Avoid using it in academic writing unless you
have a specific reason for doing so.

evidence
► Without ~~the receipts~~, we can't move forward with

our proposal.

9d Sexist and noninclusive language

Sexist and noninclusive language stereotypes and
demeans people and should be avoided. Using non-
sexist language and recognizing individuals' chosen
pronoun usage show respect and audience awareness.

In your writing, avoid referring to any profession as
exclusively made up of one gender (teachers as women
or engineers as men, for example). Avoid using gendered,
stereotypical conventions to name or identify a person.

STEREOTYPICAL LANGUAGE

After a nursing student graduates, *she* must face a
difficult state board examination. [Not all nursing
students are women.]

Running for city council are Boris Stotsky, an attor-
ney, and *Mrs.* Cynthia Jones, a professor of English
and mother of three. [The title *Mrs.* and the phrase *and
mother of three* are irrelevant.]

When a student applies for federal financial aid, *he or she* is given an FSA ID. [Not all students identify as *he* or *she*.]

Sometimes sexist language arises from the practice of using singular gendered pronouns to refer generically to persons of all genders.

SEXIST LANGUAGE

A journalist is motivated by *his* deadline.

Similarly, terms including *man* and *men* were once used to refer generically to all people of that profession or group. Current usage demands gender-neutral terms.

INAPPROPRIATE	APPROPRIATE
chairman	chairperson, chair
congressman	representative, legislator
fireman	firefighter
mankind	people, humans
to man	to operate, to staff
weatherman	meteorologist, forecaster

Revising sexist and noninclusive language When revising, some writers substitute *he or she* or *he/she*. Others alternate female pronouns with male pronouns. These strategies are wordy, can become awkward or confusing, and are not inclusive of all individuals. Instead, use the plural or revise the sentence.

It is also becoming increasingly acceptable to use the plural pronoun *they* to refer to individuals inclusively.

USING THE PLURAL

Journalists are motivated by *their* deadlines.

REVISING THE SENTENCE

A journalist is motivated by *a* deadline.

USING SINGULAR *THEY*

A journalist is motivated by *their* deadline.

NOTE: When using pronouns to refer to people, choose the pronouns that the individuals themselves would use. Some transgender, nonbinary, and gender-fluid individuals refer to themselves by new pronouns (*ze/hir*, for example), but if you are unfamiliar with such preferences, *they* and *them* are acceptable gender-neutral options.

Grammar

10 Make subjects and verbs agree.

In the present tense, verbs agree with their subjects in number (singular or plural) and in person (first, second, or third). The present-tense ending -*s* (or -*es*) is used on a verb if its subject is third-person singular; otherwise the verb takes no ending. Consider, for example, the present-tense forms of the verb *give*.

	SINGULAR	PLURAL
FIRST PERSON	I give	we give
SECOND PERSON	you give	you give
THIRD PERSON	he/she/it gives Yolanda gives	they give parents give

The verb *be* varies from this pattern; it has special forms in *both* the present and the past tense.

PRESENT-TENSE FORMS OF *BE*		PAST-TENSE FORMS OF *BE*	
I am	we are	I was	we were
you are	you are	you were	you were
he/she/it is	they are	he/she/it was	they were

This section describes particular situations that can cause problems with subject-verb agreement.

10a Words between subject and verb

Word groups often come between the subject and the verb. Such word groups, usually modifying the subject, may contain a noun that at first appears to be the subject. By mentally stripping away such modifiers, you can isolate the noun that is in fact the subject.

The *samples* on the tray in the lab *need* testing.

▶ High levels of air pollution damages the

respiratory tract.

The subject is *levels*, not *pollution*.

▶ The slaughter of pandas for their pelts ~~have~~ _{has} caused

the panda population to decline drastically.

The subject is *slaughter*, not *pandas* or *pelts*.

NOTE: Phrases beginning with expressions such as *as well as, in addition to, accompanied by, together with,* and *along with* do not make a singular subject plural: *The governor as well as his press secretary was* [not *were*] *on the plane.*

10b Subjects joined with *and*

Compound subjects joined with *and* are nearly always plural.

▶   Bleach and ammonia create̸s a toxic gas when mixed.

EXCEPTION: If the parts of the subject form a single unit, you may treat the subject as singular: *Bacon and eggs is always on the menu.*

10c Subjects joined with *or* or *nor*

With compound subjects joined with *or* or *nor,* make the verb agree with the part of the subject nearer to the verb.

▶   If an infant or a child ~~have~~ a high fever, call a doctor.
                              has

▶   Neither the chief financial officer nor the marketing managers ~~was~~ able to convince the client to reconsider.
                              were

10d Indefinite pronouns such as *someone*

Indefinite pronouns are pronouns that do not refer to specific persons or things. The following indefinite pronouns are singular: *anybody, anyone, anything, each, either, everybody, everyone, everything, neither, nobody, no one, somebody, someone, something.*

▶   Nobody who participated in the clinical trials ~~were~~ given a placebo.
                              was

▶   Each of the essays ~~have~~ been graded.
                              has

A few indefinite pronouns (*all, any, none, some*) may be singular or plural depending on the noun or

pronoun they refer to: *Some of our luggage was lost.*
Some of the rocks were slippery. None of his advice makes
sense. None of the eggs were broken.

10e Collective nouns such as *jury*

Collective nouns such as *jury, committee, audience,*
crowd, class, family, and *couple* name a group. In American English, collective nouns are nearly always treated
as singular: They emphasize the group as a unit.

▶ The board of trustees ~~meet~~ meets in Denver twice a year.

   Occasionally, to draw attention to the individual members of the group, a collective noun may be
treated as plural: *The class are debating among them-*
selves. Many writers prefer to add a clearly plural noun
such as *members: The class members are debating among*
themselves.

NOTE: In general, when a fraction or unit of measurement is used with a singular noun, treat it as singular;
when it is used with a plural noun, treat it as plural:
Three-fourths of the pie has been eaten. One-fourth of the
drivers were texting.

10f Subject after verb

Verbs ordinarily follow subjects. When this normal
order is reversed, it is easy to become confused.

▶ Of particular concern ~~is~~ are penicillin and

   tetracycline, antibiotics used to make animals

   more resistant to disease.

   The subject, *penicillin and tetracycline,* is plural.

   The subject always follows the verb in sentences
beginning with *there is* or *there are* (or *there was* or *there*
were).

▶ There ~~was~~ were a turtle and a snake in the tank.

   The subject, *turtle and snake,* is plural, so the verb must
be *were.*

10g *Who, which,* and *that*

Like most pronouns, the relative pronouns *who, which,* and *that* have antecedents, nouns or pronouns to which they refer. A relative pronoun used as the subject of a subordinate clause takes a verb that agrees with its antecedent.

ANT PN   V

Take a *train that arrives* before 6:00.

Constructions such as *one of the students who* (or *one of the things that*) may cause problems for writers. Do not assume that the antecedent must be *one*. Instead, consider the logic of the sentence.

► Our ability to use language is one of the things
   set
that ~~sets~~ us apart from animals.
      ^

> The antecedent of *that* is *things,* not *one*. Several things set us apart from animals.

When the word *only* comes before *one*, you are safe in assuming that *one* is the antecedent of the relative pronoun.

► Veronica was the only one of the first-year Spanish
                        was
students who ~~were~~ fluent enough to apply for the
            ^
exchange program.

> The antecedent of *who* is *one,* not *students*. Only one student was fluent enough.

10h Plural form, singular meaning

Words such as *athletics, economics, mathematics, physics, politics, statistics, measles,* and *news* are usually singular, despite their plural form.

       is
► Politics ~~are~~ among my mother's favorite pastimes.
          ^

EXCEPTION: Occasionally some of these words, especially *economics, mathematics, politics,* and *statistics,* have plural meanings: *Office politics often affect* *decisions about hiring and promotion. The economics of the building plan are prohibitive.*

10i Titles, company names, and words mentioned as words

Titles, company names, and words mentioned as words are singular.

▶ *Lost Cities* ~~describe~~ describes the discoveries of fifty ancient civilizations.

▶ Delmonico Brothers ~~specialize~~ specializes in organic produce and additive-free meats.

▶ *Controlled substances* ~~are~~ is a euphemism for illegal drugs.

11 Be alert to other problems with verbs.

Section 10 deals with subject-verb agreement. This section describes a few other potential problems with verbs.

11a Irregular verbs

For all regular verbs, the past-tense and past-participle forms are the same, ending in *-ed* or *-d*, so there is no danger of confusion. This is not true, however, for irregular verbs, such as the following:

BASE FORM	PAST TENSE	PAST PARTICIPLE
break	broke	broken
fly	flew	flown
go	went	gone

The past-tense form always occurs alone, without a helping verb. It expresses action that occurred entirely in the past. The past participle is used with a helping verb. It forms the perfect tenses with *has, have,* or *had;*

it forms the passive voice with *be, am, is, are, was, were, being,* or *been.*

PAST TENSE   Last July, we *went* to Beijing.

PAST PARTICIPLE   We have *gone* to Beijing twice.

When you aren't sure which verb form to choose (*went* or *gone, broke* or *broken,* and so on), look up the base form of the verb in the dictionary, which also lists any irregular forms. The chart on the next page lists some common irregular verbs.

▶ Yesterday we ~~seen~~ a film about rain forests.
                 ^saw^

Because there is no helping verb, the past-tense form *saw* is required.

▶ By the end of the day, the stock market had ~~fell~~ *fallen*

two hundred points.

Because of the helping verb *had,* the past-participle form *fallen* is required.

Distinguishing between *lie* and *lay*   Writers often confuse the various forms of *lie* (meaning "to recline or rest on a surface") and *lay* (meaning "to put or place something"). The intransitive verb *lie* does not take a direct object: *The tax forms lie on the table.* The transitive verb *lay* takes a direct object: *Please lay the tax forms on the table.*

BASE FORM	PAST TENSE	PAST PARTICIPLE	PRESENT PARTICIPLE
lie (recline)	lay	lain	lying
lay (put)	laid	laid	laying

Elizabeth was so exhausted that she *lay* down for a nap. [The past tense of *lie* ("recline") is *lay.*]

The prosecutor *laid* the photograph on a table close to the jurors. [The past tense of *lay* ("place") is *laid.*]

Letters dating from the Civil War were *lying* in the corner of the chest. [The present participle of *lie* ("rest on a surface") is *lying.*]

The patient had *lain* in an uncomfortable position all night. [The past participle of *lie* ("recline") is *lain.*]

👓 Common irregular verbs **at a glance**

BASE FORM	PAST TENSE	PAST PARTICIPLE
be	was, were	been
begin	began	begun
break	broke	broken
bring	brought	brought
choose	chose	chosen
cling	clung	clung
come	came	come
do	did	done
drink	drank	drunk
drive	drove	driven
eat	ate	eaten
fall	fell	fallen
find	found	found
get	got	gotten, got
give	gave	given
go	went	gone
hang (execute)	hanged	hanged
hang (suspend)	hung	hung
have	had	had
keep	kept	kept
know	knew	known
let (allow)	let	let
make	made	made
ride	rode	ridden
ring	rang	rung
rise (get up)	rose	risen
run	ran	run
say	said	said
see	saw	seen
send	sent	sent
set (place)	set	set
sit (be seated)	sat	sat
stand	stood	stood
steal	stole	stolen
take	took	taken
wear	wore	worn
write	wrote	written

11b Tense

Tenses indicate the time of an action in relation to the time of the speaking or writing about that action. Tenses are classified as present, past, and future, with simple, perfect, and progressive forms for each.

The most common problem with tenses—shifting from one tense to another—is discussed in 5b. Other problems with tenses are detailed in this section, after the following survey of tenses.

Simple tenses   The simple tenses indicate relatively simple time relations. The *simple present* tense is used primarily for actions occurring at the time they are being discussed or for actions occurring regularly. The *simple past* tense is used for actions completed in the past. The *simple future* tense is used for actions that will occur in the future. In the following table, the simple tenses are given for the regular verb *walk*, the irregular verb *ride*, and the highly irregular verb *be*.

SIMPLE PRESENT

SINGULAR		PLURAL	
I	walk, ride, am	we	walk, ride, are
you	walk, ride, are	you	walk, ride, are
he/she/it	walks, rides, is	they	walk, ride, are

SIMPLE PAST

SINGULAR		PLURAL	
I	walked, rode, was	we	walked, rode, were
you	walked, rode, were	you	walked, rode, were
he/she/it	walked, rode, was	they	walked, rode, were

SIMPLE FUTURE

I, you, he/she/it, we, they   will walk, ride, be

Perfect tenses   A verb in one of the perfect tenses (a form of *have* plus the past participle) expresses an action that was or will be completed at the time of another action.

PRESENT PERFECT

I, you, we, they	have walked, ridden, been
he/she/it	has walked, ridden, been

PAST PERFECT

I, you, he/she/it, we, they	had walked, ridden, been

FUTURE PERFECT

I, you, he/she/it, we, they   will have walked, ridden, been

Progressive forms   Each of the six tenses has a progressive form used to describe actions in progress. A progressive verb consists of a form of *be* followed by the present participle.

PRESENT PROGRESSIVE

I	am walking, riding, being
he/she/it	is walking, riding, being
you, we, they	are walking, riding, being

PAST PROGRESSIVE

I, he/she/it	was walking, riding, being
you, we, they	were walking, riding, being

FUTURE PROGRESSIVE

I, you, he/she/it, we, they	will be walking, riding, being

PRESENT PERFECT PROGRESSIVE

I, you, we, they	have been walking, riding, being
he/she/it	has been walking, riding, being

PAST PERFECT PROGRESSIVE

I, you, he/she/it, we, they	had been walking, riding, being

FUTURE PERFECT PROGRESSIVE

I, you, he/she/it, we, they	will have been walking, riding, being

Special uses of the present tense   Use the present tense when writing about literature or when expressing general truths.

▶ The scarlet letter ~~was~~ is a punishment placed on

 Hester's breast by the community, and yet it

 ~~was~~ is an imaginative product of Hester's own

 needlework.

▶ Galileo taught that the earth ~~revolved~~ revolves around

 the sun.

NOTE: When you are quoting, summarizing, or paraphrasing the author of a nonliterary work in MLA style, use present-tense verbs: *writes, argues*. When using APA style, use past tense or present perfect tense: *wrote, has argued.* (See p. 124 for MLA style and p. 199 for APA style.)

The past perfect tense   The past perfect tense is used for an action already completed by the time of another past action. This tense consists of a past participle preceded by *had* (*had worked, had gone*).

▶   We built our cabin forty feet above an abandoned
      had been
   quarry that ~~was~~ flooded in 1920 to create a lake.
            ^

▶   By the time dinner was served, the guest of honor
      had
   left.
   ^

11c Mood

There are three moods in English: the *indicative*, used for facts, opinions, and questions; the *imperative*, used for orders or advice; and the *subjunctive*, used to express wishes, requests, or conditions contrary to fact. For many writers, the subjunctive causes the most problems.

For wishes and in *if* clauses expressing conditions contrary to fact, the subjunctive is the past-tense form of the verb; in the case of *be*, it is always *were* (not *was*), even if the subject is singular.

I wish that Jamal *drove* more slowly late at night.

If I *were* a member of Congress, I would vote for the bill.

NOTE: Do not use the subjunctive mood in *if* clauses expressing conditions that exist or may exist: *If Danielle passes* [not *passed*] *the test, she will become a lifeguard.*

Use the subjunctive mood in *that* clauses following verbs such as *ask, insist, recommend,* and *request.* The subjunctive in such cases is the base form of the verb.

Dr. Chung insists that her students *arrive* on time.

12   Use pronouns with care.

Pronouns are words that substitute for nouns: *he, it, them, her, me,* and so on. Pronoun errors are typically related to the four topics discussed in this section:

a.   pronoun-antecedent agreement (singular vs. plural)
b.   pronoun reference (clarity)
c.   pronoun case (personal pronouns such as *I* vs. *me*)
d.   pronoun case (*who* vs. *whom*)

12a Pronoun-antecedent agreement

The antecedent of a pronoun is the word the pronoun refers to. A pronoun and its antecedent agree when they are both singular or both plural.

SINGULAR   The *doctor* finished *her* rounds.

PLURAL   The *doctors* finished *their* rounds.

Indefinite pronouns   Indefinite pronouns refer to nonspecific persons or things: *anybody, anyone, anything, each, either, everybody, everyone, everything, neither, nobody, no one, nothing, somebody, someone, something.*

    Traditionally, indefinite pronouns have been treated as singular in formal English. However, using a singular pronoun usually results in a sentence that is sexist, and the traditional alternative (*he or she*) is often considered noninclusive. (See 9d.) It is becoming increasingly acceptable in many contexts to use the gender-neutral pronoun *they* to refer to an indefinite pronoun.

    The following are usually your best options for revision:

1. Use a plural antecedent.
2. Rewrite the sentence so that no problem of agreement exists.
3. Use the plural pronoun *they* to refer to the singular antecedent or indefinite pronoun ("singular *they*").

The sentences on the next page demonstrate these revision options.

▶ If ~~anyone wants~~ to audition, ~~he or she~~ should

any singers want *they*

sign up.

▶ ~~If anyone~~ wants to audition, ~~he or she~~ should

Anyone who

sign up.

▶ If anyone wants to audition, ~~he or she~~ should

they

sign up.

Generic nouns   A generic noun represents a typical member of a group, such as a typical student, or any member of a group, such as any lawyer. Although generic nouns may seem to have plural meanings, they have traditionally been considered singular. However, you should avoid using *he* to refer to generic nouns, as in *A runner must train if he wants to excel.* (See 9d.) As with indefinite pronouns, the singular use of *they* is becoming increasingly acceptable with generic nouns.

When revising sentences with generic nouns, you will usually have the same three options as for indefinite pronouns.

▶ ~~A medical student~~ must study hard if ~~he wants~~ to

Medical students *they want*

succeed.

▶ A medical student must study hard ~~if he wants~~ to

succeed.

▶ A medical student must study hard if ~~he wants~~ to

they want

succeed.

Collective nouns   Collective nouns such as *jury, committee, audience, crowd, family,* and *team* name a group. In American English, collective nouns are usually singular because they emphasize the group functioning as a unit.

The planning *committee* granted *its* [not *their*] permission to build.

If the members of the group function individually, however, you may treat the noun as plural: *The family put their signatures on the document.* Or you might add a plural antecedent such as *members* to the sentence: *The family members put their signatures on the document.*

12b Pronoun reference

In the sentence *When Andrew got home, he went straight to bed*, the noun *Andrew* is the antecedent of the pronoun *he*. A pronoun should refer clearly to its antecedent.

Ambiguous reference Ambiguous reference occurs when the pronoun could refer to either of two possible antecedents.

▶ ~~When Aunt Harriet put the cake~~ on the table/. ~~it~~
   The cake collapsed when Aunt Harriet put it
   ~~collapsed.~~

▶ Tom told James, ~~that he had~~ won the lottery.
   "You have   "

What collapsed—the cake or the table? Who won the lottery—Tom or James? The revisions eliminate the ambiguity.

Implied reference A pronoun must refer to a specific antecedent, not to a word that is implied but not actually stated.

▶ After braiding Ann's hair, Sue decorated ~~them~~ with
   the braids
   ribbons.

Vague reference of *this*, *that*, or *which* The pronouns *this*, *that*, and *which* should ordinarily refer to specific antecedents rather than to whole ideas or sentences. When a pronoun's reference is too vague, either replace the pronoun with a noun or supply an antecedent to which the pronoun clearly refers.

▶ Television advertising has created new demands
   for prescription drugs. People respond to ~~this~~ by
   the ads
   asking for drugs they may not need.

▶   Romeo and Juliet were both too young to have
                         a fact
    acquired much wisdom, ~~and~~ that accounts for
                                    ^

    their rash actions.

Indefinite reference of *they*, *it*, or *you*   The pronoun *they* should refer to a specific antecedent. Do not
use *they* to refer indefinitely to persons who have not
been specifically mentioned.

    The board
▶   ~~They~~ announced an increase in sports fees for all
    ^

    student athletes.

The word *it* should not be used indefinitely in constructions such as *In the article, it says that . . .*

    The
▶   ~~In the~~ encyclopedia/~~it~~ states that male moths can
    ^

    smell female moths from several miles away.

The pronoun *you* is appropriate only when the
writer is addressing the reader directly: *Once you have
kneaded the dough, let it rise in a warm place.* Except in
informal contexts, *you* should not be used to mean
"anyone in general." Use a noun instead, as in the following example:

▶   Ms. Pickersgill's *Guide to Etiquette* stipulates that
    a guest
    ~~you~~ should not arrive at a party too early or leave
    ^

    too late.

12c   Case of personal pronouns (*I* vs. *me* etc.)

The personal pronouns in the following chart change
what is known as *case form* according to their grammatical function in a sentence. Pronouns functioning
as subjects or subject complements appear in the *subjective* case; those functioning as objects appear in the
objective case; and those showing ownership appear in
the *possessive* case.

	SUBJECTIVE CASE	**OBJECTIVE CASE**	**POSSESSIVE CASE**
SINGULAR	I	me	my
	you	you	your
	he/she/it	him/her/it	his/her/its
PLURAL	we	us	our
	you	you	your
	they	them	their

Pronouns in the subjective and objective cases are frequently confused. Most of the rules in this section specify when to use one or the other of these cases (*I* or *me*, *he* or *him*, and so on).

Compound word groups　You may sometimes be confused when a subject or an object appears as part of a compound structure. To test for the correct pronoun, mentally strip away all of the compound structure except the pronoun in question.

▶ While diving for pearls, Ikiko and ~~her~~ *she* found a

sunken boat.

> *Ikiko and she* is the subject of the verb *found*. Strip away the words *Ikiko and* to test for the correct pronoun: *she found* [not *her found*].

▶ The most traumatic experience for her father and

~~I~~ *me* occurred long after her operation.

> *Her father and me* is the object of the preposition *for*. Strip away the words *her father and* to test for the correct pronoun: *for me* [not *for I*].

When in doubt about the correct pronoun, some writers try to evade the choice by using a reflexive pronoun such as *myself*. Using a reflexive pronoun in such situations is nonstandard.

▶ The cabdriver gave my husband and ~~myself~~ *me* some

good tips on traveling in New Delhi.

> *My husband and me* is the indirect object of the verb *gave*.

Appositives　Appositives are noun phrases that rename nouns or pronouns. A pronoun used as an appositive has the same function (usually subject or object) as the word(s) it renames.

▶ The chief strategists, Dr. Bell and ~~me,~~ I, could not

agree on a plan.

> The appositive *Dr. Bell and I* renames the subject, *strategists*. Test: *I could not agree on a plan* [not *me could not agree on a plan*].

▶ The reporter interviewed only two witnesses, the

shopkeeper and ~~I.~~ me.

> The appositive *the shopkeeper and me* renames the direct object, *witnesses*. Test: *interviewed me* [not *interviewed I*].

Subject complements   Use subjective-case pronouns for subject complements, which rename or describe the subject and usually follow *be, am, is, are, was, were, being,* or *been.*

▶ During the Lindbergh trial, Bruno Hauptmann

repeatedly denied that the kidnapper was ~~him.~~ he.

> If *kidnapper was he* seems too stilted, rewrite the sentence: *During the Lindbergh trial, Bruno Hauptmann repeatedly denied that he was the kidnapper.*

***We* or *us* before a noun**   When deciding whether *we* or *us* should precede a noun, choose the pronoun that would be appropriate if the noun were omitted.

▶ ~~Us~~ We tenants would rather fight than move.

> Test: *We would rather fight* [not *Us would rather fight*].

▶ Management is shortchanging ~~we~~ us tenants.

> Test: *Management is shortchanging us* [not *Management is shortchanging we*].

Pronoun after *than* or *as*   When a comparison begins with *than* or *as*, your choice of pronoun will depend on your meaning. To test for the correct pronoun, finish the sentence.

▶ My brother is six years older than ~~me.~~
    I.
    ^

  Test: *older than I [am].*

▶ We respected no other candidate for city council
                                    her.
  as much as ~~she.~~
              ^

  Test: *as much as [we respected] her.*

Pronoun before or after an infinitive   An infinitive
is the word *to* followed by a verb. Both subjects and
objects of infinitives take the objective case.

                              me
▶ Ms. Wilson asked John and ~~I~~ to drive the senator
    her   ^
  and ~~she~~ to the airport.
       ^

  John and me is the subject and *senator and her* is the
  object of the infinitive *to drive.*

Pronoun or noun before a gerund   If a pronoun
modifies a gerund, use the possessive case: *my, our,
your, his, her, its, their.* A gerund is a verb form ending
in *-ing* that functions as a noun.

            your
▶ The chances of ~~you~~ being hit by lightning are
                  ^
  about two million to one.

Nouns as well as pronouns may modify gerunds. To
form the possessive case of a noun, use an apostrophe
and *-s* (*victim's*) for a singular noun or just an apostrophe (*victims'*) for a plural noun. (See also 19a.)

▶ The old order in France paid a high price for the
    aristocracy's
  ~~aristocracy~~ exploiting the lower classes.
    ^

12d *Who vs. whom*

Who, a subjective-case pronoun, is used for subjects
and subject complements. *Whom,* an objective-case
pronoun, is used for objects. The words *who* and
whom appear primarily in subordinate clauses or in
questions.

In subordinate clauses   When deciding whether to use *who* or *whom* in a subordinate clause, check for the word's function within the clause.

▶ He tells that story to ~~whomever~~ *whoever* will listen.

  Whoever is the subject of *will listen*. The entire subordinate clause *whoever will listen* is the object of the preposition *to*.

▶ You will work with our senior engineers, ~~who~~ *whom* you will meet later.

  Whom is the direct object of the verb *will meet*. This becomes clear if you restructure the clause: *you will meet whom later.* Some writers test by substituting *he* (or *she*) for *who* and *him* (or *her*) for *whom*: *you will meet him later.*

In questions   When deciding whether to use *who* or *whom* in a question, check for the word's function within the question.

▶ ~~Whom~~ *Who* was responsible for creating that computer virus?

  Who is the subject of the verb *was*.

▶ ~~Who~~ *Whom* would you nominate for council president?

  Whom is the direct object of the verb *would nominate*. This becomes clear if you restructure the question: *You would nominate whom?*

13 Use adjectives and adverbs appropriately.

Adjectives modify nouns or pronouns; adverbs modify verbs, adjectives, or other adverbs.

Many adverbs are formed by adding *-ly* to adjectives (*formal, formally*). But don't assume that all words ending in *-ly* are adverbs or that all adverbs end in *-ly*. Some adjectives end in *-ly* (*lovely, friendly*), and some adverbs don't (*always, here*). When in doubt, consult a dictionary.

13a Adjectives

Adjectives ordinarily precede the nouns they modify. But they can also function as subject complements following linking verbs (usually a form of *be*: *be, am, is, are, was, were, being, been*). When an adjective functions as a subject complement, it describes the subject.

Justice is *blind*.

Verbs such as *smell, taste, look, appear, grow*, and *feel* may also be linking. If the word following one of these verbs describes the subject, use an adjective; if the word modifies the verb, use an adverb.

ADJECTIVE   The detective looked *cautious*.

ADVERB   The detective looked *cautiously* for the fingerprints.

Linking verbs usually suggest states of being, not actions. For example, to look *cautious* suggests the state of being cautious, whereas to look *cautiously* is to perform an action in a cautious way.

▶ Lori looked ~~well~~ *good* in her new raincoat.

▶ All of us on the debate team felt ~~badly~~ *bad* about our

performance.

The verbs *looked* and *felt* suggest states of being, not actions, so they should be followed by adjectives.

13b Adverbs

Use adverbs to modify verbs, adjectives, and other adverbs. Adverbs usually answer one of these questions: When? Where? How? Why? Under what conditions? How often? To what degree?

Adjectives are often used incorrectly in place of adverbs in casual or nonstandard speech.

▶ The manager must ensure that the office runs ~~smooth~~ *smoothly* and ~~efficient.~~ *efficiently.*

▶ The chance of recovering any property lost in the
        really
fire looks ~~real~~ slim.
        ^

The incorrect use of the adjective *good* in place of
the adverb *well* is especially common in casual or nonstandard speech.

                                                          well
▶ We were delighted that Nomo had done so ~~good~~
                                                 ^
on the exam.

13c Comparatives and superlatives

Most adjectives and adverbs have three forms: the positive, the comparative, and the superlative.

POSITIVE	COMPARATIVE	SUPERLATIVE
soft	softer	softest
fast	faster	fastest
careful	more careful	most careful
bad	worse	worst
good	better	best

Comparative vs. superlative   Use the comparative
to compare two things, the superlative to compare
three or more.

                                                      better?
▶ Which of these two brands of toothpaste is ~~best?~~
                                                    ^

    most
▶ Jia is the ~~more~~ qualified of the three applicants.
   ^

Forms of comparatives and superlatives   To form
comparatives and superlatives of one-syllable adjectives, use the endings *-er* and *-est*: *smooth, smoother,
smoothest*. For adjectives with three or more syllables,
use *more* and *most* (or *less* and *least*): *exciting, more exciting, most exciting*. Two-syllable adjectives form comparatives and superlatives in both ways: *lovely, lovelier,
loveliest; helpful, more helpful, most helpful*.

Some one-syllable adverbs take the endings *-er* and
-est (*fast, faster, fastest*), but longer adverbs and all of
those ending in *-ly* use *more* and *most* or *less* and *least*
(*carefully, less carefully, least carefully*).

Double comparatives or superlatives When you have added *-er* or *-est* to an adjective or an adverb, do not also use *more* or *most* (or *less* or *least*).

▶ All the polls indicated that Gore was more ~~likelier~~ likely to win than Bush.

Absolute concepts Do not use comparatives or superlatives with absolute concepts such as *unique* or *perfect*. Either something is unique or it isn't. It is illogical to suggest that absolute concepts come in degrees.

▶ That is the most ~~unique~~ unusual wedding gown I have ever seen.

14 Repair sentence fragments.

As a rule, do not treat a piece of a sentence—a fragment—as if it were a sentence. To be a sentence, a word group must consist of at least one full independent clause. An independent clause includes a subject and a verb, and it either stands alone as a sentence or could stand alone. Although fragments are sometimes appropriate for emphasis, writers and readers do not always agree on when they are appropriate. For academic writing, you will find it more effective to write in complete sentences.

You can repair a fragment in one of two ways:

1. Pull the fragment into a nearby sentence, punctuating the new sentence correctly.
2. Rewrite the fragment as a complete sentence.

14a Fragmented clauses

A subordinate clause is patterned like a sentence, with both a subject and a verb, but it begins with a word that tells readers it cannot stand alone—a word such as *after, although, because, before, if, so that, that, though, unless, until, when, where, which,* or *who.* (For a longer list, see p. 326.)

Most fragmented clauses beg to be pulled into a sentence nearby.

▶ **Americans have come to fear the West Nile**
  because
  virus/ ~~Because~~ it is transmitted by the common
  ^
  mosquito.

If a fragmented clause cannot be attached to a nearby sentence, try rewriting it. The simplest way to turn a fragmented clause into a sentence is to delete the opening word or words that mark it as subordinate.

▶ **Uncontrolled development is taking a toll on the**
  Across
  environment. ~~So that across~~ the globe, fragile
  ^
  ecosystems are collapsing.

14b Fragmented phrases

Like subordinate clauses, certain phrases are sometimes mistaken for sentences. They are fragments if they lack a subject, a verb, or both. Often a fragmented phrase may simply be pulled into a nearby sentence.

  examining
▶ **The archaeologists worked slowly/ ~~Examining~~ and**
  ^
  labeling hundreds of pottery shards.

  The word group beginning with *Examining* is a verbal phrase, not a sentence.

                                              a
▶ **Many adults suffer silently from agoraphobia/ A**
                                              ^
  fear of the outside world.

  A fear of the outside world is an appositive phrase, not a sentence.

▶ **It has been said that there are only three**
                              jazz,
  indigenous American art forms/ ~~Jazz,~~ musical
                              ^
  comedy, and soap operas.

  The list is not a sentence. Notice how easily a colon corrects the problem. (See 18b.)

If the fragmented phrase cannot be attached to a nearby sentence, turn the phrase into a sentence. You may need to add a subject, a verb, or both.

▶ **In the training session, Jamie explained how to access our new database.** ~~Also~~ *She also taught us* **how to submit**
                    ^
reports and request vendor payments.

The revision turns the fragmented phrase into a sentence by adding a subject and a verb.

15 Revise run-on sentences.

Run-on sentences are independent clauses that have not been joined correctly. An independent clause is a word group that can stand alone as a sentence. When two independent clauses appear in one sentence, they must be joined in one of these ways:

- with a comma and a coordinating conjunction (*and, but, or, nor, for, so, yet*)
- with a semicolon (or occasionally a colon or a dash)

There are two types of run-on sentences. When a writer puts no mark of punctuation and no coordinating conjunction between independent clauses, the result is a *fused sentence*.

FUSED

┌──────── INDEPENDENT CLAUSE ────────┐┌────────
Air pollution poses risks to all humans it can be
── INDEPENDENT CLAUSE ──┐
deadly for people with asthma.

A far more common type of run-on sentence is the *comma splice*—two independent clauses joined with a comma but without a coordinating conjunction. In some comma splices, the comma appears alone.

COMMA SPLICE

Air pollution poses risks to all humans, it can be deadly for people with asthma.

In other comma splices, the comma is accompanied by a joining word, such as *however*, that is not a coordinating conjunction. (See 15b.)

COMMA SPLICE

Air pollution poses risks to all humans, however, it can be deadly for people with asthma.

To revise a run-on sentence, you have four choices:

1. Use a comma and a coordinating conjunction.
2. Use a semicolon (or, if appropriate, a colon or a dash).
3. Make the clauses into separate sentences.
4. Restructure the sentence, perhaps by subordinating one of the clauses.

REVISED WITH COMMA AND COORDINATING CONJUNCTION

Air pollution poses risks to all humans, but it can be deadly for people with asthma.

REVISED WITH SEMICOLON

Air pollution poses risks to all humans; it can be deadly for people with asthma.

REVISED WITH SEPARATE SENTENCES

Air pollution poses risks to all humans. It can be deadly for people with asthma.

REVISED BY RESTRUCTURING

Although air pollution poses risks to all humans, it can be deadly for people with asthma.

As you revise, decide which of these revision techniques will work best for a particular sentence.

15a Revision with a comma and a coordinating conjunction

When a coordinating conjunction (*and*, *but*, *or*, *nor*, *for*, *so*, *yet*) joins independent clauses, it is usually preceded by a comma.

▶ Most of his friends had made plans for their
  but
retirement, Tom had not.
          ^

15b Revision with a semicolon (or a colon or a dash)

When the independent clauses are closely related and their relation is clear without a coordinating conjunction, inserting a semicolon is an acceptable method of revision.

▶ Tragedy depicts the individual confronted with

the fact of death/; comedy depicts the adaptability

of human society.

A semicolon is required between independent clauses that have been linked with a conjunctive adverb such as *however* or *therefore* or a transitional phrase such as *in fact* or *on the contrary*. (See p. 62 for longer lists.)

▶ The timber wolf looks like a large German

shepherd/; however, the wolf has longer legs,

larger feet, and a wider head.

If the first independent clause introduces a quoted sentence, use a colon.

▶ Scholar and crime writer Carolyn Heilbrun

suggests this about the future/: "Today's shocks

are tomorrow's conventions."

Either a colon or a dash may be appropriate when the second clause summarizes or explains the first. (See 18b and 21d.)

15c Revision by separating sentences

If both independent clauses are long—or if one is a question and the other is not—consider making them separate sentences.

▶ Why should we spend money on space
                    ? We
exploration/ ~~we~~ have enough underfunded

programs here on Earth.

15d Revision by restructuring the sentence

For sentence variety, consider restructuring the run-on sentence, perhaps by turning one of the independent clauses into a subordinate clause or a phrase.

▶ One of the most famous advertising slogans is Wheaties cereal's "Breakfast of Champions," ~~it~~ *which* was penned in 1933.

▶ Mary McLeod Bethune, ~~was~~ the seventeenth child of former slaves, ~~she~~ founded the National Council of Negro Women in 1935.

16 Consider grammar topics for multilingual writers.

16a Verbs

This section offers a brief review of English verb forms and tenses and the passive voice.

Verb forms   Every main verb in English has five forms (except *be*, which has eight). These forms are used to create all of the verb tenses in English. The following list shows these forms for the regular verb *help* and the irregular verbs *give* and *be*.

	REGULAR (*HELP*)	IRREGULAR (*GIVE*)	IRREGULAR (*BE*)*
BASE FORM	help	give	be
PAST TENSE	helped	gave	was, were
PAST PARTICIPLE	helped	given	been
PRESENT PARTICIPLE	helping	giving	being
-*S* FORM	helps	gives	is

*Be also has the forms *am* and *are*, which are used in the present tense. (See also 11b.)

Verb tense   Here are descriptions of the tenses and progressive forms. See also 11b.

The simple tenses show general facts, states of being, and actions that occur regularly.

Simple present tense (base form or -s form) expresses general facts, constant states, habitual or repetitive actions, or scheduled future events: *The sun rises in the east. The plane leaves tomorrow at 6:30.*

Simple past tense (base form + -ed or -d or irregular form) is used for actions that happened at a specific time or during a specific period in the past or for repetitive actions that have ended: *She drove to Montana three years ago. When I was young, I walked to school.*

Simple future tense (will + base form) expresses actions that will occur at some time in the future and promises or predictions of future events: *I will call you next week.*

The simple progressive forms show continuing action.

Present progressive (*am, is, are* + present participle) shows actions in progress that are not expected to remain constant or future actions (with verbs such as *go, come,* or *move*): *We are building our house at the shore. They are moving tomorrow.*

Past progressive (*was, were* + present participle) shows actions in progress at a specific past time or a continuing action that was interrupted: *Roy was driving his new car yesterday. When she walked in, we were planning her party.*

Future progressive (*will* + *be* + present participle) expresses actions that will be in progress at a certain time in the future: *Nan will be flying home tomorrow.*

NOTE: Certain verbs are not normally used in the progressive: *appear, believe, belong, contain, have, hear, know, like, need, see, seem, taste, think, understand,* and *want.* There are exceptions, however, that you must notice as you encounter them: *We are thinking of buying a summer home.*

The perfect tenses show actions that happened or will happen before another time.

Present perfect tense (*have, has* + past participle) expresses actions that began in the past and continue to the present or actions that happened at an unspecific time in the past: *She has not spoken of her grandfather in a long time. They have traveled to Africa twice.*

Past perfect tense (*had* + past participle) expresses an action that began or occurred before another time in the past: *By the time Hakan was fifteen, he had learned to* *drive. I had just finished my walk when my brother drove up.*

Future perfect tense (*will* + *have* + past participle) expresses actions that will be completed before or at a specific future time: *By the time I graduate, I will have taken five film study classes.*

The perfect progressive forms show continuous past actions before another present or past time.

Present perfect progressive (*have, has* + *been* + present participle) expresses continuous actions that began in the past and continue to the present: *My sister has been living in Oregon since 2008.*

Past perfect progressive (*had* + *been* + present participle) conveys actions that began and continued in the past until some other past action: *By the time I moved to Georgia, I had been supporting myself for five years.*

Future perfect progressive (*will* + *have* + *been* + present participle) expresses actions that are or will be in progress before another specified time in the future: *By the time we reach the cashier, we will have been waiting in line for an hour.*

Modal verbs   The nine modal verbs—*can, could, may, might, must, shall, should, will,* and *would*—are used with the base form of verbs to show certainty, necessity, or possibility. Modals do not change form to indicate tense.

▶ The art museum will ~~launches~~ launch its fundraising

campaign next month.

▶ We could ~~spoke~~ speak Portuguese when we were young.

Passive voice   When a sentence is written in the passive voice, the subject receives the action instead of doing it. To form the passive voice, use a form of *be*—*am, is, are, was, were, being, be,* or *been*—followed by the past participle of the main verb. (For appropriate uses of the passive voice, see 2b.)

▶ *Dreaming in Cuban* was ~~writing~~ written by Cristina García.

▶ Senator Dixon will be defeated.

NOTE: Verbs that do not take direct objects—such as *occur, happen, sleep, die,* and *fall*—do not form the passive voice.

16b Articles (*a, an, the*)

Articles and other noun markers Articles (*a, an, the*) are part of a category of words known as *noun markers* or *determiners*. Noun markers identify the nouns that follow them. Besides articles, noun markers include possessive nouns (*Elena's, child's*); possessive pronoun/adjectives (*my, your, their*); demonstrative pronoun/adjectives (*this, that*); quantifiers (*all, few, neither, some*); and numbers (*one, twenty-six*).

> ART N
> Felix is reading a book about mythology.

> ART ADJ N
> We took an exciting trip to Alaska last summer.

When to use *a* or *an* Use *a* or *an* with singular count nouns that refer to one unspecific item (not a whole category). *Count nouns* refer to persons, places, things, or ideas that can be counted: *one girl, two girls; one city, three cities; one goose, four geese.*

▶ My professor asked me to bring *a* dictionary to class.

▶ We want to rent *an* apartment close to the lake.

When to use *the* Use *the* with most nouns that the reader can identify specifically. Usually the identity will be clear to the reader for one of the following reasons:

1. The noun has been previously mentioned.

▶ A truck cut in front of our van. When *the* truck skidded a few seconds later, we almost crashed into it.

2. A phrase or clause following the noun restricts its identity.

▶ Bryce warned me that *the* GPS in his car was not working.

3. A superlative adjective such as *best* or *most intelligent* makes the noun's identity specific. (See also 13c.)

▶ Brita had <u>the</u> best players on her team.

4. The noun describes a unique person, place, or thing.

▶ During an eclipse, one should not look directly at <u>the</u> sun.

5. The context or situation makes the noun's identity clear.

▶ Please don't slam <u>the</u> door when you leave.

6. The noun is singular and refers to a class or category of items (most often animals, musical instruments, or inventions).

▶ ~~Tin~~ <u>The tin</u> whistle is common in traditional Irish music.

When not to use articles   Do not use *a* or *an* with noncount nouns. *Noncount nouns* refer to things or abstract ideas that cannot be counted or made plural: *salt, silver, air, furniture, patience, knowledge.* (See the chart on the following page.)

To express an approximate amount of a noncount noun, use a quantifier such as *some* or *more*: *some water, enough coffee, less violence.*

▶ Ava gave us ~~an~~ information about the Peace Corps.

▶ Claudia said she had <u>some</u> ~~a~~ news that would surprise her parents.

Do not use articles with nouns that refer to all of something or something in general.

▶ ~~The kindness~~ <u>Kindness</u> is a virtue.

▶ In some parts of the world, ~~the~~ rice is preferred to all other grains.

When to use articles with proper nouns Do not use articles with most singular proper nouns: *Prime Minister Trudeau, Jamaica, Lake Huron, Ivy Street, Mount Everest.* Use *the* with most plural proper nouns: *the McGregors, the Bahamas, the Finger Lakes, the United States.* Also use *the* with large regions, oceans, rivers, and mountain ranges: *the Sahara, the Indian Ocean, the Amazon River, the Rocky Mountains.*

There are, however, many exceptions, especially with geographic names. Note exceptions when you encounter them or consult a native speaker or a dictionary.

👓 Noncount nouns **at a glance**

Food and drink
beef, bread, butter, candy, cereal, cheese, cream, meat, milk, pasta, rice, salt, sugar, wine

Nonfood substances
air, cement, coal, dirt, gasoline, gold, paper, petroleum, plastic, rain, silver, snow, soap, steel, wood, wool

Abstract nouns
advice, anger, beauty, confidence, courage, employment, fun, happiness, health, honesty, information, intelligence, knowledge, love, poverty, satisfaction, wealth

Other
biology (and other areas of study), clothing, equipment, furniture, homework, jewelry, luggage, machinery, mail, money, news, poetry, pollution, research, scenery, traffic, transportation, violence, weather, work

NOTE: A few noncount nouns can also be used as count nouns: *He had two loves: music and archery.*

16c Sentence structure

This section focuses on the major challenges that multilingual students face when writing sentences in English.

Omitted verbs   Some languages do not use linking verbs (*am*, *is*, *are*, *was*, *were*) between subjects and complements (nouns or adjectives that rename or describe the subject). Every English sentence, however, must include a verb.

▶ Jim *is* intelligent.

▶ Many streets in San Francisco *are* very steep.

Omitted subjects   Some languages do not require a subject in every sentence. Every English sentence, however, needs a subject.

▶ Your aunt is very energetic. ~~Seems~~ *She seems* young for her age.

EXCEPTION: In commands, the subject *you* is understood but not present in the sentence: *Give me the book.*

The word *it* is used as the subject of a sentence describing the weather or temperature, stating the time, indicating distance, or suggesting an environmental fact. Do not omit *it* in such sentences.

It is 9:15 a.m.

It is three hundred miles to Chicago.

In July, *it* is very hot in Arizona.

In some English sentences, the subject comes after the verb, and a placeholder (called an expletive)—*there* or *it*—comes before the verb.

  EXP V ⌐─── S ───⌐   ⌐─── S ─── V
There are many people here today. (Many people are

here today.)

  EXP V   ⌐─ S ─⌐   ⌐─ S ─⌐   V
It is important to study daily. (To study daily is

important.)

▶ As you know, *there are* many religious sects in India.

Repeated subjects, objects, and adverbs   English does not allow a subject to be repeated in its own clause.

▶ The doctor ~~she~~ advised me to cut down on salt.

Do not add a pronoun even when a word group comes between the subject and the verb.

▶ The car that had been stolen ~~it~~ was found.

Do not repeat an object or an adverb in an adjective clause. Adjective clauses begin with relative pronouns (*who, whom, whose, which, that*) or relative adverbs (*when, where*). Relative pronouns usually serve as subjects or objects in the clauses they introduce; another word in the clause cannot serve the same function. Relative adverbs should not be repeated by other adverbs later in the clause.

▶ The cat ran under the car that ~~it~~ was parked on

    the street.

The relative pronoun *that* is the subject of the adjective clause, so the pronoun *it* cannot be added as the subject.

If the clause begins with a relative adverb, do not use another adverb with the same meaning later in the clause.

▶ The office where I work ~~there~~ is close to home.

The adverb *there* cannot repeat the relative adverb *where*.

16d Prepositions showing time and place

The chart on the following page is limited to three prepositions that show time and place: *at, on,* and *in.* Not every possible use is listed in the chart, so don't be surprised when you encounter exceptions and idiomatic uses that you must learn one at a time. For example, in English, we ride *in* a car but *on* a bus, plane, train, or subway.

👓 Prepositions showing time and place at a glance

Showing time

AT   *at* a specific time: *at* 7:20, *at* dawn, *at* dinner

ON   *on* a specific day or date: *on* Tuesday, *on* June 4

IN   *in* a part of a day: *in* the afternoon, *in* the daytime [but *at* night]

   in a year or month: *in* 1999, *in* July

   in a period of time: finished *in* three hours

Showing place

AT   *at* a meeting place or location: *at* home, *at* the club

   at a specific address: living *at* 10 Oak Street

   at the edge of something: sitting *at* the desk

   at the corner of something: turning *at* the intersection

   at a target: throwing the snowball *at* Lucy

ON   *on* a surface: placed *on* the table, hanging *on* the wall

   on a street: the house *on* Spring Street

   on an electronic medium: *on* television, *on* the Internet

IN   *in* an enclosed space: *in* the garage, *in* an envelope

   in a geographic location: *in* San Diego, *in* Texas

   in a print medium: *in* a book, *in* a magazine

Punctuation

17   The comma

The comma was invented to help readers. Without it, sentence parts can collide into one another unexpectedly, causing misreadings.

CONFUSING   If you cook Elmer will do the dishes.

CONFUSING   While we were eating a rattlesnake approached our campsite.

Add commas in the logical places (after *cook* and *eating*), and suddenly all is clear. No longer is Elmer being cooked or the rattlesnake being eaten.

Various rules have evolved to prevent such misreadings and to guide readers through complex grammatical structures. Those rules are detailed in sections 17a–17i. (Section 17j explains when not to use a comma.)

17a   Before a coordinating conjunction joining independent clauses

When a coordinating conjunction connects two or more independent clauses—word groups that could stand alone as separate sentences—a comma must be placed before the conjunction. There are seven coordinating conjunctions in English: *and, but, or, nor, for, so,* and *yet.*

A comma tells readers that one independent clause has come to a close and that another is about to begin.

▶ **Jake has no talent for numbers, so he hires**
                                     ∧
   someone to prepare his taxes.

EXCEPTION: If the two independent clauses are short and there is no danger of misreading, the comma may be left out.

   The plane took off and we were on our way.

NOTE: As a rule, do *not* use a comma with a coordinating conjunction that joins only two words, phrases, or subordinate clauses. (See 17j. See also 17c for commas with coordinating conjunctions joining three or more elements.)

17b After an introductory clause or phrase

A comma tells readers that an introductory clause or phrase has come to a close and that the main part of the sentence is about to begin. The most common introductory clauses and phrases function as adverbs. Such word groups usually tell when, where, how, why, or under what conditions the main action of the sentence occurred.

▶ **When Arthur ran his first marathon, he was**
^
pleased to finish in under four hours.

▶ **During the past decade, scientists have made**
^
important discoveries about how humans form

memories.

▶ **Buried under layers of younger rocks, the earth's**
^
oldest rocks contain no fossils.

EXCEPTION: The comma may be omitted after a short adverb clause or phrase if there is no danger of misreading: *In no time we were at 2,800 feet.*

NOTE: Other introductory word groups include transitional expressions and absolute phrases (see 17f).

17c Between items in a series

In a series of three or more items (words, phrases, or clauses), use a comma between all items, including the last two.

▶ **Langston Hughes's poetry is concerned with pride,**

social justice, and the African American experience.
^

Although some writers view the last comma in a series as optional, most experts advise using it because its omission can result in ambiguity or misreading.

▶ **My uncle willed me all of his property, houses,**
^
and boats.

Did the uncle will his property *and* houses *and* boats—or simply his property, consisting of houses and boats? If the former meaning is intended, a comma prevents ambiguity.

17d Between coordinate adjectives

When two or more adjectives each modify a noun separately, they are coordinate.

> Roberto is a *warm, gentle, affectionate* father.

If the adjectives can be joined with *and*, the adjectives are coordinate: *warm* and *gentle* and *affectionate*.

NOTE: Do not use a comma between cumulative adjectives, those that do not each modify the noun separately.

> *Three large gray* shapes moved slowly toward us.

Cumulative adjectives cannot be joined with *and* (not *three and large and gray shapes*).

17e To set off a nonrestrictive element, but not a restrictive element

A *restrictive* element defines or limits the meaning of the word it modifies; it is therefore essential to the meaning of the sentence and is not set off with commas. A *nonrestrictive* element describes a word whose meaning is clear without it. Because it is not essential to the meaning of the sentence, it is set off with commas.

RESTRICTIVE (NO COMMAS)

The campers need clothes *that are durable.*

NONRESTRICTIVE (WITH COMMAS)

The campers need sturdy shoes, *which are expensive.*

If you remove a restrictive element from a sentence, the meaning changes significantly, becoming more general than intended. The writer of the first sample sentence does not mean that the campers need clothes in general. The meaning is more restricted: The campers need *durable* clothes.

If you remove a nonrestrictive element from a sentence, the meaning does not change significantly. Some information may be lost, but the defining characteristics of the person or thing described remain the same: The campers need *sturdy shoes,* and these happen to be expensive.

Elements that may be restrictive or nonrestrictive include adjective clauses, adjective phrases, and appositives.

Adjective clauses   Adjective clauses, which usually follow the noun or pronoun they describe, begin with a relative pronoun (*who, whom, whose, which, that*) or with a relative adverb (*when, where*). When an adjective clause is nonrestrictive, set it off with commas; when it is restrictive, omit the commas.

NONRESTRICTIVE CLAUSE (WITH COMMAS)

▶ The Kyoto Protocol, which was adopted in 1997,

aims to reduce greenhouse gases.

RESTRICTIVE CLAUSE (NO COMMAS)

▶ The giant panda/ that was born at the National

Zoo in 2013/ was sent to China in 2017.

NOTE: Use *that* only with restrictive clauses. Many writers use *which* only with nonrestrictive clauses, but usage varies.

Adjective phrases   Prepositional or verbal phrases functioning as adjectives may be restrictive or nonrestrictive. Nonrestrictive phrases are set off with commas; restrictive phrases are not.

NONRESTRICTIVE PHRASE (WITH COMMAS)

▶ The helicopter, with its million-candlepower

spotlight illuminating the area, circled above.

RESTRICTIVE PHRASE (NO COMMAS)

▶ One corner of the attic was filled with newspapers/

dating from the 1920s.

Appositives   An appositive is a noun or pronoun that renames a nearby noun. Nonrestrictive appositives are set off with commas; restrictive appositives are not.

NONRESTRICTIVE APPOSITIVE (WITH COMMAS)

▶   Darwin's most important book, *On the Origin of*
                                  ∧
    Species, was the result of many years of research.
            ∧

RESTRICTIVE APPOSITIVE (NO COMMAS)

▶   Selections from the book / *Democracy and Education* /

    were read aloud in class.

17f To set off transitional and parenthetical expressions, absolute phrases, and word groups expressing contrast

Transitional expressions   Transitional expressions serve as bridges between sentences or parts of sentences. They include conjunctive adverbs such as *however*, *therefore*, and *moreover* and transitional phrases such as *for example* and *as a matter of fact*. For more examples, see page 62.

When a transitional expression appears between independent clauses in a compound sentence, it is preceded by a semicolon and is usually followed by a comma.

▶   Minh did not understand our language; moreover,
                                              ∧
    he was unfamiliar with our customs.

When a transitional expression appears at the beginning of a sentence or in the middle of an independent clause, it is usually set off with commas.

▶   In fact, stock values rose after the company's press
          ∧
    release.

▶   Natural foods are not always salt-free; celery, for
                                                   ∧
    example, is relatively high in sodium.
           ∧

Parenthetical expressions Expressions that provide only supplemental information and interrupt the flow of a sentence should be set off with commas.

▶ Evolution, so far as we know, doesn't work this way.
^   ^

Absolute phrases An absolute phrase consists of a noun followed by a participle or participial phrase. It modifies the whole sentence and should be set off with commas.

┌──────── ABSOLUTE PHRASE ────────┐
    N PARTICIPLE

The sun appearing for the first time all week, we were

at last able to begin the archaeological dig.

Word groups expressing contrast Sharp contrasts beginning with words such as *not* and *unlike* are set off with commas.

▶ Unlike Robert, Celia loved poetry slams.
^

17g To set off nouns of direct address, the words *yes* and *no,* interrogative tags, and mild interjections

▶ Forgive me, Angela, for forgetting our meeting.
^   ^

▶ Yes, the loan will probably be approved.
^

▶ The film was faithful to the book, wasn't it?
^

▶ Well, cases like this are difficult to decide.
^

17h To set off direct quotations introduced with expressions such as *he said*

▶ Gladwell asserts, "Those who are successful . . .
^

are most likely to be given the kinds of special

opportunities that lead to further success" (30).

17i With dates, addresses, and titles

Dates   In dates, set off the year from the rest of the sentence with a pair of commas.

▶ On December 12, 1890, orders were sent out for

the arrest of Sitting Bull.

EXCEPTION: Commas are not needed if the date is inverted or if only the month and year are given: *15 April 2018; January 2020.*

Addresses   The elements of an address or a place name are separated by commas. A zip code, however, is not preceded by a comma.

▶ The teen group met at 708 Spring Street, Washington,

IL 61571.

Titles   If a title follows a name, set off the title with a pair of commas.

▶ Sandra Barnes, MD, has been appointed to the

board of trustees.

17j Misuses of the comma

Do not use commas unless you have good reasons for using them. In particular, avoid using commas in the following situations:

WITH A COORDINATING CONJUNCTION JOINING ONLY TWO WORDS, PHRASES, OR SUBORDINATE CLAUSES

▶ Marie Curie discovered radium/ and later applied

her work on radioactivity to medicine.

TO SEPARATE A VERB FROM ITS SUBJECT

▶ Zoos large enough to give the animals freedom to

roam/ are becoming more popular.

BETWEEN CUMULATIVE ADJECTIVES (See 17d.)

▶ We found an old / maroon hatbox.

TO SET OFF RESTRICTIVE ELEMENTS (See 17e.)

▶ Drivers / who think they own the road / make cycling a dangerous sport.

▶ Margaret Mead's book / *Coming of Age in Samoa* / caused controversy when it was published.

AFTER A COORDINATING CONJUNCTION

▶ TV talk shows are sometimes performed live, but / more often they are taped.

AFTER *SUCH AS* OR *LIKE*

▶ Bacterial infections such as / methicillin-resistant *Staphylococcus aureus* (MRSA) have become a serious concern in hospitals.

BEFORE *THAN*

▶ Touring Crete was more thrilling for us / than visiting the Greek islands frequented by the rich.

BEFORE A PARENTHESIS

▶ At InterComm, Sylvia began at the bottom / (with only a cubicle and a swivel chair), but within three years she had been promoted to supervisor.

TO SET OFF AN INDIRECT (REPORTED) QUOTATION

▶ Samuel Goldwyn once said / that a verbal contract isn't worth the paper it's written on.

WITH A QUESTION MARK OR AN EXCLAMATION POINT

▶ "Why don't you try it? /" she coaxed.

18   The semicolon and the colon

18a   The semicolon

The semicolon is used between independent clauses not joined with a coordinating conjunction. It can also be used between items in a series containing internal punctuation.

The semicolon is never used between elements of unequal grammatical rank.

Between independent clauses   When two independent clauses appear in one sentence, they are usually linked with a comma and a coordinating conjunction (*and*, *but*, *or*, *nor*, *for*, *so*, *yet*). The coordinating conjunction signals the relation between the clauses. If the relation is clear without a conjunction, a writer may choose to connect the clauses with a semicolon instead.

> In film, a low-angle shot makes the subject look powerful; a high-angle shot does just the opposite.

A writer may also connect the clauses with a semicolon and a conjunctive adverb such as *however* or a transitional phrase such as *for example*.

> Many corals grow very gradually; in fact, the creation of a coral reef can take centuries.

CONJUNCTIVE ADVERBS

accordingly, also, anyway, besides, certainly, consequently, conversely, finally, furthermore, hence, however, incidentally, indeed, instead, likewise, meanwhile, moreover, nevertheless, next, nonetheless, now, otherwise, similarly, specifically, still, subsequently, then, therefore, thus

TRANSITIONAL PHRASES

after all, as a matter of fact, as a result, at any rate, at the same time, even so, for example, for instance, in addition, in conclusion, in fact, in other words, in the first place, on the contrary

NOTE: A semicolon must be used whenever a coordinating conjunction does not appear between independent clauses. To use only a comma—or to use a comma and a conjunctive adverb or transitional expression—creates an error known as a *comma splice*. (See 15.)

Between items in a series containing internal punctuation   Three or more items in a series are usually separated by commas. If one or more of the items contain internal punctuation, a writer may use semicolons for clarity.

> Science suggests that you can improve your memory by sleeping seven to eight hours a day; using mnemonics, self-testing, and visualization techniques; and including water, berries, and fish in your diet.

Misuses of the semicolon   Do not use a semicolon in the following situations:

BETWEEN A SUBORDINATE CLAUSE AND THE REST OF THE SENTENCE

▶ Although children's literature was added to the National Book Awards in 1969; it has had its own award, the Newbery Medal, since 1922.

BETWEEN AN APPOSITIVE AND THE WORD IT REFERS TO

▶ The scientists were fascinated by the species *Argyroneta aquatica*; a spider that lives underwater.

TO INTRODUCE A LIST

▶ Some birds are flightless; emus, penguins, and ostriches.

BETWEEN INDEPENDENT CLAUSES JOINED BY *AND*, *BUT*, *OR*, *NOR*, *FOR*, *SO*, OR *YET*

▶ Five of the applicants had worked with spreadsheets; but only one was familiar with database management.

18b The colon

Main uses of the colon　A colon can be used after an independent clause to direct readers' attention to a list, an appositive, or a quotation.

A LIST

The daily exercise routine should include the following: twenty knee bends, fifty leg lifts, and five minutes of running in place.

AN APPOSITIVE

My roommate seems to live on two things: snacks and social media.

A QUOTATION

Consider the words of Benjamin Franklin: "There never was a good war or a bad peace."

TIP: For other ways of introducing quotations, see 20d.

A colon may also be used between independent clauses if the second clause summarizes or explains the first clause.

Faith is like love: It cannot be forced.

NOTE: When an independent clause follows a colon, begin the independent clause with a capital letter. Some disciplines use a lowercase letter; see 34a, 39a, and 44a for variations.

Conventional uses

SALUTATION IN A LETTER　Dear Editor:

HOURS AND MINUTES　5:30 p.m.

PROPORTIONS　The ratio of women to men was 2:1.

TITLE AND SUBTITLE　*Alvin Ailey: A Life in Dance*

BIBLIOGRAPHIC ENTRIES　Boston: Bedford/St. Martin's, 2016

CITATIONS OF SACRED TEXTS　Luke 2:14, Qur'an 67:3

NOTE: MLA recommends a period in citations of sacred texts: Luke 2.14, Qur'an 67.3.

Misuses of the colon   A colon must be preceded by an independent clause. Therefore, avoid using it in the following situations:

BETWEEN A VERB AND ITS OBJECT OR COMPLEMENT

▶   Some important vitamins found in vegetables are:

 vitamin A, thiamine, niacin, and vitamin C.

BETWEEN A PREPOSITION AND ITS OBJECT

▶   The heart's two pumps each consist of: an upper

 chamber, or atrium, and a lower chamber, or

 ventricle.

AFTER *SUCH AS*, *INCLUDING*, OR *FOR EXAMPLE*

▶   The NCAA regulates college sports, including:

 basketball, softball, and football.

19   The apostrophe

The apostrophe indicates possession and marks contractions. In addition, it has a few conventional uses.

19a To indicate possession

The apostrophe is used to indicate that a noun or an indefinite pronoun is possessive. Possessives usually indicate ownership, as in *Tim's hat* or *the writer's desk*. Frequently, however, ownership is only loosely implied: *the tree's roots, a day's work.* If you are not sure whether a word is possessive, try turning it into an *of* phrase: *the roots of the tree, the work of a day.*

When to add -'s   Add -'s if the noun does not end in -s or if the noun is singular and ends in -s or an s sound.

> Luck often propels a rock musician's career.

> Thank you for refunding the children's money.

> Lois's sister spent last year in India.

> Her article presents an overview of Marx's teachings.

EXCEPTION: To avoid potentially awkward pronunciation, some writers use only an apostrophe with a single noun ending in -s: *Sophocles'*.

When to add only an apostrophe   If the noun is plural and ends in -s, add only an apostrophe.

> Both diplomats' briefcases were searched by guards.

Joint possession   To show joint possession, use -'s (or -s') with the last noun only; to show individual possession, make all nouns possessive.

> Have you seen Joyce and Greg's new camper?

> Hernando's and Maria's expectations were quite different.

Compound nouns   If a noun is compound, use -'s (or -s') with the last element.

> My father-in-law's memoir about his childhood in Sri Lanka was published in October.

Indefinite pronouns such as *someone*   Use -'s to indicate that an indefinite pronoun is possessive. Indefinite pronouns refer to no specific person or thing: *anyone, everyone, someone, no one,* and so on.

> Someone's raincoat has been left in the classroom.

NOTE: Possessive pronouns (*its, his,* and so on) do not use an apostrophe. (See 19d.)

19b To mark contractions

In a contraction, an apostrophe takes the place of one or more missing letters.

It's a shame that Frank can't go on the tour.

It's stands for *it is, can't* for *cannot*.
The apostrophe is also used to mark the omission of the first two digits of a year (*the class of '13*) or years (*the '60s generation*).

19c Conventional uses

An apostrophe typically is not used to pluralize numbers, abbreviations, letters, or words mentioned as words. Note the few exceptions and be consistent in your writing.

Plural of numbers and abbreviations   Do not use an apostrophe in the plural of any numbers (including decades) or of any abbreviations.

Peggy skated nearly perfect figure 8s.

The 1920s are known as the Jazz Age.

Plural of letters   Italicize the letter and use roman (regular) font style for the -*s* ending.

Two large *J*s were painted on the door.

To avoid misreading, you may use an apostrophe with some letters: two *A*'s in biology.

Plural of words mentioned as words   Italicize the word and use roman (regular) font style for the -*s* ending.

We've heard enough *maybe*s.

Words mentioned as words may also appear in quotation marks. When you choose this option, use the apostrophe.

We've heard enough "maybe's."

19d   Misuses of the apostrophe

Do not use an apostrophe in the following situations:

WITH NOUNS THAT ARE PLURAL BUT NOT POSSESSIVE

▶   Some ~~outpatient's~~ have special parking permits.

    outpatients

IN THE POSSESSIVE PRONOUNS *ITS, WHOSE, HIS, HERS, OURS,*
YOURS, **AND** *THEIRS*

▶   Each area has ~~it's~~ own conference room.

    its

▶   We attended a reading by Amy Tan, ~~who's~~ work

    whose

focuses on the Chinese immigration experience.

It's means "it is"; *who's* means "who is" (see 19b).
Possessive pronouns such as *its* and *whose* contain no
apostrophes.

20   Quotation marks

Quotation marks are used to enclose direct quotations.
They are also used around some titles and to set off
words used as words.

20a   To enclose direct quotations

Direct quotations of a person's words, whether spoken
or written, must be in quotation marks.

"Twitter," according to social media researcher
Jameson Brown, "is the best social network for brand
to customer engagement."

Use single quotation marks to enclose a quotation
within a quotation.

Marshall notes that Peabody's school focused on "not
merely 'teaching' but 'educating children morally and
spiritually as well as intellectually from the first'" (107).

EXCEPTIONS: Do not use quotation marks around
indirect quotations, which report what a person said

without using the person's exact words: *The mediator pledged to find a compromise even though negotiations had broken down.*

When a long quotation has been set off from the text by indenting, quotation marks are not needed. (See pp. 121, 196–97, and 259.)

20b Around titles of short works

Use quotation marks around titles of short works such as articles, poems, short stories, songs, television and radio episodes, and chapters or subdivisions of long works.

> James Baldwin's story "Sonny's Blues" is about two brothers who come to understand each other's suffering.

NOTE: Titles of long works such as books, plays, television and radio series, films, magazines, and so on are put in italics. (See pp. 82–83.)

20c To set off words used as words

Although words used as words are often italicized (see p. 83), some styles (including APA style) recommend using quotation marks. Use one method or the other consistently.

> The words "affect" and "effect" are frequently confused.

20d Other punctuation with quotation marks

This section describes the conventions American publishers use in placing various marks of punctuation inside or outside quotation marks. It also explains how to punctuate when introducing quoted material.

Periods and commas   Place periods and commas inside quotation marks.

> "I'm here for my service-learning project," I told the teacher. "I'd like to become a reading specialist."

This rule applies to single and double quotation marks, and it applies to quotation marks around words, phrases, and clauses.

EXCEPTION: In MLA- and APA-style parenthetical in-text citations, the period follows the citation in parentheses. MLA: *According to Cole, "The instruments of science have vastly extended our senses" (53).* APA: *According to Cole (1999), "The instruments of science have vastly extended our senses" (p. 53).*

Colons and semicolons   Put colons and semicolons outside quotation marks.

> Harold wrote, "I regret that I cannot attend the fund-raiser for AIDS research"; his letter, however, came with a substantial contribution.

Question marks and exclamation points   Put question marks and exclamation points inside quotation marks unless they apply to the whole sentence.

> Professor Abrams asked us on the first day of class, "What are your three goals for the course?"

> Have you heard the old proverb "Do not climb the hill until you reach it"?

In the first sentence, the question mark applies only to the quoted question. In the second sentence, the question mark applies to the whole sentence.

Introducing quoted material   After a word group introducing a quotation, choose a colon, a comma, or no punctuation at all, whichever is appropriate in context.

Formal introduction   If a quotation has been formally introduced, a colon is appropriate. A formal introduction is a full independent clause, not just an expression such as *he said* or *she writes.*

> Thomas Friedman provides a challenging yet optimistic view of the future: "We need to get back to work on our country and on our planet. The hour is late, the stakes couldn't be higher, the project couldn't be harder, the payoff couldn't be greater" (25).

Signal phrase   If a quotation is introduced with an expression such as *she argues* or *he explained*—or is followed by such an expression—a comma is needed.

> Mark Twain once declared, "In the spring I have counted one hundred and thirty-six different kinds of weather within four and twenty hours" (55).

"Unless another war is prevented it is likely to bring destruction on a scale never before held possible," Einstein wrote in the aftermath of the atomic bomb (29).

Blended quotation   When a quotation is blended into the writer's own sentence, either a comma or no punctuation is appropriate, depending on the way the quotation fits into the sentence structure.

> The future champion could, as he put it, "float like a butterfly and sting like a bee."

> Virginia Woolf wrote in 1928 that "a woman must have money and a room of her own if she is to write fiction" (4).

Beginning of sentence   If a quotation appears at the beginning of a sentence, use a comma after it unless the quotation ends with a question mark or an exclamation point.

> "I've always thought of myself as a reporter," American poet Gwendolyn Brooks stated (162).

> "What is it?" she asked, bracing herself.

Interrupted quotation   If a quoted sentence is interrupted by explanatory words, use commas to set off the explanatory words.

> "With regard to air travel," Stephen Ambrose notes, "Jefferson was a full century ahead of the curve" (53).

If two successive quoted sentences from the same source are interrupted by explanatory words, use a comma before the explanatory words and a period after them.

> "Everyone agrees journalists must tell the truth," Bill Kovach and Tom Rosenstiel write. "Yet people are befuddled about what 'the truth' means" (37).

20e Misuses of quotation marks

Do not use quotation marks to draw attention to familiar slang, to disown trite expressions, or to justify an attempt at humor.

▶   The economist emphasized that 5 percent was a

⁄"ballpark figure.⁄"

21 Other punctuation marks

21a The period

Use a period to end all sentences except direct questions or genuine exclamations.

> The therapist asked whether the session was beneficial.

A period is conventionally used with personal titles, Latin abbreviations, and designations for time.

Mr.	i.e.	a.m. (or AM)
Ms.	e.g.	p.m. (or PM)
Dr.	etc.	

NOTE: If a sentence ends with a period marking an abbreviation, do not add a second period.

> Periods are not used with most other abbreviations.

CA	UNESCO	UCLA	BCE	BS
NY	AFL-CIO	IRS	USA	PhD

21b The question mark

Use a question mark after a direct question.

> What is the horsepower of a 747 engine?

NOTE: Use a period, not a question mark, after an indirect question, one that is reported rather than asked directly.

> He asked me who was teaching the psychology course this year.

21c The exclamation point

Use an exclamation point after a sentence that expresses exceptional feeling or deserves special emphasis.

> When Gloria entered the room, I turned on the lights, and we all yelled, "Surprise!"

Do not overuse the exclamation point.

▶ In the fisherman's memory, the fish lives on,

increasing in length and weight each year, until it

is big enough to shade a fishing boat⌣.

This sentence is emphatic enough without an exclamation point.

21d The dash

The dash may be used to set off parenthetical material that deserves special emphasis. When typing, use two hyphens to form a dash (- -), with no spaces before or after the dash.

Use a dash to introduce a list, to signal a restatement or an amplification, or to indicate a striking shift in tone or thought.

> Peter decided to focus on his priorities—applying to graduate school, getting financial aid, and finding a roommate.

> Kiere took a few steps back, came running full speed, kicked a mighty kick—and missed the ball.

In the first example, the writer could also use a colon. (See 18b.) The colon is more formal than the dash and not quite as dramatic.

Use a pair of dashes to set off parenthetical material that deserves special emphasis or to set off an appositive that contains commas.

> Everything in the classroom—from the pencils on the desks to the books on the shelves—was in perfect order.

> In my hometown, people's basic needs—food, clothing, and shelter—are less costly than in Denver.

21e Parentheses

Parenthetical phrases   Use parentheses to enclose supplemental material, minor digressions, and afterthoughts.

> Nurses record patients' vital signs (temperature, pulse, and blood pressure) several times a day.

Abbreviations Use parentheses around an abbreviation following the spelled-out form the first time you mention a term. Use the abbreviation alone in subsequent references.

> Data from the Uniform Crime Reports (UCR) indicate that homicide rates have been declining. Because most murders are reported to the police, the data from the UCR are widely viewed as a valid indicator of homicide rates.

Labels in a series Use parentheses to enclose letters or numbers labeling items in a series.

> Freudians recognize three parts to a person's psyche: (a) the unconscious id, where basic drives reside; (b) the ego, which controls many of our conscious decisions; and (c) the superego, which regulates behavior according to internalized societal expectations.

Citations Parentheses are used around page numbers in in-text citations and, in APA style, around dates in in-text citations and the reference list. (See also 33a, 38a, and 38b.)

NOTE: Do not overuse parentheses. Often a sentence reads more gracefully without them.

▶ **Research shows that seventeen million** ^from^ **~~(estimates run as high as~~** ^to^ **twenty-three million~~)~~ Americans have diabetes.**

21f Brackets

Use brackets to enclose any words or phrases you have inserted into an otherwise word-for-word quotation.

> *Audubon* reports that "if there are not enough young to balance deaths, the end of the species [California condor] is inevitable" (4).

The *Audubon* article did not contain the words *California condor* in the sentence quoted.

The Latin word "sic" in brackets indicates that an error in a quoted sentence appears in the original source.

> According to the review, the book was "an important contribution to gender studies, suceeding [sic] where others have fallen short."

NOTE: APA and *Chicago* use italics for the word "sic" (but not for the brackets). MLA uses regular (roman) font. See pages 196, 258, and 121, respectively.

21g The ellipsis

Use an ellipsis mark, three spaced periods, to indicate that you have deleted words from an otherwise direct quotation.

> Shute acknowledges that treatment for autism can be expensive: "Sensory integration therapy . . . can cost up to $200 an hour" (82).

If you delete a full sentence or more in the middle of a quoted passage, use a period before the ellipsis.

NOTE: Do not use an ellipsis at the beginning of a quotation. Readers will understand that the quoted material is taken from a longer passage. If you have cut some words from the end of the final quoted sentence, however, MLA style requires an ellipsis.

21h The slash

Use the slash to separate two or three lines of poetry that have been run into your text. Add a space both before and after the slash. (For more than three lines of poetry, see p. 131.)

> In the opening lines of "Jordan," George Herbert pokes fun at popular poems of his time: "Who says that fictions only and false hair / Become a verse? Is there in truth no beauty?"

Use the slash sparingly, if at all, to separate options: *pass/fail, producer/director.* Put no space around the slash. Avoid using the awkward construction *and/ or,* as well as using *he/she* and *him/her* to solve sexist language problems. (See 9d.)

Mechanics

22 Capitalization

In addition to the following guidelines, a good dictionary can help you decide when to use capital letters.

22a Proper vs. common nouns

Proper nouns and words derived from them are capitalized; common nouns are not. Proper nouns name specific persons, places, and things. All other nouns are common nouns.

The following types of words are usually capitalized: names of deities, religions, religious followers, and sacred books; words of family relationship used as names; particular places; nationalities and their languages, races, and tribes; educational institutions and departments and specific courses; government departments and organizations and political parties; historical movements, periods, events, and documents; and trade names.

PROPER NOUNS	COMMON NOUNS
God (used as a name)	a god
Uncle Pedro	my uncle
Dad (used as a name)	my dad
Lake Superior	a large lake
the South	a southern state
University of Wisconsin	a state university
the Democratic Party	a political party
the Enlightenment	the eighteenth century
Advil	a painkiller

Months, holidays, and days of the week are capitalized: *May, Labor Day, Monday.* The seasons and numbers of the days of the month are not: *summer, the fifth of June.*

EXCEPTION: Capitalize *Fourth of July* (or *July Fourth*) when referring to the holiday.

Names of school subjects are capitalized only if they are names of languages: *geology, history, English, French.* Names of particular courses are capitalized: *Geology 101, Principles of Economics.*

NOTE: Do not capitalize common nouns to make them seem important: *Our company is currently hiring technical support staff* [not *Company, Technical Support Staff*].

22b Titles with proper names

Capitalize a title when used as part of a proper name but usually not when used alone.

> Prof. Margaret Burnes; Dr. Sinyee Sein; John Scott Williams Jr.; Anne Tilton, LLD
>
> District Attorney Mill was ruled out of order.
>
> The district attorney was elected for a two-year term.

Usage varies when the title of an important public figure is used alone: *The president* [or *President*] *vetoed the bill.*

22c Titles of works

In titles and subtitles, all major words—nouns, pronouns, verbs, adjectives, and adverbs—should be capitalized. Minor words—articles, prepositions, and coordinating conjunctions—are not capitalized unless they are the first or last word of a title or subtitle. (In APA style, capitalize all words of four or more letters in titles. See 39a.)

> *The Impossible Theater: A Manifesto*
>
> *A River Runs through It*
>
> "I Want to Hold Your Hand"

Titles of works are handled differently in the APA reference list. See "Preparing the list of references" in 39a.

22d First word of a sentence or quoted sentence

The first word of a sentence should be capitalized. Also capitalize the first word of a quoted sentence within a sentence, but not the first word of a quoted phrase.

> Loveless writes, "If failing schools are ever to be turned around, much more must be learned about how schools age as institutions" (25).

Steven Pinker has written that one important element of good writing is "attention to the readers' vantage point" (26).

If a quoted sentence is interrupted by explanatory words, do not capitalize the first word after the interruption.

"When we all think alike," he said, "no one is thinking."

When a sentence appears within parentheses, capitalize the first word unless the parentheses appear within another sentence.

Early detection of breast cancer increases survival rates. (See table 2.)

Early detection of breast cancer increases survival rates (see table 2).

22e First word following a colon

When a group of words following a colon can stand on its own as a complete sentence, MLA recommends using lowercase for the first word in most situations, whereas APA calls for capitalizing it.

MLA STYLE

Clinical trials revealed a problem: a high percentage of participants reported severe headaches.

APA STYLE

Clinical trials revealed a problem: A high percentage of participants reported severe headaches.

Always use lowercase for the first word of a list or an appositive that follows a colon.

Students were divided into two groups: residents and commuters.

22f Abbreviations

Capitalize abbreviations for departments and agencies of government, other organizations, and corporations; capitalize trade names and the call letters of radio and television stations.

EPA, FBI, DKNY, IBM, WERS, KNBC-TV

23 Abbreviations, numbers, and italics

23a Abbreviations

Use abbreviations only when they are clearly appropriate.

Appropriate abbreviations   Use standard abbreviations for titles immediately before and after proper names.

TITLES BEFORE PROPER NAMES	TITLES AFTER PROPER NAMES
Ms. Nancy Linehan	Thomas Hines Sr.
Mr. Raphael Zabala	Valda Coimbra, PhD
Dr. Margaret Simmons	Robert Simkowski, MD
Rev. John Stone	Mia Chin, LLD

Do not abbreviate a title if it is not used with a proper name: *My history professor* [not *prof.*] *was an expert on naval warfare.*

Familiar abbreviations for the names of organizations, corporations, and countries are also acceptable: *CIA, FBI, NAACP, EPA, YMCA, NBC, USA.*

When using an unfamiliar abbreviation (such as *NASW* for National Association of Social Workers) or a potentially ambiguous abbreviation (such as *AMA*, which can refer to either the American Medical Association or the American Management Association), write the full name followed by the abbreviation in parentheses at the first mention of the name. Then use just the abbreviation throughout the rest of the paper.

Inappropriate abbreviations   In formal writing, abbreviations for the following are not commonly accepted.

DAYS OF THE WEEK   Monday (*not* Mon.)

HOLIDAYS   Christmas (*not* Xmas)

MONTHS   January, February (*not* Jan., Feb.)

COURSES OF STUDY   political science (*not* poli. sci.)

STATES AND COUNTRIES   Florida (*not* FL or Fla.)

Although Latin abbreviations are appropriate in footnotes and bibliographies and in informal writing, use the appropriate English phrases in formal writing.

e.g. (Latin *exempli gratia*, "for example")

et al. (Latin *et alii*, "and others")

etc. (Latin *et cetera*, "and so forth")

i.e. (Latin *id est*, "that is")

N.B. (Latin *nota bene*, "note well")

Units of measurement   Use abbreviations for units of measurement when they appear with numerals; spell out the units when they are used alone or when they are used with spelled-out numbers. (See also 23b.)

Results were measured in pounds.

Runners in the 5-km race had to contend with pouring rain.

23b Numbers

Spell out numbers of one or two words. Use numerals for numbers that require more than two words to spell out.

▶ The 1980 eruption of Mount St. Helens blasted ash
  sixteen   230
  16̶ miles into the sky and devastated ~~two hundred~~
  ^   ^
  ~~thirty~~ square miles of land.

If a sentence begins with a number, spell out the number or rewrite the sentence.

  One hundred fifty
▶ 1̶5̶0̶ children in our program need expensive
  ^
  dental treatment.

Academic styles vary for handling numbers in the text of a paper. In the humanities, MLA and *Chicago* spell out numbers below 101 and large round numbers (*forty million*); they use numerals for specific numbers above one hundred (*234*). In the social sciences and the sciences, APA and CSE spell out the numbers one through nine in most situations and use numerals for all other numbers.

Generally, numerals are acceptable for the following:

DATES July 4, 1776; 56 BC; 30 CE

ADDRESSES 77 Latches Lane, 519 West 42nd Street

PERCENTAGES 55 percent (or 55%)

FRACTIONS, DECIMALS ⅞, 0.047

SCORES 7 to 3, 21–18

STATISTICS average age 37

SURVEYS 4 out of 5

EXACT AMOUNTS OF MONEY $105.37

DIVISIONS OF BOOKS volume 3, chapter 4, page 189

DIVISIONS OF PLAYS act 3, scene 3 (or act III, scene iii)

TIME OF DAY 4:00 p.m., 1:30 a.m.

23c Italics

This section describes conventional uses for italics: for titles of works; names of ships, aircraft, and spacecraft; foreign words; and words as words.

Titles of works Titles of the following types of works should be italicized:

TITLES OF BOOKS *The Color Purple, The Round House*

MAGAZINES *Time, Scientific American, Slate*

NEWSPAPERS the *Baltimore Sun,* the *Orlando Sentinel*

PAMPHLETS *Common Sense, Facts about Marijuana*

LONG POEMS *The Waste Land, Paradise Lost*

PLAYS *King Lear, Wicked*

FILMS *Casablanca, Argo*

TELEVISION PROGRAMS *The Voice, Frontline*

RADIO PROGRAMS *All Things Considered*

PODCAST SERIES *Embedded*

MUSICAL COMPOSITIONS *Porgy and Bess*

WORKS OF VISUAL ART *American Gothic*

VIDEO GAMES *Dragon Age, Call of Duty*

DATABASES OR WEBSITES [MLA] *JSTOR, Google*

COMPUTER SOFTWARE OR APP [MLA] *Photoshop, Instagram*

Sometimes guidelines for italics vary among the style guides (MLA, APA, and *Chicago*). See also the style section your instructor has assigned.

The titles of other works—including short stories, essays, songs, and short poems—are enclosed in quotation marks. (See 20b.)

NOTE: Do not use italics when referring to the Bible; the titles of books in the Bible (Genesis, not *Genesis*); the titles of legal documents (the Constitution, not the *Constitution*); or the titles of your own papers.

Non-English words   Italicize non-English words used in an English sentence.

> I wished my German teacher a *gute Reise* before his flight.

EXCEPTION: Do not italicize foreign words that have become part of the English language—"laissez-faire," "fait accompli," "modus operandi," or "per diem," for example.

Words as words etc.   Italicize words used as words, letters mentioned as letters, and numbers mentioned as numbers.

> Tomás assured us that the chemicals could probably be safely mixed, but his *probably* stuck in our minds.

> Some toddlers have trouble pronouncing the letters *f* and *s*.

> A big *3* was painted on the stage door.

NOTE: APA style recommends using quotation marks instead of italics to set off words mentioned as words and letters mentioned as letters, but neither italics nor quotation marks for numerals mentioned as numerals. (See 20c.) An exception is that italics are used for key terms that are being defined.

> Social scientists use the term *androgyny* to describe a blending of traditionally masculine and feminine traits.

Inappropriate italics   Italicizing to emphasize words or ideas is often ineffective and should be used sparingly.

24   Hyphenation

In addition to the following guidelines, a dictionary will help you make decisions about hyphenation.

24a Compound words

The dictionary will tell you whether to treat a compound word as a hyphenated compound (*water-repellent*), as one word (*waterproof*), or as two words (*water table*). If the compound word is not in the dictionary, treat it as two words.

24b Words functioning together as an adjective

When two or more words function together as an adjective before a noun, connect them with a hyphen. Generally, do not use a hyphen when such compounds follow the noun.

▶   Pat Hobbs is not yet a well-known candidate.
                                      ^

▶   After our television campaign, Pat Hobbs will be

    well/known.

Do not use a hyphen to connect *-ly* adverbs to the words they modify.

▶   A slowly/moving truck tied up traffic.

NOTE: In a series of hyphenated adjectives modifying the same noun, hyphens are suspended: *Do you prefer first-, second-, or third-class tickets?*

24c Conventional uses

Fractions, prefixes, etc. Hyphenate the written form of fractions and of compound numbers from twenty-one to ninety-nine. Also use a hyphen with the prefixes *all-, ex-,* and *self-* and with the suffix *-elect*.

▶ One-fourth of my income goes toward paying
  ^
  rent.

▶ The charity is funding more self-help projects.
                                         ^

Hyphenation at ends of lines Only words that already contain a hyphen should be broken at the end of a line of text. If your word processor automatically breaks words at the ends of lines, disable that setting.

Email addresses, URLs, and DOIs need special attention when they must break in the text of a paper or in a bibliographic citation. Do not insert a hyphen. Consult the guidelines for MLA, APA, *Chicago*, or CSE style (34a, 39a, 44a, or 46b, respectively).

Research

A college research assignment asks you to pose questions worth exploring, read widely in search of possible answers, interpret what you read, draw reasoned conclusions, and support those conclusions with evidence. It asks you to enter a research conversation by being *in* conversation with other writers and thinkers who have explored and studied your topic.

As you listen to and learn from the voices already in the conversation, you'll find entry points where you can add your own insights and ideas. Take time to discover what has been written about your topic and to uncover what's missing and needs to be questioned and researched.

This section and the color-coded sections that follow—MLA (red), APA (green), *Chicago* (purple), and CSE (turquoise)—will help you write your essay and document your sources in the style your instructor requires.

25 Posing a research question

▶ How to enter a research conversation **88**
▶ Testing a research question at a glance **89**

Every research project starts with questions. Try using *who*, *what*, *why*, and *how* to form possible research questions for your project:

- **How** can nutritional labels be redesigned so that they inform rather than confuse consumers?
- **Why** are boys diagnosed with attention deficit disorder more often than girls are?
- **What** happens to the arts without public funding?

As you draft possible questions, choose those that are focused (not too broad), challenging (not just factual), and grounded (not too speculative) as entry points into a research conversation.

25a Choosing a focused question

If your initial question is too broad given the length of the essay you plan to write, look for ways to narrow and focus your question.

TOO BROAD	FOCUSED
What are the benefits of higher tariffs on imported cars?	How will higher tariffs on imported cars create new auto-industry jobs and make US carmakers more profitable?

HOW TO Enter a research conversation

A college research project asks you to be in conversation with writers and researchers who have studied your topic — responding to their ideas and arguments and contributing your own insights to move the conversation forward. As you ask preliminary research questions, you may wonder where and how to step into a research conversation.

1 **Identify the experts and ideas in the conversation.** Ask: Who are the major writers and most influential people researching your topic? What are their credentials? What positions have they taken? How and why do the experts disagree?

2 **Identify gaps in the conversation.** What is missing? Where are the gaps in the existing research? What questions haven't been asked yet? What positions need to be challenged?

3 **Try using a sentence guide,** which acts as a sentence starter to help you find an entry point. For more examples of sentence guides, see page 125.

- Key details that have been overlooked in this debate are . . .

- Researchers have drawn conclusion X from the evidence, but one could also draw conclusion Y.

25b Choosing a debatable question

Your research project will be more interesting if you ask a question that is open to debate, not a question that leads to a report or a list of facts. A *why* or *how* question most often leads to a researched argument and engages you and your readers in a debate with multiple perspectives.

TOO FACTUAL	DEBATABLE
What percentage of state police departments use body cameras?	How has the widespread use of body cameras changed encounters between officers and civilians?

25c Choosing a question grounded in evidence

For most college courses, the central argument of a research project should be grounded in evidence, not in personal preferences or opinions. Your question should lead you to evidence, not to a defense of your opinions.

TOO DEPENDENT ON PERSONAL OPINION	GROUNDED IN EVIDENCE
Do medical scientists have the right to experiment on animals?	How have technological breakthroughs made medical experiments on animals increasingly unnecessary?

6ổ Testing a research question at a glance

As you draft possible research questions, explore your topic from multiple perspectives and let your curiosity drive your project. Ask yourself:

- Does the question allow you to research a topic that interests you? Is it a topic that will engage readers?
- Can you show your audience why the question needs to be asked and why the answer is worth knowing?
- Is the research question flexible enough to allow for many possible answers? Can you articulate possible ways to answer it?

The answer to all of these questions should be "yes."

26 Finding appropriate sources

Before you search for sources, think about what kinds of sources might be appropriate for your project. Considering the kinds of sources you need will help you develop a research strategy—a systematic plan for locating sources. Try to cast a wide net in your search strategy to learn about what aspects of your topic are generating the most debate.

No single search strategy works for every topic. For some topics, it may be useful to search for information in newspapers, government publications, and websites. For others, the best sources might be scholarly journals, books, research reports, and specialized reference works.

👓 Primary and secondary sources at a glance

As you search for sources, determine whether each one you consider is a primary or a secondary source.

Primary source
letter, diary, film, legislative bill, laboratory study, field research report, speech, eyewitness account, poem, short story

Secondary source
commentary, review, or interpretation of a primary source by another writer

Although a primary source is not necessarily more reliable than a secondary source, it has the advantage of being a firsthand account. You can better evaluate what a secondary source says if you have read any primary source it discusses.

26a Using the library

Your college library's website links to databases and other references containing articles, studies, and reports written by scholars and scientists. Use your

HOW TO Go beyond a Google search

Good research involves going beyond the information available from a quick Google search. You might start with Google to gain an overview of your topic, but relying on the search engine to choose your sources isn't a research strategy. To locate reliable, authoritative sources, be strategic about *how* and *where* to search.

1 **Familiarize yourself with the research conversation.** Identify the current debate about the topic you have chosen and the most influential writers and experts in the debate. Which experts or sources are cited repeatedly? Where is the research conversation happening: In scholarly sources? in government agencies? in popular media?

2 **Generate keywords to focus your search.** Use specific words and combinations when you search. Be flexible and try new words and phrases as you encounter them in your research. Add a word such as *debate*, *disagreements*, *controversies*, *proponents*, or *opponents* to track down various positions in the research conversation. Use questions such as *when*, *how*, and *why* to refine a search.

3 **Search discipline-specific databases available through your school library** to locate carefully chosen scholarly (peer-reviewed) content that doesn't appear in search results on the open web. Use databases such as *JSTOR* and *Academic Search Premier*, designed for academic researchers, to locate sources in influential publications.

4 **If your topic has been in the news, try *CQ Researcher*,** available through most college libraries. Its brief articles provide pro/con arguments on current controversies in criminal justice, law, environment, technology, health, and education.

5 **Explore the Pew Research Center site (pewresearch.org),** which presents original research and nonpartisan discussions of findings and trends in a wide range of academic fields.

library's resources, designed for academic researchers, to find the most authoritative sources for your project.

26b   Using the web

When conducting searches, use terms and phrases—keywords—that are as specific as possible to describe your topic and focus your search. The keywords you enter into a search engine will determine the quality of the results you see, so avoid general words that will yield millions of unproductive results. To narrow your search, experiment with specific words, combinations of words, dates, and other criteria. If, for example, your research question focuses on legislation to regulate healthy eating choices, search for ".gov" sites and sort by the most recent results to identify current government publications on food regulations.

👓 Smart searching **at a glance**

For currency. If you need current information and up-to-date statistics, news outlets such as *The New York Times*, *The Washington Post,* and the BBC; think tanks; and government agencies may provide appropriate sources for your research. When using Google, limit a search to the most recent year, month, week, or day.

For authority. Keep an eye out for experts being cited in sources you examine. Following the trail of citations can lead you to sources by those experts — or the organizations they represent — that may be helpful. You can limit a search by type of website or type of source. For instance, type *site:.gov* after a search term to find government sources or *filetype:pdf* to locate reports and papers available as PDF files.

For scholarship. Use a library database to look for scholarly sources, including reports of original research written by the people who conducted it, and for authors who are experts and academics. Read the abstract of a long article or the article's introductory paragraphs and conclusion to see if the source is worth further investigation.

For context. Books often provide more in-depth coverage and context than articles. You may find a single chapter or even a few pages that are just what you need to gain a deeper perspective about the background of your topic or about related important research.

26c Using bibliographies and citations

Scholarly books and articles list the works the author has cited, usually at the end. These lists are useful shortcuts to additional reliable sources on your topic. Let one source lead you to the next. Following the trail of citations may lead you to helpful sources and a network of relevant research about your topic.

27 Managing information; avoiding plagiarism

▶ How to avoid plagiarizing from the web **94**
▶ How to take notes responsibly **96**
▶ Integrating and citing sources to avoid plagiarism **97**

An effective researcher is a good record keeper. Whether you decide to keep records on paper or on your computer or another device, you will need methods for managing information: maintaining a working bibliography, keeping track of source materials, and taking notes without plagiarizing your sources. (For more on avoiding plagiarism, see 30 for MLA style, 36 for APA style, and 41 for *Chicago* style.)

27a Maintaining a working bibliography

Keep a record of sources you read or view. This record, called a *working bibliography*, will help you keep track of publication information for the sources you might use so that you can easily refer to them as you write and compile a list of works cited. The format of this list depends on the documentation style you are using. (For MLA style, see 33b; for APA style, see 38b; for *Chicago* style, see 43c; for CSE style, see 45c.)

27b Keeping track of source materials

Save a copy of each potential source as you conduct your research. Many database services allow you to email, text, save, or print citations or full texts, and you can easily download, bookmark, or take screenshots of information from the web.

HOW TO

Avoid plagiarizing from the web

1 **Understand what plagiarism is.** When you use another author's intellectual property — language, visuals, or ideas — in your own writing without giving proper credit, you engage in a kind of academic dishonesty called *plagiarism*.

2 **Treat online sources as someone else's intellectual property.** Language, data, or images that you find online must be cited, even if the material is in the public domain (which includes older works no longer protected by copyright law), is publicly accessible on free sites or social media, or is on a government website.

3 **Keep track of words and ideas borrowed from sources.** When you copy and paste passages from online sources, put quotation marks around any text that you have copied. Develop a system for distinguishing and labeling your words and ideas from anything you've summarized, paraphrased, or quoted.

4 **Create a complete bibliographic entry for each source** to keep track of publication information. From the start of your research project, maintain accurate records for all online sources you read or view.

Working with photocopies, printouts, screenshots, or files—as opposed to relying on memory or hastily written notes—lets you annotate the source as you read. You also reduce the chance of unintentional plagiarism, since you will be able to compare your use of a source in your essay with the actual source, not just with your notes.

27c Taking notes responsibly; avoiding unintentional plagiarism

Plagiarism, using someone's words or ideas without giving credit, is often accidental. After spending so much time spent thinking through your topic and reading sources, it's easy to forget where a helpful idea came from or that the idea wasn't yours to begin with. Even if you half-copy the author's sentences—either by mixing the author's phrases with your own without using quotation marks or by plugging synonyms into the author's sentence structure—you are plagiarizing.

Summarizing information, paraphrasing ideas, and quoting exact language are three ways of taking notes to avoid plagiarism.

Summarizing   A summary, written in your own words, condenses information and captures main ideas, reducing a chapter to a short paragraph or a paragraph to a single sentence.

Paraphrasing   Like a summary, a paraphrase is written in your own words, but it restates information in roughly the same number of words as the original source, using different sentence structure.

Quoting   A quotation consists of the exact words from a source. Put all quoted material in quotation marks.

HOW TO **Take notes responsibly**

1 **Understand the ideas in the source.** Start by determining the purpose and meaning of the source. Focus on the author's overall ideas. Ask: What is the argument? What is the evidence?

2 **Keep the source close by to check for accuracy,** but resist the temptation to look at the source as you take notes — except when you are quoting.

3 **Use quotation marks around any borrowed words or phrases.** Copy the words exactly and keep complete bibliographic information for each source.

4 **Develop an organized system** to distinguish your insights and ideas from those of the source. Think about what you've read as you take notes by indicating your agreements, disagreements, and questions. Take time to note how you might use a source and what it will contribute to the answer to your research question.

5 **Create a method to label** when you have summarized a text or its data or paraphrased or quoted an author's words.

6 **Record complete bibliographic information for each source** so that you can cite it accurately and find it easily.

Integrating and citing sources to avoid plagiarism

Source text

Our language is constantly changing. Like the Mississippi, it keeps forging new channels and abandoning old ones, picking up debris, depositing unwanted silt, and frequently bursting its banks. In every generation there are people who deplore changes in the language and many who wish to stop its flow. But if our language stopped changing it would mean that American society had ceased to be dynamic, innovative, pulsing with life — that the great river had frozen up.

— Robert MacNeil and William Cran, *Do You Speak American?*, p. 1

NOTE: The examples in this chart follow MLA style (see 33). For information on APA, *Chicago*, and CSE styles, see 38, 43, and 45, respectively.

- **If you are using an exact sentence from a source,** with no changes, *put quotation marks around the sentence. Use a signal phrase and include a page number in parentheses.*

  MacNeil and Cran write, "Our language is constantly changing" (1).

- **If you are using a few exact words from the source** but not an entire sentence, *put quotation marks around the exact words that you have used from the source. Use a signal phrase and include a page number in parentheses.*

  Some people, according to MacNeil and Cran, "deplore changes in the language" (1).

- **If you are using near-exact words from the source but changing some word forms** (*I* to *she*, *walk* to *walked*) or adding words to clarify and make the quotation flow with your own text, *put quotation marks around the quoted words and put brackets around the changes you have introduced. Include a signal phrase and follow the quotation with the page number in parentheses.*

  MacNeil and Cran compare the English language to the Mississippi River, which "forg[es] new channels and abandon[s] old ones" (1).

Continued ➔

> ## Integrating and citing sources to avoid plagiarism (*continued*)
>
> - **If you are paraphrasing or summarizing the source,** using the author's ideas but not any of the author's exact words, *introduce the ideas with a signal phrase and put the page number at the end of your sentence. Do not use quotation marks.* (See 30, 36, and 41.)
>
>   MacNeil and Cran argue that changes in the English language are natural and that they represent cultural progress (1).
>
> - **If you have used the source's sentence structure** but substituted a few synonyms for the author's words, *STOP! This is a form of plagiarism even if you use a signal phrase and a page number. Change your sentence by using one of the techniques given in this chart or in sections 31, 37, or 42.*
>
>   **PLAGIARIZED**
>   MacNeil and Cran claim that, like a river, English creates new waterways and discards old ones.
>
>   **INTEGRATED AND CITED CORRECTLY**
>   MacNeil and Cran claim, "Like the Mississippi, [English] keeps forging new channels and abandoning old ones" (1).

28 Evaluating sources

You will often locate far more potential sources on your topic than you will have time to read. Your challenge then is to determine what kinds of sources you need—and what you need these sources to do—and to select a reasonable number of trustworthy sources.

How you plan to use sources will affect how you evaluate them. You can use sources to

- provide background information or context for your topic
- explain terms or concepts that your readers might not understand
- provide evidence for your argument
- lend authority to your argument
- offer counterevidence and counterargument

28a Evaluating the reliability and usefulness of a source

The following questions will help you judge the reliability and usefulness of sources you might use to support your research project:

Relevance   Is the source clearly related to your research topic and your argument? Will your readers understand why you've included the source in your paper? How will the source help you clarify or support your position?

👓 Determining if a source is scholarly at a glance

Scholarly sources are written by experts for a knowledgeable audience and usually go into more depth than books and articles written for a general audience. Scholarly sources are sometimes called *peer-reviewed* or *refereed* because the work is evaluated by experts in the field before publication.

To determine if a source is scholarly, look for the following:

- Formal language and presentation
- Authors who are academics or scientists
- Footnotes or a bibliography documenting the works cited in the source
- Original research and interpretation (rather than a summary of other people's work)
- A description of research methods or a review of related research (in the sciences or social sciences)

NOTE: In some databases, searches can be limited to show only peer-reviewed or refereed journals.

Currency   How recent is the source? Is the information up to date? Does your research topic require current information? Will your research benefit from consulting older sources, including primary sources from a historical period?

Credibility   Where does the source come from? Who created it? What are the author's credentials? How accurate and trustworthy is the information? If the source is authored by an organization, what research has the organization done to support its claims? Are the source's ideas and research cited by other experts? Is it a scholarly or popular source?

Bias   Does the author endorse political or religious views that could affect objectivity? Is evidence and counterevidence presented in a fair and objective way? Is the author engaging in a scholarly debate or giving a personal point of view?

28b Reading with an open mind and a critical eye

As you begin reading the sources you have chosen, keep an open mind. Do not let your personal beliefs prevent you from listening to new ideas and opposing viewpoints. Be curious about the wide range of positions in the research conversation you are entering.

Read carefully to understand a source. Read skeptically to question a source. And read evaluatively to consider how a source will contribute to your research project. Ask questions such as these:

- What is the purpose of the source? Why was it written and for whom?
- What is the author's central argument, or thesis?
- How does the author support this argument—with relevant and sufficient evidence or with just a few anecdotal examples?
- Are any statistics reported in the source consistent with those you encounter in other sources? Have they been used fairly? Does the author explain where the statistics come from?
- Are any of the author's assumptions questionable?
- Does the author consider opposing arguments and refute them persuasively?

Detect false and misleading sources

Sources can distort information or spread misinformation by taking information out of context or by promoting opinions as facts. As you evaluate sources, determine authenticity: Can the information be verified? Is the source reliable? You can verify facts and quotations by reading multiple sources and gathering a variety of perspectives. Because information and misinformation live side by side on the web, you need to read critically to determine the truth.

1 **Consider the source.** Is more than one source covering the topic? Is the author anonymous or named? What can you learn about the author's credentials and the mission of a site from checking the "About Us" page? Does the site present only one side of an issue? Be skeptical if the source is the only one reporting the story.

2 **Examine the source's language and visual clues.** Does the headline use sensational (shocking or emotional) language? Is the language of the source offensive? Is the screen cluttered with text in ALL CAPS and unprofessional web design?

3 **Question the seriousness of the source.** Is it possible that the source is satirical and humorous and is not intended to be read as factual?

4 **Fact-check the information.** Can the facts be objectively verified? If the conclusions of a research study are cited, find the study to verify; if an authority is quoted, research the original source of the quotation, if possible, to see whether the quotation was taken out of context. Also, be skeptical if a source reports a research study but doesn't quote the study's principal investigator or other respected researchers.

5 **Pay attention to the URL.** Established news organizations have standard domain names. Fake sites often use web addresses that imitate the addresses of real sites, such as "Newslo" or "com.co," and package information with misinformation to make the site look authentic. Among the more credible sites are those sponsored by institutions of higher education (.edu), nonprofit groups (.org), and government agencies (.gov).

6 **Note your biases.** If an article makes you angry or challenges your beliefs, or if it confirms your beliefs by ignoring evidence to the contrary, take notice, and try to be as objective as possible. Learn about an issue from reliable sources and from multiple perspectives.

6⊖ Scholarly sources at a glance

1. Formal presentation with abstract and research methods

2. Includes review of previous research studies

3. Reports original research

4. Includes references

5. Multiple authors with academic credentials

FIRST PAGE OF ARTICLE

Cyberbullying: Using Virtual Scenarios to Educate and Raise Awareness

Vivian H. Wright, Joy J. Burnham, Christopher T. Inman, and Heather N. Ogorchock **5**

1 *Abstract*

This study examined cyberbullying in three distinct phases to facilitate a multifaceted understanding of cyberbullying. The phases included (a) a quantitative survey, (b) a qualitative focus group, and (c) development of educational scenarios/simulations (within the Second Life virtual environment). Phase III was based on adolescent feedback about cyberbullying from Phases I and II of this study. In all three phases, adolescent reactions to cyberbullying were examined and reported to raise awareness and to educate others about cyberbullying. Results from scenario development indicate that simulations created in a virtual environment are engaging and have the potential to be powerful tools in helping schools address problems such as cyberbullying education and prevention. (Keywords: cyberbullying, virtual worlds, Second Life, teacher education, counselor education)

cyberbullying, this study sought to examine cyberbullying through three phases: (a) a quantitative survey, (b) a qualitative focus group, and (c) development of the educational scenarios/simulations (i.e., using virtual world avatars similar to those used in Linden Lab's (1993) Second Life (SL; http://secondlife.com) based on adolescent feedback from Phases I and II of this study. Adolescent reactions to cyberbullying in all three phases of this study were examined and reported with two aims in mind: (a) to raise awareness of cyberbullying, and (b) to educate others about cyberbullying.

Introduction

Cyberbullying has gained attention and recognition in recent years (Beale & Hall, 2007; Carney, 2008; Casey-Canon, Hayward, & Gowen, 2001; Kowalski & Limber, 2007; Li, 2007; Shariff, 2005). The increased interest and awareness of cyberbullying relates to such factors as the national media attention after several published cyberbullying tragedies (Maag, 2007; Stelter, 2008; Zifcak, 2006), the attenuation of communication between individuals when using technology and computer networks as communication facilitators and mediators, the expansion of technology use among youth who may access and use technology and the easy access available to youth, presently there remains much to understand about how cyberbullying and its possible links to adolescents. Because cyberbullying occurs through interpersonal systems (i.e., home, school, and other), teachers, parents, school professionals" (Li, 2007, p. 1778), and mental health providers must not only be made aware of cyberbullying and its consequences, but must also have access to ways to deal with this growing concern.

Two years ago, cyberbullying was considered to be a "new territory" for exploration (Li, 2007, p. 1778) because there was limited information about bullying through "electronic means" (Li, p. 1780). In contrast, today studies on cyberbullying, including some descriptions of the more cyberbullying incidences (Maag, 2007; Stelter, 2008; Zifcak, 2006), are becoming more prevalent (Beale & Hall, 2007; Carney, 2008; Kowalski & Limber, 2007; Li, 2007). At this time, there is a need to raise awareness about the effects of cyberbullying and to create educational opportunities to serve multiple audiences (i.e., teachers, teacher educators, school administrators, school counselors, mental health professionals, students, parents) in the quest to identify and hopefully prevent cyberbullying in the future. Consequently, to facilitate a multifaceted understanding of

Defining Cyberbullying

Cyberbullying has been described as a traumatic experience that can lead to physical, cognitive, emotional, and social consequences (Carney, 2008; Casey-Canon et al., 2001; Patchin & Hinduja, 2006). Cyberbullying has been defined as "bullying through the e-mail, instant messaging, in a chat room, on a website, or though digital messages or images sent to a cell phone" (Kowalski & Limber, 2007, p. 822). There are numerous methods to engage in cyberbullying, including e-mail, instant messaging, online gaming, chat rooms, and text messaging (Beale & Hall, 2007; Li, 2007). In addition, cyberbullying appears in different forms than traditional bullying. For example, Beale and Hall (2007), Mason (2007), and Willard (2008) found that at least seven different types of cyberbullying exist, including:

2 Research suggests that cyberbullying has distinct gender and age differences. According to the literature, girls are more likely to be online and to cyberbully (Beale & Hall, 2007; Kowalski & Limber, 2007; Li, 2006, 2007). This finding is "opposite of what happens on line," where boys are

- information
- Exclusion: excluding someone purposefully

Research suggests that cyberbullying has distinct gender and age differences. According to the literature, girls are more likely to be online and more likely to bully than girls (Beale & Hall, p. 8). Age also appears to be a factor in cyberbullying. Cyberbullying increases in the elementary years, peaks during the middle school years, and declines in the high school years (Beale & Hall). Based on the literature, cyberbullying is a growing concern among middle school-aged children (Beale & Hall; Hinduja & Patchin, 2008; Kowalski & Limber, 2007; Li, 2007; Pellegrini & Bartini, 2000; Smith, Mahdavi, Carvalho, & Tippett, 2006; Williams & Guerra, 2007). Of the middle school grades, 6th grade students are usually the

Volume 26/ Number 1 Fall 2009 Journal of Computing in Teacher Education 35
Copyright © 2009 ISTE (International Society for Technology in Education), 800.336.5191 (U.S. & Canada) or 541.302.3777 (Int'l), iste@iste.org, www.iste.org

EXCERPTS FROM OTHER PAGES

3 Table 2: Percentage of Students Who Experienced Cyberbullying through Various Methods

	E-mail	Facebook	MySpace	Cell Phone	Online Video	Chat Rooms
Victim	35.3%	11.8%	52.9%	50%	14.7%	11.8%
Bully	17.6%	0%	70.6%	47.1%	11.8%	5.9%

4 **References**

Bainbridge, W. S. (2007, July). The scientific research potential of virtual worlds. *Science, 317,* 472–476.

Beale, A., & Hall, K. (2007, September/October). Cyberbullying:

5 *Vivian H. Wright is an associate professor of instructional technology at the University of Alabama. In addition to teaching in the graduate program, Dr. Wright works with teacher educators on innovative ways to infuse technology in the curriculum to*

6∂ Popular sources at a glance

1. Eye-catching title
2. Written by a staff reporter, not an expert
3. Presents anecdotes about the topic
4. Sources are named, but no formal works cited list appears
5. Presents a summary of research but no original research

ONLINE ARTICLE

Part of complete coverage on
Bullying   SPECIAL REPORT: BULLYING

When bullying goes high-tech

by Elizabeth Landau, CNN **2**
updated 2:12 PM EDT, Mon April 15, 2013

STORY HIGHLIGHTS
- As many as 25% of teenagers have experienced cyberbullying
- Among young people, it's rare that an online bully will be a total stranger
- Researchers are working on apps and algorithms to detect and report bullying online

(CNN) — Brandon Turley didn't have friends in sixth grade. He would often eat alone at lunch, having recently switched to his school without knowing anyone.

While browsing MySpace one day, he saw that someone from school had posted a bulletin — a message visible to multiple people — declaring that Turley was a "fag." Students he had never even spoken with wrote on it, too, saying they agreed.

EXCERPT FROM A LATER SECTION

A pervasive problem
As many as 25% of teenagers have experienced cyberbullying at some point, said Justin W. Patchin, who studies the phenomenon at the University of Wisconsin-Eau Claire. He and colleagues have conducted formal surveys of 15,000 middle and high school students throughout the United States, and found that about 10% of teens have been victims of cyberbullying in the last 30 days.

28c Assessing web sources with special care

Before using a web source in your project, make sure you know who created the material and for what purpose. Sources with reliable information can stand up to scrutiny. Ask questions such as these:

Authorship

- Is there an author? You may need to do some clicking and scrolling to find the author's name. Check the home page or an "About This Site" link.

- Can you tell whether the author is knowledgeable and credible? If the author's qualifications aren't listed on the site, look for links to the author's home page, which may provide evidence of any expertise.

Sponsorship

- Who, if anyone, sponsors the site? The sponsor of a site is often named and described on the home page.

- What does the URL tell you? The domain name extension often indicates the type of group hosting the site: commercial (.com), educational (.edu), non-profit (.org), governmental (.gov), military (.mil), or network (.net). A domain name extension may also indicate a country of origin: .uk (United Kingdom) or .jp (Japan), for instance.

Purpose and audience

- Why was the site created: To argue a position? To sell a product? To inform readers?

- Who is the site's intended audience?

Currency

- How current is the site? Check for the date of publication or the date of the latest update.

- How current are the site's links? If many of the links to other sites no longer work, the site may be too dated for your purposes.

28d Constructing an annotated bibliography

Constructing an annotated bibliography allows you to summarize, evaluate, and record publication information for your sources before drafting your research paper. You summarize each source to understand its main ideas; you evaluate each source to assess how it contributes to your research project; and you record bibliographic information to keep track of publication details for each source.

Take the following steps for each source in your annotated bibliography:

- **RECORD** Using the documentation style your assignment requires, record the publication information for your source.

- **SUMMARIZE** Start by identifying the purpose and thesis of the source and the author's credentials. Summarize the source's main ideas and the evidence used to support those ideas. Summarizing gives you an opportunity to test your understanding of the source's meaning.

- **EVALUATE** Ask yourself what role a source might play and how it will contribute to your argument. Did it shape your thinking? Provide key evidence? Lend authority? Offer a counterargument? Evaluate how and why the source is useful to help you answer your research question and support your position.

SAMPLE ANNOTATED BIBLIOGRAPHY ENTRY (MLA STYLE)

Resnik, David. "Trans Fat Bans and Human Freedom." | Record
The American Journal of Bioethics, vol. 10, no.
3, Mar. 2010, pp. 27–32.

In this scholarly article, bioethicist David | Summarize
Resnik argues that bans on unhealthy
foods threaten our personal freedom. He
claims that researchers don't have enough
evidence to know whether banning trans
fats will save lives or money; all we know
is that such bans restrict dietary choices.
Resnik explains why most Americans oppose
food restrictions, noting our multiethnic
and regional food traditions as well as our

Summarize   resistance to government limitations on personal freedoms. He acknowledges that few people would miss eating trans fats, but he fears that bans on such substances could lead to widespread restrictions on red meat, sugary sodas, and other foods known to have harmful effects.

Evaluate   Resnik offers a well-reasoned argument, but he goes too far by insisting that all proposed food restrictions will do more harm than good. This article contributes important perspectives on American resistance to government intervention in food choice and counters arguments in other sources that support the idea of food legislation to advance public health.

6∂ Annotated bibliographies **at a glance**

- **An organized list of sources arranged in alphabetical order by author** (or by title for works with no author) includes complete bibliographic information for each source.

- **A brief annotation or note for each source**, typically no longer than one paragraph, contains a summary and an evaluation. The annotation may be written in full sentences or as brief notes; check with your instructor for preferences.

- **The summary** of each source states the work's main ideas and key points and identifies the author's qualifications. The summary is written in present tense, third person, directly and concisely.

- **The evaluation** of the source's role and usefulness includes an assessment of the source's strengths and limitations, the author's qualifications and expertise, and the function of the source in helping you answer your research question.

MLA Papers

In English and other humanities courses, you may be asked to document your sources with the Modern Language Association (MLA) system of citations described in section 33. When writing an MLA paper that draws on sources, you will need to (1) support a thesis, (2) cite your sources and avoid plagiarism, and (3) integrate quotations and other source material effectively.

29 Supporting a thesis

▶ How to test your thesis **109**

Most research assignments ask you to form a thesis, or main idea, and to support that thesis with well-organized evidence.

29a Forming a thesis statement

Once you have read a variety of sources and considered your subject from different perspectives, you are ready to form a thesis—a one-sentence (or occasionally a two-sentence) statement of your central idea. The thesis states your position—an informed answer to your research question—about which reasonable people might disagree. Usually your thesis will appear at the end of the first paragraph (see p. 179).

As you learn more about your subject, your ideas may change, and your thesis will evolve, too. You can revise your initial thesis (or *working thesis*) as you draft.

In a research paper, your thesis will answer the central question that you pose, as in the following examples:

PUBLIC POLICY QUESTION

Should the government enact laws to regulate healthy eating choices?

THESIS

In the name of public health and safety, governments have the responsibility to shape health policies and to regulate healthy eating choices, especially since doing so offers a potentially large social benefit for a relatively small cost.

Test your thesis

When drafting and revising a thesis statement, make sure that it's suitable for your writing purpose and that you can successfully develop it with the sources available to you. The following guidelines will help you develop an effective thesis statement:

1 **A thesis should answer a research question and take a position that needs to be argued and supported.** It should not be a fact or a description. Make sure your position is debatable by considering other possible viewpoints and answers to your research question.

2 **A thesis should match the scope of the research project.** If your thesis is too broad, explore a subtopic of your original topic. If your thesis is too narrow, ask a research question that has more than one answer.

3 **A thesis should be focused.** Avoid vague words such as *interesting* or *good*. Use specific language and make sure readers know your position.

4 **A thesis should stand up to the "So what?" test.** Ask yourself why readers should be interested in your essay and care about your thesis.

LITERATURE QUESTION

What does Stephen Crane's short story "The Open Boat" reveal about the relationship between humans and nature?

THESIS

In Stephen Crane's gripping tale "The Open Boat," four men lost at sea discover not only that nature is indifferent to their fate but also that their own particular talents make little difference as they struggle for survival.

MEDIA STUDIES QUESTION

How does the shift from print to online news change the way readers engage with the news?

THESIS

The shift from print to online news provides opportunities for readers to become more engaged with the news, to hold journalists account-able, and to participate as producers, not simply as consumers.

Each of these thesis statements takes a stand on a debatable issue — an issue about which thoughtful, well-meaning people might disagree. In your paper, you will need to persuade such people — your readers — that your view is worth taking seriously.

29b Organizing your ideas

The body of your paper will consist of evidence in support of your thesis. Try sketching a plan to focus and organize your ideas, as student writer Sophie Harba did in this informal outline.

- Debates about the government's role in regulating food have a long history in the United States.

- Some experts argue that we should focus on the dangers of unhealthy eating habits and on preventing chronic diseases linked to diet.

- But food regulations are not a popular solution because many Americans object to government restrictions on personal choice.

- Food regulations designed to prevent chronic disease don't ask Americans to give up their freedom; they ask Americans to see health as a matter of public good.

After you have written a rough draft, a more formal outline can help you test and adjust the organization of your argument.

29c Using sources to inform and support your argument

As you consider the source materials you have gathered, ask yourself what you learned from each source and how the source might function to answer your research question. Sources can play many different roles to support your thesis and develop your argument.

Providing background information or context Describe a study or offer a statistic to help readers grasp the significance of your topic or understand generalizations about it.

Explaining terms or concepts Explain words, phrases, or ideas that might be unfamiliar to your readers. Quoting or paraphrasing a source can help you define terms and concepts in accessible language.

Supporting your claims Back up your assertions with facts, examples, and other evidence from your research.

Lending authority to your argument Expert opinion can give weight to your argument, but don't rely on experts to make your argument for you. Construct your argument in your own words and cite authorities in the field to support your position.

Anticipating and countering objections Do not ignore sources that seem to contradict your position or that offer arguments different from your own. Instead, use them to give voice to opposing points of view and to state potential objections to your argument before you counter them.

30 Avoiding plagiarism

▶ How to be a responsible research writer **115**

In a research paper, you draw on the work of other writers. To be fair and responsible, you must document their contributions by citing your sources. When you acknowledge and document your sources, you avoid plagiarism, a form of academic dishonesty. In general, these three acts are considered plagiarism:

1. failing to cite quotations and borrowed ideas
2. failing to enclose borrowed language in quotation marks
3. failing to put summaries and paraphrases in your own words

30a Citing quotations and borrowed ideas

When you cite sources, you give credit to writers from whom you've borrowed words and ideas. You must cite anything you borrow from a source, including direct quotations; statistics and other specific facts; visuals such as cartoons, graphs, and diagrams; and any ideas you present in a summary or a paraphrase. Your citation guides readers quickly to the source of a quoted, paraphrased, or summarized idea so that they can find and read the original source.

The only exception is common knowledge — information your readers likely already know or could easily find in general sources. When you have seen information repeatedly in your reading, you don't need to cite it. However, when information has appeared in only one or two sources, when it is highly specific (as with statistics), or when it is controversial, you should cite the source. If you're not sure whether you need to cite something, check with your instructor.

30b Using the MLA citation system to lead readers to your sources

MLA style requires you to use in-text citations within your paper to credit your sources and to refer your readers to more detailed citations of the sources in the works cited list at the end of your paper. Here, briefly, is how the MLA citation system usually works:

1. The source is introduced by a signal phrase that names its author.
2. The material being cited is followed by a page number in parentheses (unless the source is unpaginated).
3. At the end of the paper, a list of works cited, arranged alphabetically by authors' last names (or by titles if no authors are listed), gives complete publication information for the source.

IN-TEXT CITATION

Bioethicist David Resnik emphasizes that such policies "open
the door to excessive government control over food, which
could restrict dietary choices, interfere with cultural, ethnic,
and religious traditions, and exacerbate socioeconomic
inequalities" (31).

ENTRY IN THE LIST OF WORKS CITED

Resnik, David. "Trans Fat Bans and Human Freedom." *American
Journal of Bioethics*, vol. 10, no. 3, Mar. 2010, pp. 27–32.

NOTE: This basic MLA format varies for different types
of sources. For a detailed discussion and other models,
see 33.

30c Using quotation marks around borrowed language

To indicate that you are using a source's exact phrases
or sentences, you must enclose them in quotation
marks unless they have been set off from the text by
indenting (see p. 121). To omit the quotation marks
is to claim—falsely—that the language is your own.
Such an omission is plagiarism even if you have cited
the source. In the example below, the highlighted
strings of words have been copied directly from the
source without quotation marks.

ORIGINAL SOURCE

Although these policies may have a positive impact
on human health, they open the door to excessive
government control over food, which could restrict
dietary choices, interfere with cultural, ethnic, and
religious traditions, and exacerbate socioeconomic
inequalities.

—David Resnik, "Trans Fat Bans
and Human Freedom," p. 31

PLAGIARISM

Bioethicist David Resnik points out that policies to ban trans
fats may protect human health, but they open the door to
excessive government control over food, which might limit
available food options and interfere with cultural, ethnic, and
religious traditions (31).

BORROWED LANGUAGE IN QUOTATION MARKS

Bioethicist David Resnik points out that policies to ban trans fats may protect human health, but "they open the door to excessive government control over food," which might limit available food options and "interfere with cultural, ethnic, and religious traditions" (31).

30d Putting summaries and paraphrases in your own words

A summary condenses information from a source; a paraphrase conveys the information using roughly the same number of words as the original source. When you summarize or paraphrase, it is not enough to name the source. You must also restate the source's meaning in your own words and sentence structure. Half-copying the author's sentences either by using the author's phrases in your own sentences without quotation marks or by plugging synonyms into the author's sentence structure is a form of plagiarism.

The paraphrase below is plagiarized—even though the source is cited—because the paraphrase borrows too much of its language from the original. The high-lighted strings of words have been copied exactly (without quotation marks), and the writer has echoed the sentence structure of the source, merely substituting some synonyms (underlined).

ORIGINAL SOURCE

[A]ntiobesity laws encounter strong opposition from some quarters on the grounds that they constitute paternalistic intervention into lifestyle choices and enfeeble the notion of personal responsibility. Such arguments echo those made in the early days of tobacco regulation.

—Michelle M. Mello et al., "Obesity—the New Frontier of Public Health Law," p. 2602

PLAGIARISM: UNACCEPTABLE BORROWING

Health policy experts Mello and others argue that antiobesity laws encounter strong opposition from some people because they interfere with lifestyle choices and decrease the feeling of personal responsibility. These debates mirror those made in the early days of tobacco regulation (2602).

Be a responsible research writer

Using good citation habits is the best way to demonstrate that you are a responsible researcher.

1 Cite your sources as you write drafts. Don't wait until your final draft is complete to include in-text citations. Include a citation when you quote from a source, when you summarize or paraphrase, and when you borrow facts that are not common knowledge.

2 Check each quotation, summary, and paraphrase against the source to make sure you aren't misrepresenting the source. For paraphrases, also be sure that your language and sentence structure differ from those in the original passage.

3 Place quotation marks around direct quotations, both in your notes and in your drafts.

4 Provide a full citation in your works cited list. It is not sufficient to cite a source only in the body of your paper; you must also provide complete publication information for each source in a list of works cited.

To avoid plagiarizing an author's language, resist the temptation to look at the source while you are summarizing or paraphrasing. After you've restated the author's ideas in your own words, return to the source and check that you haven't used the author's language or sentence structure or misrepresented the author's ideas.

ACCEPTABLE PARAPHRASE

As health policy experts Mello and others point out, opposition to food and beverage regulation is similar to the opposition to early tobacco legislation: the public views the issue as one of personal responsibility rather than one requiring government intervention (2602).

31 Integrating sources

Quotations, summaries, paraphrases, and facts will help you develop your argument, but they cannot speak for you. Readers should always know who is speaking in your paper—you or your source. You can use several strategies to integrate sources into your paper while maintaining your own voice.

31a Summarizing and paraphrasing effectively

Summarizing   When you summarize a source, you express another writer's ideas in your own words, condensing the author's key points and using fewer words than the author did.

WHEN TO SUMMARIZE

• When a passage is lengthy and you want to condense a chapter to a short paragraph or a paragraph to a single sentence

• When you want to state the source's main ideas simply and briefly in your own words

- When you want to compare arguments or ideas from various sources
- When you want to provide readers with an understanding of the source's argument before you respond to it or launch your own argument

Paraphrasing   When you paraphrase, you express an author's ideas in your own words, using approximately the same number of words and details as in the source.

WHEN TO PARAPHRASE

- When the ideas and information are important but the author's exact words are not needed
- When you want to restate the source's ideas in your own words
- When you need to simplify or explain a technical or complicated source

31b Using quotations effectively

When you quote a source, you borrow some of the author's exact words and enclose them in quotation marks. Quotation marks show your readers that both the idea and the words belong to the author.

WHEN TO USE QUOTATIONS

- When language is especially vivid or expressive
- When exact wording is needed for accuracy
- When it is important to let the debaters of an issue explain their positions in their own words
- When the words of an authority lend weight to an argument
- When the language of a source is the topic of your discussion

Limiting your use of quotations   Keep the emphasis on your own ideas. It is not always necessary to quote full sentences from a source. Often you can integrate words or phrases from a source into your own sentence structure.

Resnik acknowledges that his argument relies on "slippery slope" thinking, but he insists that "social and political pressures" regarding food regulations make his concerns valid (31).

Paraphrase effectively

A paraphrase shows your readers that you understand a source and can explain it to them. When you choose to paraphrase a passage, you use the information and ideas of a source for your own purpose — to provide background information, explain a concept, or advance your argument — and yet maintain your voice. It is challenging to write a paraphrase that isn't a word-for-word translation of the original source and doesn't imitate the source's sentence structure. These strategies will help you paraphrase effectively.

1 **Understand the source.** Identify the source's key points and argument. Test your understanding by asking questions: What is being said? Why and how is it being said? Look up words you don't know to help you understand whole ideas.

ORIGINAL
People's vision of the world has broadened with the advent of global media such as television and the Internet. Those thinking about going elsewhere can see what the alternatives are and appear to have fewer inhibitions about resettling.

> — Darrell M. West, *Brain Gain: Rethinking U.S. Immigration Policy*, Brookings Institution Press, 2011, p. 5

STUDENT'S NOTES
–TV and Internet have opened our eyes, our minds
–We can imagine making big moves (country to country) as we never could before; the web offers a preview
–"resettling" = moving to a new location, out of the familiar region
– Lessens the anxiety about starting over in a new place

2 **Use your own vocabulary and sentence structure** to convey the source's information. Check to make sure there is no overlap in vocabulary or sentence structure with the original.

> Since TV and the web can offer a preview of life in other places, people feel less uncertainty and anxiety about making moves from one area of the world to another.

3 Use a signal phrase to identify the source (*According to X, _____, or X argues that _____*).

> West argues that since TV and the web can offer a preview of life in other places, people feel less uncertainty and anxiety about making moves from one area of the world to another.

4 Include a citation to give credit to the source. Even though the words are yours, you need to give credit for the idea. Here, the author's name and the page number on which the original passage appeared are listed.

> West argues that since TV and the web can offer a preview of life in other places, people feel less uncertainty and anxiety about making moves from one area of the world to another (5).

NOTE: If you choose to use exact language from the source in a paraphrase, be sure to put quotation marks around any borrowed words or phrases.

> West argues that since TV and the web can offer a preview of life in other places, people "have fewer inhibitions" about making moves from one area of the world to another (5).

Using the ellipsis mark To condense a quoted passage, you can use an ellipsis—a series of three spaced periods—to indicate that you have omitted words. What remains must be grammatically complete.

In Mississippi, legislators passed "a ban on bans — a law that forbids . . . local restrictions on food or drink" (Conly A23).

The writer has omitted from the source the words *municipalities to place* before *local restrictions* to condense the quoted material.

If you want to leave out one or more full sentences, use a period before the ellipsis.

Legal scholars Gostin and Gostin argue that "individuals have limited willpower to defer immediate gratification for longer-term health benefits. . . . A person understands that high-fat foods or a sedentary lifestyle will cause adverse health effects, or that excessive spending or gambling will cause financial hardship, but it is not always easy to refrain" (217).

Ordinarily, do not use an ellipsis at the beginning or at the end of a quotation. Your readers will understand that you have taken the quoted material from a longer passage. The only exception occurs when you have dropped words at the end of the final quoted sentence. In such cases, put an ellipsis before the closing quotation mark and the parenthetical reference.

USING SOURCES RESPONSIBLY: Make sure that omissions and ellipses do not distort the meaning of your source.

6∂ Punctuating quotations at a glance

Integrating sources smoothly into your own sentences is easier when you follow guidelines about using periods, commas, and question marks with quotation marks.

Quotation with no page number, author mentioned in sentence

- The ban, according to MacMillan, "gave consumers a healthier default option."
- The ban "gave consumers a healthier default option," according to MacMillan.

Quotation with no page number, author's name in parentheses

- The ban "gave consumers a healthier default option" (Macmillan).

Quotation with page number

- Fortin notes that instead of a ban, the FDA "took a more moderate approach" (113).

Quotation within a writer's own question

- Why did the FDA choose "a more moderate approach" (Fortin 113)?

Quotation that is itself a question

- Fortin begins with a key question: "Why do we have food laws?" (3).

Long quotation

Hilts argues that Americans have faith in the FDA:

> The Roper Organization has tracked the FDA and government issues consistently, and found that among all government agencies, the FDA has been among the most popular, and routinely number one among regulatory agencies. (295)

NOTE: APA-style citations also require the source's year of publication. See 38a.

Using brackets   Brackets allow you to insert your own words into quoted material to clarify a confusing reference or to keep a sentence grammatical in your context.

Neergaard and Agiesta argue that "a new poll finds people are split on how much the government should do to help [find solutions to the national health crisis] — and most draw the line at attempts to force healthier eating."

To indicate an error such as a misspelling in a quotation, insert [sic] with brackets around it right after the error.

Setting off long quotations   When you quote more than four typed lines of a paragraph or more than three lines of poetry, set off the quotation by indenting it one-half inch from the left margin.

Long quotations should be introduced by an informative sentence, usually followed by a colon. Quotation marks are unnecessary because the indented format tells readers that the passage is taken word-for-word from the source. At the end of an indented quotation, the parenthetical citation goes outside the final mark of punctuation. See page 120 for an example.

31c Using signal phrases to integrate sources

When you include a paraphrase, summary, or direct quotation of another writer's work in your paper, prepare your readers for it with introductory words called a *signal phrase*. A signal phrase usually names the author of the source, provides some context for the source material (such as the author's credentials), and helps readers distinguish your ideas from those of the source. (See the chart on page 124 for a list of verbs commonly used in signal phrases.)

Marking boundaries   Readers need to move smoothly from your words to the words of a source. Avoid dropping a quotation into the text without warning. Provide a clear signal phrase, including at least the author's name, to indicate the boundary between your words and the source's words.

DROPPED QUOTATION

Laws designed to prevent chronic disease by promoting healthier food and beverage consumption also have potential economic benefits. "[A] 1% reduction in the intake of saturated fat across the population would prevent more than 30,000 cases of coronary heart disease annually and would save more than a billion dollars in health care costs" (Nestle 7).

QUOTATION WITH SIGNAL PHRASE

Laws designed to prevent chronic disease by promoting healthier food and beverage consumption also have potential economic benefits. Marion Nestle, New York University professor of nutrition and public health, notes that "a 1% reduction in the intake of saturated fat across the population would prevent more than 30,000 cases of coronary heart disease annually and would save more than a billion dollars in health care costs" (7).

Establishing authority The first time you mention a source, include in the signal phrase the author's title, credentials, or experience to help your readers recognize the source's authority and your own credibility as a responsible researcher who has located reliable sources.

SOURCE WITH NO CREDENTIALS

Michael Pollan notes that "[t]he Centers for Disease Control estimates that fully three quarters of US health care spending goes to treat chronic diseases, most of which are preventable and linked to diet: heart disease, stroke, type 2 diabetes, and at least a third of all cancers."

SOURCE WITH CREDENTIALS

Journalist Michael Pollan, who has written extensively about Americans' unhealthy eating habits, notes that "[t]he Centers for Disease Control estimates that fully three quarters of US health care spending goes to treat chronic diseases, most of which are preventable and linked to diet: heart disease, stroke, type 2 diabetes, and at least a third of all cancers."

Introducing summaries and paraphrases Introduce most summaries and paraphrases with a signal phrase that names the author and places the material in the context of your argument. Readers will then understand that everything between the signal phrase and the parenthetical citation summarizes or paraphrases the cited source.

Without the signal phrase (highlighted) in the following example, readers might think that only the quotation at the end is being cited, when in fact the whole paragraph is based on the source.

To improve public health, advocates such as Bowdoin College philosophy professor Sarah Conly contend that it is the government's duty to prevent people from making harmful choices, whenever feasible and whenever public benefits outweigh the costs. In response to critics who claim that laws aimed at stopping us from eating whatever we want are an assault on our freedom of choice, Conly asserts that "laws aren't designed for each one of us individually" (A23).

Sometimes a summary or a paraphrase does not require a signal phrase. When the context makes clear where the cited material begins, you may omit the signal phrase and include the author's last name in parentheses.

According to a nationwide poll, seventy-five percent of Americans are opposed to laws that restrict or put limitations on access to healthy foods (Neergaard and Agiesta).

Integrating statistics and other facts   When you cite a statistic or another specific fact, a signal phrase is often not necessary. Readers usually will understand that the citation refers to the statistic or fact (not the whole paragraph.)

Seat belt use saved an average of more than fourteen thousand lives per year in the United States between 2000 and 2010 (United States, Department of Transportation 231).

Putting source material in context   Readers should not have to guess why source material appears in your paper. A signal phrase can help you connect your own ideas with those of another writer by clarifying how the source will contribute to your paper. For guidance on integrating source material with your own sentences, see the box on page 125.

𝟞𝟃 Signal phrases **at a glance** MLA

To avoid monotony, try to vary both the language and the placement of your signal phrases.

Model signal phrases

Michael Pollan, who has written extensively about Americans' unhealthy eating habits, argues . . .

Marion Nestle, New York University professor of nutrition and public health, notes . . .

As health policy experts Mello and others point out, ". . ."

In response to critics, Conley offers a persuasive counterargument: ". . ."

Bioethicist David Resnik emphasizes ". . ."

Verbs in signal phrases

Are you providing background, explaining a concept, supporting a claim, lending authority, or refuting a belief? Choose a verb that is appropriate for the way you are using the source.

acknowledges	contends	insists
adds	declares	notes
admits	denies	observes
agrees	describes	points out
argues	disputes	refutes
asserts	emphasizes	rejects
believes	endorses	reports
claims	grants	responds
compares	illustrates	suggests
confirms	implies	writes

NOTE: In MLA style, use the present tense or present perfect tense (*argues* or *has argued*) to introduce source material unless you include a date or other marker that specifies the time of the original author's writing.

If you use another writer's words, you must explain how they relate to your argument. Quotations don't speak for themselves; you must create a context for readers. Sandwich each quotation between sentences of your own, introducing the quotation with a signal phrase and following it with interpretive comments that link the quotation to your paper's argument.

QUOTATION WITH EFFECTIVE CONTEXT (QUOTATION SANDWICH)

In response to critics who claim that laws aimed at stopping us from eating whatever we want are an assault on our freedom of choice, Conly offers a persuasive counterargument:

> [L]aws aren't designed for each one of us individually. Some of us can drive safely at 90 miles per hour, but we're bound by the same laws as the people who can't, because individual speeding laws aren't practical. Giving up a little liberty is something we agree to when we agree to live in a democratic society that is governed by laws. (A23)

As Conly suggests, we need to change our either/or thinking (either we have complete freedom of choice *or* we have govern-ment regulations and lose our freedom) and instead see health as a matter of public good, not individual liberty.

6∂ Using sentence guides **at a glance**

These guides act as academic sentence starters. They show you how to use signal phrases in sen-tences to make clear to your reader whose ideas you're presenting — your own or those you have encountered in a source.

Presenting others' ideas The following language will help you demonstrate your understanding of a source by summarizing the views or arguments of its author:

X argues that _____.

X and Y emphasize the need for _____.

Presenting direct quotations To introduce the exact words of a source, you might try phrases like these:

X describes the problem this way: "_____."

Y argues in favor of the policy, pointing out that "_____."

Continued ➔

6∂ Using sentence guides at a glance
(continued)

Presenting alternative ideas At times you will have to synthesize the ideas of multiple sources before you introduce your own:

While X and Y have asked an important question, Z suggests that we should be asking a different question: _____?

X has argued that Y's research findings rest upon questionable assumptions _____ and _____.

Presenting your own ideas by agreeing or extending You may agree with the author of a source but want to add your own voice to extend the point or go deeper. The following phrases could be useful:

X's argument is convincing because _____.

Y claimed that _____. But isn't it also true that _____?

Presenting your own ideas by disagreeing and questioning College writing assignments encourage you to show your understanding of a subject but also to question or challenge ideas and conclusions about the subject. This language can help:

X's claims about _____ are misguided.

Y insists that _____, but perhaps she is asking the wrong question.

Presenting and countering objections to your argument To anticipate objections that readers might make, try the following sentence guides:

Not everyone will endorse this argument; some may argue instead that _____.

Some will object to this proposal on the grounds that _____.

NOTE: If you are following APA style, include the year of publication after the source's name and use past tense or present perfect tense (*emphasized* or *have emphasized*). See 37.

31d Synthesizing sources

When you synthesize multiple sources in a research paper, you create a conversation about your research topic. You show readers that your argument is based on your analysis and is not just a series of quotations and paraphrases strung together. The thread of your argument should be easy to identify and to understand, with or without your sources.

In the sample synthesis below, Sophie Harba uses her own analyses to shape the conversation among her sources. She does not simply string quotations together or allow sources to overwhelm her writing. She finds commonalities among her sources, acknowledges the contributions of others in the research conversation, and shows readers, in her own voice, how the various sources support her argument.

SAMPLE SYNTHESIS

❶ Why is the public largely resistant to laws that would limit unhealthy choices or penalize those choices with so-called fat taxes? Many consumers and civil rights advocates find such laws to be an unreasonable restriction on individual freedom of choice. As health policy experts Mello and others point out, opposition to food and beverage regulation is similar to the opposition to early tobacco legislation: the public views the issue as one of personal responsibility rather than one requiring **❸** government intervention (2602). In other words, if people eat unhealthy food and become ill as a result, that is their choice. But those who favor legislation claim that freedom of choice is a myth because of the strong influence of food and beverage industry marketing on consumers' **❹** dietary habits. According to one nonprofit health advocacy group, food and beverage companies spend roughly two billion dollars per year marketing directly to children. As a result, kids see about four thousand ads per year encouraging them to consume unhealthy

Student writer (❶)

Source 1 (❷)

Student writer (❸)

Source 2 (❹)

Continued ➜

---

1 Student writer Sophie Harba sets up her synthesis with a question.

2 A signal phrase indicates how the source contributes to Harba's argument and shows that the idea that follows is not her own.

3 Harba interprets a paraphrased source.

4 Harba uses a source to support her counterargument.

food and drinks ("Facts"). As was the case with   **Student writer**
antismoking laws passed in recent decades, taxes
and legal restrictions on junk food sales could
help to counter the strong marketing messages
that promote unhealthy products.

The United States has a history of
state and local public health laws that have
successfully promoted a particular behavior by
punishing an undesirable behavior. The decline
in tobacco use as a result of antismoking taxes
and laws is perhaps the most obvious example.
Another example is legislation requiring the use
of seat belts, which have significantly reduced
❺ fatalities in car crashes. One government agency | Source 3
reports that seat belt use saved an average of
more than fourteen thousand lives per year
in the United States between 2000 and 2010
(United States, Department of Transportation
231). Perhaps seat belt laws have public support
because the cost of wearing a seat belt is small,   **Student writer**
especially when compared with the benefit of
saving fourteen thousand lives per year.

---

5 Harba extends the argument with a statistic and follows it with an interpretive comment.

6a Synthesizing sources **at a glance**

When synthesizing sources, ask yourself:

- How do your sources address your research question? How do they support the points you want to make?

- How do your sources speak to one another? Do they support, extend, or counter each other? What common information or arguments do you see among your sources?

- Is your own argument easy to identify and to understand, with or without your sources?

32 Integrating literary quotations

When you are writing about literary works, the advice in section 31 about integrating quotations generally applies. This section provides guidance for situations that are unique to literary quotations. Parenthetical citations at the ends of examples are written in MLA style (see pp. 143–45 for specific guidelines on citing literary works).

32a Introducing quotations from literary works

When writing about a single work of literature, you do not need to include the author's name each time you quote from the work. Mention the author's name in the introduction to your paper; then refer, as appropriate, to the narrator of a story, the speaker of a poem, or the characters in a play. Do not confuse the author of the work with the narrator, speaker, or characters.

CONFUSING

Poet Andrew Marvell describes his fear of death like this: "But at my back I always hear / Time's wingèd chariot hurrying near" (21–22).

REVISED

Addressing his beloved in an attempt to win her sexual favors, the speaker of the poem argues that death gives them no time to waste: "But at my back I always hear / Time's wingèd chariot hurrying near" (21–22).

32b Avoiding shifts in tense

Because it is conventional to write about literature in the present tense (see p. 27) and because literary works often use other tenses, you will need to exercise some care when weaving quotations into your own text. A first-draft attempt may result in an awkward shift, as it did for one student who was writing about Nadine Gordimer's short story "Friday's Footprint."

TENSE SHIFT

When Rita sees Johnny's relaxed attitude, "she blushed, like a wave of illness" (159).

To avoid the distracting shift from present tense (*sees*) to past tense (*blushed*), the writer decided to paraphrase the reference to Rita's blushing and reduce the length of the quotation.

REVISED

When Rita sees Johnny's relaxed attitude, she is overcome with embarrassment, "like a wave of illness" (159).

The writer could have changed the quotation to the present tense, using brackets to indicate the change: *When Rita sees Johnny's relaxed attitude, "she blushe[s], like a wave of illness" (159).* (See also p. 121 for the use of brackets.)

32c Formatting and citing literary passages

MLA guidelines for formatting and citing quotations differ somewhat for short stories or novels, poems, and plays.

Short stories or novels If a quotation from a short story or a novel takes up four or fewer typed lines in your paper, put it in quotation marks and run it into the text of your essay. Include a page number in parentheses after the quotation.

The narrator of Eudora Welty's "Why I Live at the P.O.," known to us only as "Sister," makes many catty remarks about her enemies. For example, she calls Mr. Whitaker "this photographer with the pop-eyes" (46).

If a quotation from a short story or a novel is five typed lines or longer in your paper, set the quotation off from the text by indenting it one-half inch from the left margin; do not use quotation marks. (See also p. 121.) Put the page number in parentheses after the final mark of punctuation.

Sister's tale begins with "I," and she makes every event revolve around herself, even her sister's marriage:

> I was getting along fine with Mama, Papa-Daddy, and Uncle Rondo until my sister Stella-Rondo just separated from her husband and came back home again.

Mr. Whitaker! Of course I went with Mr. Whitaker first, when he first appeared here in China Grove, taking "Pose Yourself" photos, and Stella-Rondo broke us up. (46)

Poems   Enclose quotations of three or fewer lines of poetry in quotation marks within your text, and indicate line breaks with a slash with a space on each side. (Indicate a break between stanzas with a double slash.) Include line numbers in parentheses at the end of the quotation. For the first reference in the paper, use the word "lines." For following references, use just numbers.

The opening of Lewis Carroll's "The Aged Aged Man" strikes a conversational tone: "I'll tell thee everything I can; / There's little to relate" (lines 1–2).

When you quote four or more lines of poetry, set the quotation off from the text by indenting it one-half inch and omit the quotation marks. Put the line number(s) in parentheses after the final mark of punctuation.

In the second stanza of his poem "London," William Blake argues that the city's inhabitants are bound to their plight by urban regulations and their inability to see beyond their own suffering:

> In every cry of every Man,
> In every Infants cry of fear,
> In every voice: in every ban,
> The mind-forg'd manacles I hear (lines 5–8)

Plays   If a quotation from a play takes up four or fewer typed lines in your paper and is spoken by only one character, put quotation marks around it and run it into the text of your paper. Whenever possible, include the act number, scene number, and line number(s) in parentheses at the end of the quotation. Separate the numbers with periods and use arabic numerals unless your instructor prefers roman numerals.

Two attendants silently watch as the sleepwalking Lady Macbeth subconsciously struggles with her guilt: "Here's the smell of the blood still. All the perfumes of Arabia will not sweeten this little hand" (5.1.50–51).

33 MLA documentation style

In English and other humanities classes, you may be asked to use the MLA (Modern Language Association) system for documenting sources, which is set forth in the *MLA Handbook*, 9th edition (MLA, 2021). MLA recommends in-text citations (33a) that refer readers to a list of works cited at the end of the paper (33b).

🔊 MLA documentation at a glance

The MLA system of documentation requires an in-text citation and a works cited entry for each source you use in a paper. These parts work together to credit your sources and to help readers find the sources for themselves. For each source you use, you should have

- an **in-text citation**, made up of two elements: a *signal phrase* and a *parenthetical citation*. These elements introduce the source, name the author, and provide a page number for the information (if the source is paginated). (See 33a for how to use in-text citations in different situations.) The information in the in-text citation points readers to

- the **works cited entry** in your works cited list at the end of the paper. Each entry includes the full bibliographic information for the source, such as the author, title, date, and publisher or URL or DOI. (See 33b for what information to include for different types of sources.)

In each example below—the first a paraphrase from a paginated academic journal, the second a quotation from an unpaginated online magazine—the information that connects the two parts is underlined.

IN-TEXT CITATION (within the body of your paper)

Provost and Gerber explain that bureaucrats are often hesitant to create environmental regulations because of a lack of solid scientific data, or the inability to interpret that data, understand its consequences, and translate it into policy (330–31).

WORKS CITED ENTRY (in a list at the end of your paper)

Provost, Colin, and Brian J. Gerber. "Political Control and Policy-Making Uncertainty in Executive Orders: The Implementation of Environmental Justice Policy." *Journal of Public Policy,* vol. 39 no. 2, June 2019, pp. 329–58, https://doi.org/10.1017 /S0143814X18000077.

IN-TEXT CITATION

Weaver points out that the five-month trip taken by the Donner party in 1847 "could be done in under two hours by a Honda Accord today, assuming normal traffic, while a plane from Springfield, Ill., their starting point, to Sacramento would zoom over their whole route in half a day, including layover."

WORKS CITED ENTRY

Weaver, Caity. "We're All in This Together: The Particular Sheen of America by Amtrak." *The New York Times Magazine,* 20 Mar. 2019, www.nytimes.com/interactive /2019/03/20/magazine/train-across-america -amtrak.html.

33a MLA in-text citations

MLA in-text citations are made with a combination of signal phrases and parenthetical references. A signal phrase introduces information taken from a source (a quotation, summary, paraphrase, or fact); usually the signal phrase includes the author's name. The parenthetical reference comes after the cited material, often at the end of the sentence. It includes at least a page number (except for unpaginated sources, such as those found on the web). In the models in this section, the elements of the in-text citation are highlighted.

General guidelines for signal phrases and page numbers   Items 1–5 explain how the MLA system usually works for all sources—in print, on the web, in other media, and with or without authors and page numbers. Items 6–25 give variations on the basic guidelines.

List of MLA in-text citation models

List of MLA works cited models

Continued ➜

● **1. Author named in a signal phrase**   Ordinarily, introduce the material being cited with a signal phrase that includes the author's name. In addition to preparing readers for the source, the signal phrase allows you to keep the parenthetical citation brief.

> According to Lorine Goodwin, a food historian, nineteenth-century reformers who sought to purify the food supply were called "fanatics" and "radicals" by critics who argued that consumers should be free to buy and eat what they want (77).

The signal phrase *According to Lorine Goodwin* names the author; the parenthetical citation gives the number of the page on which the quoted words may be found.

Notice that the period follows the parenthetical citation. When a quotation ends with a question mark or an exclamation point, leave the end punctuation inside the quotation mark and add a period at the end of your sentence, after the parenthetical citation.

> Burgess asks a critical question: "How can we think differently about food labeling?" (51).

● **2. Author named in parentheses**   If you do not give the author's name in a signal phrase, put the last name in parentheses with the page number (if the source has one). Use no punctuation between the name and the page number: (Moran 351).

> According to a nationwide poll, seventy-five percent of Americans are opposed to laws that restrict or put limitations on access to unhealthy foods (Neergaard and Agiesta).

● **3. Author unknown**   If a source has no author, the works cited entry will begin with the title. In your in-text citation, either use the complete title in a signal phrase or use a short form of the title in parentheses. Titles of books and other long works are italicized; titles of articles and other short works are put in quotation marks.

> As a result, kids see nearly four thousand ads per year encouraging them to eat unhealthy food and drinks ("Facts").

NOTE: If the author is a corporation or a government agency, see items 8 and 16.

● **4. Page number unknown**   Do not include the page number if a work lacks page numbers, as is the case with many web sources. Do not use page numbers from a printout from a website. (When the pages of a web source are stable, as in PDF files, supply a page number in your in-text citation.)

> Michael Pollan points out that "cheap food" actually has "significant costs — to the environment, to public health, to the public purse, even to the culture."

If a source has numbered paragraphs or sections, use "par." (or "pars.") or "sec." (or "secs.") in the parentheses: (Smith, par. 4). If you cite an audiovisual source (such as a video), include a time stamp for the material you have quoted or paraphrased: (00:08:31–40).

● **5. One-page source**   If the source is one page long, do not include the page number in your in-text citation. You should, however, include the page number in your works cited list entry.

> Sarah Conly uses John Stuart Mill's "harm principle" to argue that citizens need their government to intervene to prevent them from taking harmful actions — such as driving too fast or buying unhealthy foods — out of ignorance of the harm they can do. But government intervention may overstep in the case of food choices.

Variations on the general guidelines   Items 6–25 describe the MLA guidelines for handling a variety of situations not covered in items 1–5.

● **6. Two authors**   Name the authors in a signal phrase, as in the following example, or include their last names in the parenthetical citation: (Gostin and Gostin 214).

> As legal scholars Gostin and Gostin explain, "[I]nterventions that do not pose a truly significant burden on individual liberty" are justified if they "go a long way towards safeguarding the health and well-being of the populace" (214).

● **7. Three or more authors**   In a parenthetical citation, give the first author's name followed by "et al." (Latin for "and others"). In a signal phrase, give the first author's name followed by a phrase such as "and others."

> The clinical trials were extended for two years, and only after results were reviewed by an independent panel did the researchers publish their findings (Blaine et al. 35). Researchers Blaine and others note that clinical trial results were reviewed by an independent panel (35).

● **8. Organization as author**   When the author is a corporation or an organization, name that author either in the signal phrase or in the parenthetical citation. (For a government agency as author, see item 16.)

> The American Diabetes Association estimates that the cost of diagnosed diabetes in the United States in 2012 was $245 billion.

In the list of works cited, the American Diabetes Association is treated as the author and alphabetized under *A*. When you give the organization name in the text, spell out the name; when you use it in parentheses, shorten the name to the first noun and any preceding adjectives, removing initial articles (*A, An, The*).

> The cost of diagnosed diabetes in the United States in 2012 was estimated at $245 billion (American Diabetes).

● **9. Authors with the same last name**   If your list of works cited includes works by two or more authors with the same last name, include the author's first name in the signal phrase or first initial in the parentheses.

> One approach to the problem is to introduce nutrition literacy at the elementary level in public schools (E. Chen 15).

● **10. Two or more works by the same author**   Mention the title of the work in the signal phrase or include a short version of the title in the parentheses.

> The American Diabetes Association tracks trends in diabetes across age groups. In 2012, more than 200,000 children and adolescents had diabetes ("Fast Facts"). Because of an expected dramatic increase in diabetes in young people over the next forty years, the association encourages "strategies for implementing childhood obesity prevention programs and primary prevention programs for youth at risk of developing type 2 diabetes" ("Number").

Titles of articles and other short works are placed in quotation marks; titles of books and other long works are italicized.

In the rare case when both the author's name and a short title must be given in parentheses, separate them with a comma.

> Researchers have estimated that "the number of youth with type 2 [diabetes] could quadruple and the number with type 1 could triple" by 2050, "with an increasing proportion of youth with diabetes from minority populations" (American Diabetes, "Number").

● **11. Two or more works in one citation**   To cite more than one source in the parentheses, list the authors (or titles) in alphabetical order and separate them with semicolons.

> The prevalence of early-onset type 2 diabetes has been well documented (Finn 68; Sharma 2037; Whitaker 118).

● **12. Repeated citations from the same source** When you are writing about a single work, you do not need to include the author's name each time you quote from or paraphrase the work. After you mention the author's name at the beginning of your paper, you may include just the page number in your parenthetical citations.

> Family expectations are at the heart of *Everything I Never Told You*, a debut novel in which a daughter shrinks from a mother who forces her to read books on science and medicine "to inspire her, to show her what she could accomplish" (Ng 73). But teenage Lydia commits herself to standing up to her overbearing mother, promising that "she will tell her mother: enough" (274).

In a paper with multiple sources, if you are citing a source more than once in a paragraph, you may omit the author's name after the first mention in the paragraph as long as it is clear that you are still referring to the same source.

● **13. Encyclopedia or dictionary entry** When an encyclopedia or dictionary entry does not have an author, either in your text or in your parenthetical citation, mention the entry and give the number of the page on which the entry may be found.

> The word *crocodile* has a complex etymology ("Crocodile" 139).

● **14. Entire work** Use the author's name in a signal phrase or a parenthetical citation. There is no need to use a page number.

> Pollan explores the issues surrounding food production and consumption from a political angle.

● **15. Selection in an anthology or a collection** Put the name of the author of the selection (not the editor of the anthology) in the signal phrase or the parentheses.

> In "Love Is a Fallacy," the narrator's logical teachings disintegrate when Polly declares that she should date Petey because "[h]e's got a raccoon coat" (Shulman 372).

In the list of works cited, the work is alphabetized under *Shulman*, the author of the story, not under the name of the editor of the anthology. (See item 29 in 33b.)

● **16. Government document** In a signal phrase, include the name of the agency or governing body as given in the works cited list. In a parenthetical citation, shorten the name.

> In fact, the amount of money the United States spends to treat chronic illnesses is increasing so rapidly that the Centers for Disease Control has labeled chronic disease "the public health challenge of the 21st century" (National Center 1).

If you cite more than one agency or department from the same government in your essay, you may choose to standardize the names by beginning with the governing nation (see item 57 in 33b). In that case, when shortening names of government agencies, give enough of the name to differentiate the authors: (United States, Department of Transportation); (United States, Environmental Protection).

● **17. Historical document**   When you discuss a historic document such as the U.S. Constitution in your writing, provide the document title, neither italicized nor in quotation marks, along with relevant article and section numbers. In parenthetical citations, use abbreviations such as "art." and "sec."

> While the Constitution provides for the formation of new states (art. 4, sec. 3), it does not explicitly allow or prohibit the secession of states.

Titles of constitutions and other historical documents are treated differently in the works cited list (see item 57 in 33b).

● **18. Legal source**   For a legislative act (law) or court case, name the act or case either in a signal phrase or in parentheses. Italicize the names of cases but not the names of acts. (See also items 58 and 59 in 33b.)

> The CARES Act of 2020 provided loans for small businesses.

> *Dred Scott v. Sandford*, which concluded that both free and enslaved Black people could not be citizens of the United States, may have been the US Supreme Court's worst decision.

● **19. Visual such as a table, a chart, or another graphic**   To cite a visual that has a figure number in the original source, use the abbreviation "fig." and the number in place of a page number in your parenthetical citation: (Manning, fig. 4). If you refer to the figure in your text, spell out the word "figure."

To cite a visual that appears in a print source without a figure number, use the visual's title or a description in your text and cite the author and page number as for any other source.

For a visual not in a print source, identify the visual in your text and then in parentheses use the first element in the works cited entry: the artist's or photographer's name or the title of the work. (See items 51–55 in 33b.)

> Photographs such as *Woman Aircraft Worker* (Bransby) and *Women Welders* (Parks) demonstrate the US government's attempt to document the contributions of women during World War II.

● **20. Personal communication and social media** Cite personal letters, personal interviews, email messages, and social media posts by the name listed in the works cited entry, as you would for any other source. Identify the type of source in your text if you think it is necessary for clarity. (See items 60–64 in 33b.)

● **21. Web source** Your in-text citation for a source from the web should follow the same guidelines as for other sources. If the source lacks page numbers but has numbered paragraphs, sections, or divisions, use those numbers with the appropriate abbreviation in your parenthetical citation: "par.," "sec.," "ch.," "pt.," and so on. Do not add such numbers if the source itself does not use them; simply give the author or title in your in-text citation.

> Sanjay Gupta, CNN chief medical correspondent, explains that "limited access to fresh, affordable, healthy food" is one of America's most pressing health problems.

● **22. Indirect source (source quoted in another source)** When a writer's or a speaker's quoted words appear in a source written by someone else, begin the parenthetical citation with the abbreviation "qtd. in." In the following example, Gostin and Gostin are the authors of the source given in the works cited list; their work contains a quotation by Beauchamp.

> Public health researcher Dan Beauchamp has said that "public health practices are communal in nature, and concerned with the well-being of the community as a whole and not just the well-being of any particular person" (qtd. in Gostin and Gostin 217).

Literary works and sacred texts Literary works and sacred texts are usually available in a variety of editions. Your list of works cited will specify which edition you are using, and your in-text citation will usually consist of a page number from the edition you consulted (see item 23). When possible, give enough information so that readers can locate the cited passage in any edition of the work, as described below.

● **23. Literary work without line numbers** If a literary work has numbered divisions, include the page number followed by a semicolon and the section, part, or chapter number(s). For a play, include the act/and or scene numbers after the page number: (37; sc. 1).

> In utter despair, Dostoyevsky's character Mitya wonders aloud about the "terrible tragedies realism inflicts on people" (376; bk. 8, ch. 2).

● **24. Verse play or poem** For verse plays, give act, scene, and line numbers. Use arabic numerals and separate the numbers with periods.

> In Shakespeare's *King Lear*, Gloucester learns a profound lesson from a tragic experience: "A man may see how this world goes / with no eyes" (4.2.148–49).

For a poem, cite the part, stanza, and line numbers, if it has them, separated by periods.

> The Green Knight claims to approach King Arthur's court "because the praise of you, prince, is puffed so high, / And your manor and your men are considered so magnificent" (1.12.258–59).

For poems that are not divided into numbered parts or stanzas, use line numbers. For the first citation, use the word "lines": (lines 5–8). Thereafter use just the numbers: (12–13).

● **25. Sacred text** When citing a sacred text such as the Bible or the Qur'an, name the edition you are using in your works cited entry (see item 33 in 33b). In your parenthetical citation, give the book and then the chapter and verse (or their equivalent), separated with a period. Common abbreviations for books of the Bible are acceptable.

Consider the words of Solomon: "If your enemy is hungry, give him bread to eat; and if he is thirsty, give him water to drink" (*Oxford Annotated Bible*, Prov. 25.21).

The title of a sacred work is italicized when it refers to a specific edition of the work, as in the preceding example. If you refer to the book in a general sense in your text, neither italicize it nor put it in quotation marks.

The Bible and the Qur'an provide allegories that help readers understand how to lead a moral life.

33b MLA list of works cited

▶ List of MLA works cited models **134–36**
▶ The works cited list at a glance **148–50**

Your list of works cited guides readers to the sources you have quoted, summarized, and paraphrased. Ask yourself: *What would readers need to know to find this source for themselves?* Usually, you will provide basic information common to most sources, such as author, title, publisher, publication date, and location (page numbers or URL, for example).

You'll find the models in this section organized by type (article, book, website, and so on). But even if you aren't sure exactly what type of source you have (*Is this a blog post or an article?*), you can follow two general principles:

Gather key publication information about the source—the citation elements.

Organize the basic information about the source using what MLA calls "containers."

The author's name and the title of the work are needed for most sources and are the first two pieces of information to gather. For the remaining pieces of information, you might find it helpful to think about whether the work is contained within one or more larger works. Some sources are self-contained. Others are nested in larger containers. The diagram on the next page illustrates these containers.

Self-contained
a *book*
a *film*

One container
an *article* in a scholarly journal
a *poem* in a collection of poetry
a *video* posted to YouTube
a *fact sheet* on a government website

Two containers
an *article* in a journal within a database (JSTOR etc.)
an *episode* from a TV series within a streaming service (Netflix etc.)

Keep in mind that most sources won't include all of the following pieces of information, so gather only those that are relevant to and available for your source.

Author.

Title of source.

Title of container,

Contributors,

Version (or edition),

Number(s),

Publisher,

Date,

Location (page numbers, URL, DOI, etc.).

If there is a second container, gather the same information for it (if available). →

Title of container 2,

Contributors,

Version (or edition),

Number(s),

Publisher,

Date,

Location.

WORKS CITED ENTRY, ONE CONTAINER (SELECTION IN AN ANTHOLOGY)

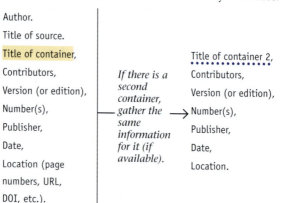

author: Eisenberg, Deborah. title of selection: "Some Other, Better Otto." title of collection: *New American*

Stories, container 1 — contributor: edited by Ben Marcus, publisher: Vintage Books, year: 2015,

location (pages): pp. 94–136.

WORKS CITED ENTRY, TWO CONTAINERS (ARTICLE IN A JOURNAL IN A DATABASE)

author | title of article
Coles, Kimberly Anne. "The Matter of Belief in John Donne's

container 1
journal title | volume, issue
Holy Sonnets." *Renaissance Quarterly*, vol. 68, no. 3,

container 2
date | location (pages) | database title | location (DOI)
fall 2015, pp. 899–931. *JSTOR*, https://doi.org/10.1086/683855.

Once you've gathered the relevant and available information about a source, you will organize the elements using the list above as your guideline. Note the punctuation after each element in that list. In this section you will find many examples of how elements and containers are combined to create works cited entries.

General guidelines for listing authors The formatting of authors' names in items 1–11 applies to all sources—books, articles, websites—in print, on the web, or in other media. For more models of specific source types, see items 12–64.

● **1. Single author**

author: last name first | title (book) | publisher
Bowker, Gordon. *James Joyce: A New Biography*. Farrar, Straus

year
and Giroux, 2012.

● **2. Two authors**

first author: last name first | second author: in typical order | title (book)
Gourevitch, Philip, and Errol Morris. *Standard Operating*

publisher | year
Procedure. Penguin Books, 2008.

👓 The works cited list **at a glance**

In the list of works cited, include only sources that you have quoted, summarized, or paraphrased in your paper. Although not all elements will apply to every source, you can adapt the guidelines and models in this section to any type of source you encounter in your research.

Gathering information and organizing entries

The elements needed for a works cited entry are the following:

- The author (if a work has one)
- The title
- The title of the larger work in which the source is located, if it is contained in a larger work (or "container" — see pp. 145–47)
- As much of the following information as is available about the source and the container: editor, translator, director, or performer; version or edition; number(s) (such as volume and issue); publisher; date of publication; and location of the source (page numbers, URL, DOI, and so on).

Authors

- Arrange the list alphabetically by authors' last names or by titles for works with no authors.
- For the first author, list the last name first, followed by a comma and the first name. Put a second author's name in typical order (first name followed by last name). For three or more authors, use "et al." after the first author's name.
- Spell out "editor," "translator," "edited by," and so on.

Titles

- Capitalize all words in titles except articles (*a*, *an*, *the*), prepositions, coordinating conjunctions, and the *to* in infinitives — unless the word is first or last in the title or subtitle.

- Use quotation marks for titles of articles and other short works. Place single quotation marks around a quoted term or a title of a short work that appears within an article title; italicize a term or title that is normally italicized.

- Italicize titles of books and other long works. If a book title contains another title that is normally italicized, neither italicize the internal title nor place it in quotation marks. If the title within the title is normally put in quotation marks, retain the quotation marks and italicize the entire book title.

Publication information

- Use the complete version of publishers' names, except for terms such as "Inc." and "Co."; retain terms such as "Books" and "Press." For university publishers, use "U" and "P" for "University" and "Press."

- For a book, take the name of the publisher from the title page (or from the copyright page if it is not on the title page). For a website, the publisher might be at the bottom of a page or on the "About" page. If a work has two or more publishers, separate the names with slashes.

- If the title of a website and the publisher are the same or similar, give the title of the site but omit the publisher.

Dates

- For a book, give the most recent year found on the title page or the copyright page. For an article from a periodical, use the most specific date listed in the source.

- For a web source, use the posting date, copyright date, or update date. If no date is listed, give your date of access at the end: Accessed 24 Feb. 2021.

- Abbreviate all months except May, June, and July and give the date in inverted form: 13 Mar. 2021.

Continued ➡

> ## 👓 The works cited list **at a glance**
> (*continued*)
>
> ### Page numbers
>
> - For most articles and other short works, give page numbers when they are available, preceded by "pp." (or "p." for only one page).
> - If a short work does not appear on consecutive pages, give the number of the first page followed by a plus sign: 35+.
>
> ### URLs and DOIs
>
> - Give a DOI (digital object identifier) if a source has one. Include the protocol and host (*https://doi.org/*).
> - If a source does not have a DOI, include a permalink if the website provides one.
> - If a source does not have a permalink or a DOI, include the full URL for the source. Copy the URL directly from your browser. It is optional to remove the protocol (*http://* or *https://*) when you do not need to provide live links for your readers. Do not insert any line breaks or hyphens into the URL.
> - If a URL is longer than three lines on the works cited page, you may shorten it, leaving at least the website host (for example, *cnn.com* or *www.usda .gov*) in the entry.

● **3. Three or more authors**   Name the first author followed by "et al." (Latin for "and others"). For in-text citations, see item 7 in 33a.

first author:
last name first   "et al." for
other authors   title (book)   publisher

Cunningham, Stewart, et al. *Media Economics*. Palgrave Macmillan,

year

2015.

● **4. Organization or company as author** Begin with the organization name, removing any initial articles (*A, An, The*).

author: organization
name, not abbreviated   title (book)

Human Rights Watch. *World Report of 2015: Events of 2014.*
publisher   year

Seven Stories Press, 2015.

● **5. No author listed**

article title   publication

"CEO Activism in America Is Risky Business." *The Economist,*
date   URL

17 Apr. 2021, www.economist.com/business/2021/04/14

/ceo-activism-in-america-is-risky-business.

NOTE: In web sources, often the author's name is available but is not easy to find. It may appear at the end of a web page, in tiny print, or on another page of the site, such as the home page. Also, an organization or a government may be the author (see items 4 and 56).

● **6. Two or more works by the same author or group of authors** Alphabetize the works by title (ignoring the article *A, An,* or *The* at the beginning of a title). Use the author's name or authors' names for the first entry; for subsequent entries, use three hyphens or dashes and a period.

Coates, Ta-Nehisi. *Between the World and Me.* Spiegel and Grau, 2015.

---. *We Were Eight Years in Power: An American Tragedy.* One
World, 2018.

Eaton-Robb, Pat, and Susan Haigh. "Pandemic May Lead to Long-
Term Changes in School Calendar." *AP News*, 15 Apr. 2021,
apnews.com/article/pandemics-connecticut-ned-lamont
-975d41076ae6b985030c133614685f33.

---. "Rock Star Van Zandt Helping Connecticut Students Re-engage."
AP News, 20 Apr. 2021, apnews.com/article/health-music
-education-arts-and-entertainment-entertainment
-5b038c218b30863d76031134db46fa5d.

● **7. Editor or translator**   Begin with the editor's or translator's name. After the name, add "editor" or "translator" (or "editors" or "translators").

first editor: last   second editor:
  name first   in typical order   title (book)

Horner, Avril, and Anne Rowe, editors. *Living on Paper: Letters*
                                        publisher   year

    from Iris Murdoch, 1934–1995. Princeton UP, 2016.

● **8. Author with editor or translator**   Begin with the name of the author. Place the editor's or translator's name after the title.

    author: last   translator: in
    name first   title (book)   typical order

Ullmann, Regina. *The Country Road: Stories*. Translated by Kurt Beals,
                 publisher   year

  New Directions Publishing, 2015.

● **9. Graphic narrative or other illustrated work**   If a work has both an author and an illustrator, the order in your citation will depend on which of those persons you emphasize in your paper.

Gaiman, Neil. *The Sandman: Overture*. Illustrated by
    J. H. William III, DC Comics, 2015.

Wenzel, David, illustrator. *The Hobbit*. By J. R. R. Tolkien,
    Ballantine Books, 2012.

● **10. Author using a pseudonym (pen name)**   Give the author's name as it appears in the source, followed by the author's real name, if available, in brackets. Alternatively, you may start with the real name followed by "*published as*" and the pen name in brackets: Franklin, Benjamin [*published as* Richard Saunders].

Saunders, Richard [Benajmin Franklin]. "Poor Richard, 1773."
    1773. *Founders Online*, National Archives, founders
    .archives.gov/documents/Franklin/01-01-02-0093.

Answer the basic question "Who is the author?"

PROBLEM: Sometimes when you need to cite a source, it's not clear who the author is. This is especially true for sources on the web and other nonprint sources, which may have been created by one person and uploaded by a different person or an organization. Whom do you cite as the author in such a case? How do you determine who *is* the author?

EXAMPLE: The video "Surfing the Web on the Job" (see below) was uploaded to YouTube by CBSNewsOnline. Is the person or organization that uploads the video the author of the video? Not necessarily.

STRATEGY: After you view or listen to the source a few times, ask yourself whether you can tell who is chiefly responsible for creating the content in the source. It could be an organization. It could be an identifiable individual. This video consists entirely of reporting by Daniel Sieberg, so in this case the author is Sieberg.

Surfing the Web on The Job

CBSNewsOnline · 42,491 videos

▶ Subscribe   85,736

Uploaded on Nov 12, 2009
As the Internet continues to emerge as a critical facet of everyday life, CBS News' Daniel Sieberg reports that companies are cracking down on employees' personal Web use.

CITATION: To cite the source, you would use the basic MLA guidelines for a video found on the web (item 42).

author: last name first — title of video — website title
Sieberg, Daniel. "Surfing the Web on the Job." *YouTube*,
upload information — upload date
uploaded by CBSNewsOnline, 12 Nov. 2009,
URL
www.youtube.com/watch?v=1wLhNwY-enY.

● **11. Screen name or social media account**   Start with the account display name, followed by the screen name or handle (if available) in brackets. If the account name and handle are very similar (for example, ACLU SoCal and @ACLU_SoCal), omit the handle.

Gay, Roxane [@rgay]. "The shortness of cultural memory is
   always astonishing." *Twitter*, 25 Apr. 2021, twitter.com
   /rgay/status/1386507940601995274?.

Articles and other short works

● **12. Basic format for an article or other short work**

a. Print

author:
last name first ⎴ article title ⎴ journal title ⎴

Tilman, David. "Food and Health of a Full Earth." *Daedalus*,

volume, issue ⎴ date ⎴ page(s) ⎴
   vol. 144, no. 4, fall 2015, pp. 5–7.

b. Web

author:
last name first ⎴ title of short work ⎴

Florez, Nina.   "Chicago Rally Held in Support of Colombian

title of website ⎴ date ⎴ URL ⎴
   Protesters." *NBC 5 Chicago*, 9 May 2021, www.nbcchicago

.com/news/local/chicago-rallies-held-in-support-of

-colombian-protesters/2505612.

c. Database

first author: last name first ⎴ second author: in typical order ⎴ article title ⎴

Harris, Ashleigh May, and Nicklas Hållén. "African Street Literature:

A Method for an Emergent Form beyond World Literature."
journal title ⎴ volume, issue ⎴ date ⎴
Research in African Literatures, vol. 51, no. 2, summer 2020,

page(s) ⎴ database title ⎴ DOI ⎴
pp. 1–26. *JSTOR*, https://doi.org/10.2979/reseafrilite.51.2.01.

● **13. Article in a journal**

a. Print

author: last name first / article title / journal title

Matchie, Thomas. "Law versus Love in *The Round House*." *The Midwest*

volume, issue / date / page(s)

Quarterly, vol. 56, no. 4, summer 2015, pp. 353–64.

b. Online journal

author: last name first / article title

McGuire, Meg. "Women, Healing, and Social Community:

journal title / volume, issue

Cyberfeminist Activities on Reddit." *Kairos*, vol. 25, no. 2,

date / URL

spring 2021, kairos.technorhetoric.net/25.2/topoi

/mcguire/index.html.

c. Database

author: last name first / article title

Maier, Jessica. "A 'True Likeness': The Renaissance City Portrait."

journal title / volume, issue / date

Renaissance Quarterly, vol. 65, no. 3, fall 2012,

page(s) / database title / DOI

pp. 711–52. *JSTOR*, https://doi.org/10.1086/668300.

● **14. Article in a magazine**

author: last name first / article title / magazine title

Owusu, Nadia. "Head Wraps." *The New York Times Magazine*,

date / page(s)

7 Mar. 2021, p. 20.

Stuart, Tessa. "New Study Suggests Burning Fossil Fuels
Contributed to 1 in 5 Deaths in 2018." *Rolling Stone*, 17 Feb.
2021, www.rollingstone.com/politics/politics-news/fossil
-fuels-air-pollution-premature-deaths-statistics-1127586/.

Guerrero, Desirée. "All Genders, Period." *The Advocate*, no.
1105, Oct.–Nov. 2019, p. 31. *ProQuest*, www-proquest
-com.proxy3.noblenet.org/docview/2488268993.

6ð Citation at a glance

Article in an online journal MLA

To cite an article in an online journal in MLA style, include the following elements:

1. Author(s) of article
2. Title and subtitle of article
3. Title of journal
4. Volume and issue numbers
5. Date of publication (including month or season, if any)
6. Page number(s) of article, if given
7. DOI or permalink, if available; otherwise, URL to article

FIRST PAGE OF ONLINE JOURNAL ARTICLE

WORKS CITED ENTRY FOR AN ARTICLE IN AN ONLINE JOURNAL

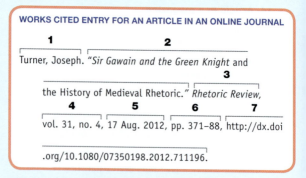

For more on citing online articles in MLA style, see item 12b.

6∂ Citation at a glance

Article from a database MLA

To cite an article from a database in MLA style, include the following elements:

1. Author(s) of article
2. Title and subtitle of article
3. Title of journal, magazine, or newspaper
4. Volume and issue numbers (for journal)
5. Date of publication (including month or season, if any)
6. Page number(s) of article, if any
7. Name of database
8. DOI or permalink, if available; otherwise, URL to article

DATABASE RECORD

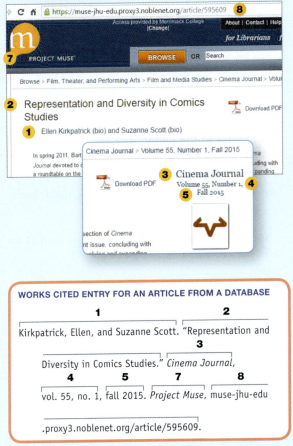

WORKS CITED ENTRY FOR AN ARTICLE FROM A DATABASE

Kirkpatrick, Ellen, and Suzanne Scott. "Representation and

Diversity in Comics Studies." *Cinema Journal,*

vol. 55, no. 1, fall 2015. *Project Muse,* muse-jhu-edu

.proxy3.noblenet.org/article/595609.

For more on citing articles from databases in MLA style, see items 12c and 13c.

● **15. Article in a newspaper**

author: last
name first

article title

Bray, Hiawatha. "As Toys Get Smarter, Privacy Issues Emerge."

newspaper title   date   page(s)

The Boston Globe, 10 Dec. 2015, p. C1.

Jones, Ayana. "Chamber of Commerce Program to Boost Black-
    Owned Businesses." *The Philadelphia Tribune*, 21 Apr.
    2021, www.phillytrib.com/news/business/chamber-of
    -commerce-program-to-boost-black-owned-businesses
    /article_6b14ae2f-5db2-5a59-8a67-8bbf974da451.html.

● **16. Editorial or opinion**   You may add the word
"Editorial" or "Op-ed" to the end of the entry if it is
not clear from the author or title of the source.

Kansas City Star Editorial Board. "Kansas Considers Lowering
    Concealed Carry Age to 18. Why It's Wrong for Many
    Reasons." *The Kansas City Star*, 9 Mar. 2021, www.kansascity
    .com/opinion/editorials/article249793143.html.

● **17. Letter to the editor**   Use the label "Letter" as
the title if the letter is untitled. Otherwise, cite as an
article.

Carasso, Roger. Letter. *The New York Times*, 4 Apr. 2021, Sunday
    Book Review sec., p. 5.

● **18. Comment on an online article**   See item 11 for
more on screen names.

author:
screen
name   label   article title & author   website title

satch. Comment on "No Compassion," by Roy Edroso." *Alicublog*,

date & time   URL to comment

20 Mar. 2021, 9:50 a.m., disq.us/p/2fu0ulk.

● **19. Book review**

Jopanda, Wayne Silao. Review of *America Is Not the Heart*, by
    Elaine Castillo. *Alon: Journal for Filipinx American and
    Diasporic Studies*, vol. 1, no. 1, Mar. 2021, pp. 106–08.
    eScholarship, https://escholarship.org/uc/item/0d44t8wx.

Della Subin, Anna. "It Has Burned My Heart." *London Review
of Books*, 22 Oct. 2015, www.lrb.co.uk/v37/n20
/anna-della-subin/it-has-burned-my-heart.

● 20. Film review or other review

Bramesco, Charles. "Honeyland Couches an Apocalyptic Warning
in a Beekeeping Documentary." *The A.V. Club*, G/O Media,
23 July 2019, film.avclub.com/honeyland-couches-an
-apocalyptic-warning-in-a-beekeepin-1836624795.

Turley, Bethani. Review of *Born in a Ballroom*, directed by
Clara Lehman and Jonathan Lacocque. *The Journal of
American Folklore*, vol. 134, no. 532, spring 2021,
pp. 239–41. *JSTOR*, www.jstor.org/stable/10.5406
/jamerfolk.134.532.0239.

● 21. Performance review

Stout, Gene. "The Ebullient Florence + the Machine Give
KeyArena a Workout." *The Seattle Times*, 28 Oct. 2015,
www.seattletimes.com/entertainment/music/the-ebullient
-florence-the-machine-give-keyarena-a-workout.

● 22. Interview

Harjo, Joy. "The First Native American U.S. Poet Laureate
on How Poetry Can Counter Hate." Interview by Olivia
B. Waxman. *Time*, 22 Aug. 2019, time.com/5658443
/joy-harjo-poet-interview/.

Kendi, Ibram X. Interview by Eric Deggans. *Life Kit*, NPR, 24
Oct. 2020.

Freedman, Sasha. Video interview with the author. 10 Nov. 2020.

● 23. Article in a dictionary or an encyclopedia (including a wiki)

Robinson, Lisa Clayton. "Harlem Writers Guild." *Africana: The
Encyclopedia of the African and African American Experience*,
edited by Kwame Anthony Appiah and Henry Louis Gates Jr.,
2nd ed., Oxford UP, 2005, p. 163.

"House Music." *Wikipedia: The Free Encyclopedia*, Wikimedia
Foundation, 8 Apr. 2021, en.wikipedia.org/wiki
/House_music.

● **24. Letter in a collection**   List the title as it appears in the collection (or, if untitled, "Letter to" and the recipient).

Murdoch, Iris. Letter to Raymond Queneau. 7 Aug. 1946. *Living on Paper: Letters from Iris Murdoch, 1934–1995*, edited by Avril Horner and Anne Rowe, Princeton UP, 2016, pp. 76–78.

Oblinger, Maggie. "Letter from Maggie Oblinger to Charlie Thomas, March 31, 1895." 31 Mar. 1895. *Prairie Settlement: Nebraska Photographs and Family Letters, 1862-1912*, Library of Congress / American Memory, memory.loc.gov/cgi-bin/query/r?ammem/ps :@field(DOCID+l306)#l3060001.

Books and other long works

▶ Citation at a glance: Book **161**
▶ Citation at a glance: Selection from an anthology or a collection **164**

● **25. Basic format for a book**

a. Print book or e-book   If you have used an e-book, indicate "e-book ed." before the publisher's name.

author: last   book
name first   title   publisher   year
Porter, Max. *Lanny*. Graywolf Press, 2019.

Beard, Mary. *SPQR: A History of Ancient Rome*. E-book ed., Liveright Publishing, 2015.

b. Web   Give whatever print publication information is available for the work, followed by the title of the website and the URL.

author: last
name first   book title
Piketty, Thomas. *Capital in the Twenty-First Century*. Translated
translator: in
typical order   publisher   year   website title
by Arthur Goldhammer, Harvard UP, 2014. *Google Books*,
URL
books.google.com/books?isbn=0674369556.

6ð Citation at a glance

Book MLA

To cite a print book in MLA style, include the following elements:

1. Author(s)
2. Title and subtitle
3. Publisher
4. Year of publication (latest year)

TITLE PAGE

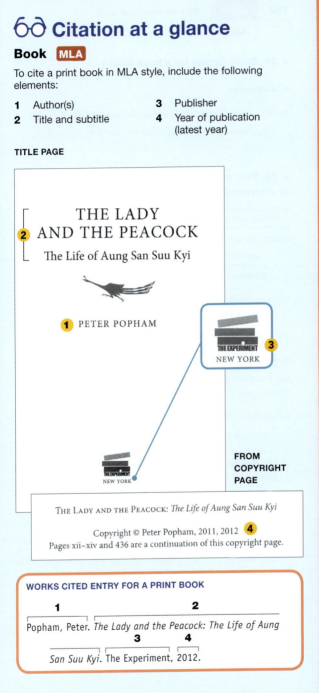

THE LADY AND THE PEACOCK

The Life of Aung San Suu Kyi

1 PETER POPHAM

3 THE EXPERIMENT
NEW YORK

FROM COPYRIGHT PAGE

THE LADY AND THE PEACOCK: *The Life of Aung San Suu Kyi*

Copyright © Peter Popham, 2011, 2012 **4**
Pages xii–xiv and 436 are a continuation of this copyright page.

WORKS CITED ENTRY FOR A PRINT BOOK

  1   **2**

Popham, Peter. *The Lady and the Peacock: The Life of Aung*
                     3   **4**

San Suu Kyi. The Experiment, 2012.

For more on citing books in MLA style, see items 25–32.

● **25. Basic format for a book** (*cont.*)

c. Audiobook

de Hart, Jane Sherron. *Ruth Bader Ginsburg: A Life.* Narrated
    by Suzanne Toren, audiobook ed., Random House Audio,
    2018.

● **26. Part of a book (foreword, introduction, preface,
or afterword)**

author of foreword: book
last name first   part   book title   author of book:
in normal order

Coates, Ta-Nehisi. Foreword. *The Origin of Others,* by Toni Morrison,

publisher   year   page(s)

   Harvard UP, 2017, pp. vii–xvii.

Sullivan, John Jeremiah. "The Ill-Defined Plot." Introduction.
    The Best American Essays 2014, edited by Sullivan,
    Houghton Mifflin Harcourt, 2014, pp. xvii–xxvi.

● **27. Book in a language other than English**   Capitalize the title according to the conventions of the book's
language.

Vargas Llosa, Mario. *El sueño del celta* [*The Dream of the Celt*].
    Alfaguara Ediciones, 2010.

● **28. Entire anthology or collection**   An anthology is
a collection of works on a common theme, often with
different authors for the selections and usually with an
editor for the entire volume.

editor: last   title of
name first   anthology   publisher   year

Marcus, Ben, editor. *New American Stories.* Vintage Books, 2015.

Vendler, Helen, editor. *Poems, Poets, Poetry: An Introduction
    and Anthology.* 3rd ed., Bedford/St. Martin's, 2018.

● **29. One selection from an anthology or a collection**

author of selection — title of selection — title of anthology

Sayrafiezadeh, Saïd. "Paranoia." *New American Stories,* edited

editor(s) of anthology — publisher — year — page(s)

by Ben Marcus, Vintage Books, 2015, pp. 3–29.

● **30. Two or more selections from an anthology or a collection** Provide an entry for the entire anthology (see item 28) and a shortened entry for each selection.

author of selection — title of selection — editor(s) of anthology — page(s)

Eisenberg, Deborah. "Some Other, Better Otto." Marcus, pp. 94–136.

editor of anthology — title of anthology — publisher — year

Marcus, Ben, editor. *New American Stories*. Vintage Books, 2015.

author of selection — title of selection — editor(s) of anthology — page(s)

Sayrafiezadeh, Saïd. "Paranoia." Marcus, pp. 3–29.

● **31. Edition other than the first** If the book has a translator or an editor in addition to the author, give the name of the translator or editor (if any) before the edition number (see item 8 for a book with an editor or a translator).

Eagleton, Terry. *Literary Theory: An Introduction*. 3rd ed., U of
Minnesota P, 2008.

● **32. Multivolume work** Include the total number of volumes at the end of the entry, using the abbreviation "vols."

Cather, Willa. *Willa Cather: The Complete Fiction and Other
Writings*. Edited by Sharon O'Brien, Library of America,
1987–92. 3 vols.

If you cite only one volume in your paper, include volume's title (if the volumes are individually titled), date of publication, and number.

Cather, Willa. *Willa Cather: Later Novels*. Edited by Sharon
O'Brien, Library of America, 1990. Vol. 2 of *Willa Cather:
The Complete Fiction and Other Writings*.

6∂ Citation at a glance

Selection from an anthology or a collection `MLA`

To cite a selection from an anthology in MLA style, include the following elements:

1. Author(s) of selection
2. Title and subtitle of selection
3. Title and subtitle of anthology
4. Editor(s) of anthology
5. Publisher
6. Year of publication
7. Page number(s) of selection

TITLE PAGE OF ANTHOLOGY

FIRST PAGE OF SELECTION

CHAPTER 3

Technology's Quiet Revolution for Women 2

Isobel Coleman 1

THE UNFINISHED
REVOLUTION 3

VOICES FROM THE GLOBAL FIGHT
FOR WOMEN'S RIGHTS

the eve of Egypt's January 2011 revolution, I happened to be in
airo, having dinner with Gamila Ismail, a longtime Egyptian
al activist who had spent decades opposing the Mubarak
"What will happen tomorrow?" I asked her, referring to the

EDITED BY MINKY WORDEN 4

sweek named her as one of "150 Women Who Shake the World."

41 ● 41 7

5

Seven Stories Press
NEW YORK

6

Copyright © 2012 by Minky Worden
Individual chapters © 2012 by each author

7

Seven Stories Press
NEW YORK

FROM COPYRIGHT PAGE

WORKS CITED ENTRY FOR A SELECTION FROM AN ANTHOLOGY

1
2

Coleman, Isobel. "Technology's Quiet Revolution for Women."

3

The Unfinished Revolution: Voices from the Global

4

Fight for Women's Rights, edited by Minky Worden,

5 6 7

Seven Stories Press, 2012, pp. 41–49.

For more on citing selections from anthologies in MLA style, see items 28–30.

● **33. Sacred text**   Give the title of the edition (taken from the title page), italicized. Add the name of the version, if there is one, before the publisher.

The Oxford Annotated Bible with the Apocrypha. Edited by
  Herbert G. May and Bruce M. Metzger, Revised Standard
  Version, Oxford UP, 1965.

Qur'an: The Final Testament. Translated by Rashad Khalifa,
  Authorized English Version with Arabic Text, Universal
  Unity, 2000.

● **34. Dissertation**

Kabugi, Magana J. *The Souls of Black Colleges: Cultural Production, Ideology, and Identity at Historically Black Colleges
  and Universities*. 2020. Vanderbilt U, PhD dissertation.
  Vanderbilt University Institutional Repository, hdl.handle
  .net/1803/16103.

Websites and parts of websites

▶ Citation at a glance: Work from a website **167**

● **35. An entire website**   Include the website's sponsor or publisher and the update date. If the website
name is the same or similar to the publisher, do not
include it; if no date is provided, include the date
you accessed the source (see the second example in
item 36).

title of website   publisher
⌐‾‾‾‾‾‾‾‾‾⌐   ⌐‾‾‾‾‾‾‾‾‾‾‾‾‾‾‾‾‾‾‾‾‾‾‾‾‾‾‾‾‾‾‾‾‾‾‾‾
Lift Every Voice. Library of America / Schomburg Center for

                              date   URL
‾‾‾‾‾‾‾‾‾‾‾‾‾‾‾‾‾‾‾‾‾‾‾‾⌐   ⌐‾‾‾⌐   ⌐‾‾‾‾‾‾‾‾‾‾‾‾‾‾‾‾‾‾‾‾‾‾‾
Research in Black Culture, 2020, africanamericanpoetry.org/.

title of website   publisher date   URL
⌐‾‾‾‾‾‾‾‾‾‾‾⌐   ⌐‾‾‾‾‾‾‾⌐ ⌐‾‾‾⌐   ⌐‾‾‾‾‾‾‾‾‾‾‾‾‾‾‾‾‾‾‾‾‾‾‾‾‾‾
The Newton Project. U of Sussex, 2021, www.newtonproject.ox.ac.uk/.

● **36. Work from a website** The titles of short works, such as articles or individual web pages, are placed in quotation marks. Titles of long works, such as books and reports, are italicized. If a book's original publication date is not available, include the date of online publication.

author: last
name first · · · · · · · · · · · · · · · · title of short work
Gallagher, Sean. "The Last Nomads of the Tibetan Plateau."

· · · · · · title of website · · · · · · · · · · date
Pulitzer Center on Crisis Reporting, 25 Oct. 2012,
· · · · · · · · · · · · · · · · · · URL
pulitzercenter.org/reporting/china-glaciers-global-warming

-climate-change-ecosystem-tibetan-plateau-grasslands-nomads.

· · · · · title of short work · · · · · · · · · · title of website
"Social and Historical Context: Vitality." *Arapesh Grammar and*
· publisher
Digital Language Archive Project, Institute for Advanced
· URL
Technology in the Humanities, www.arapesh.org/socio

· · · · · · · · · · · · · · · · · · access date for
· · · · · · · · · · · · · · · · · · undated site
_historical_context_vitality.php. Accessed 22 Mar. 2021.

author · · title of long work · · · · · · · · · · translator
Euripides. *The Trojan Women*. Translated by Gilbert Murray,
· · · · · · · · book
· · · · · · · · publication
publisher · · · date · · · · · website title · · · · · · URL
Oxford UP, 1915. *Internet Sacred Text Archive*, www.sacred

-texts.com/cla/eurip/trojan.htm.

6∂ Citation at a glance

Work from a website MLA

To cite a work from a website in MLA style, include the following elements:

1 Author(s) of work, if any
2 Title and subtitle
3 Title of website
4 Publisher of website (unless it is the same as the title of site)
5 Update date
6 URL of page
7 Date of access (if no update date on site)

INTERNAL PAGE FROM A WEBSITE

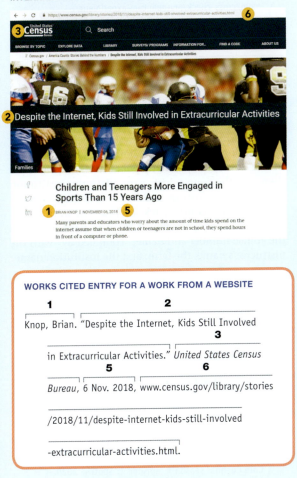

WORKS CITED ENTRY FOR A WORK FROM A WEBSITE

    1   **2**

Knop, Brian. "Despite the Internet, Kids Still Involved

                                   3

in Extracurricular Activities." *United States Census*

      5   **6**

Bureau, 6 Nov. 2018, www.census.gov/library/stories

/2018/11/despite-internet-kids-still-involved

-extracurricular-activities.html.

For more on citing sources from websites in MLA style, see item 36.

● **37. Blog post** To cite a comment on a blog, follow the guidelines in item 18.

author: last
name first   title of blog post   title of blog

Horgan, John. "My Quantum Experiment." *Cross-Check,*

publisher   date   URL

Scientific American, 5 June 2020, blogs.scientificamerican

.com/cross-check/my-quantum-experiment/.

author:
last name
first   title of blog post   title of blog   date

Edroso, Roy. "No Compassion." *Alicublog,* 18 Mar. 2021,

URL

alicublog.blogspot.com/2021/03/no-compassion.html.

● **38. Course materials** For materials posted to an online learning management system, include as much information as is available about the source (author, title or description, and any publication information); then give the course, instructor, platform, institution name, date of posting, and URL. For materials delivered in a PDF course pack, include the author and title of the work; the words "Course pack for" with the course number and name; "compiled by" with the instructor's name; the term; and the institution name.

Rose, Mike. "Blue Collar Brilliance." Introduction to College

Writing, taught by Melanie Li. *Blackboard,* Merrimack

College, 9 Sept. 2020, blackboard.merrimack.edu/ultra/

courses/_25745_1/cl/readings.

Audio, visual, and multimedia sources

● **39. Podcast series or episode**

episode title   series title   contributor

"Childish Gambino: *Because the Internet.*" *Dissect,* hosted by

episode number   production company   date

Cole Cuchna, season 7, episode 1, Spotify, 2020.

streaming service

Spotify app.

Dolly Parton's America. Hosted by Jad Abumrad, produced and

reported by Shima Oliaee, WNYC Studios, 2019, www

.wnycstudios.org/podcasts/dolly-partons-america.

● **40. Film**   Generally, begin the entry with the title, followed by the director, as in the first example. If your paper emphasizes one or more people involved with the film, you may begin with those names, as in the second example.

director: name in
normal order

film title

Judas and the Black Messiah. Directed by Shaka King,

release
distributor | date

Warner Bros. Pictures, 2021.

director: last
name first | film title | distributor

Kubrick, Stanley, director. *A Clockwork Orange*. Hawk Films /

release | streaming
date | service

Warner Bros. Pictures, 1971. *Netflix*, www.netflix.com.

● **41. Supplementary material accompanying a film**
Begin with the title of the supplementary material and the names of any important contributors. End with information about the film, as in item 40, and about the location of the supplementary material.

"Sweeney's London." Produced by Eric Young. *Sweeney Todd:*

The Demon Barber of Fleet Street, directed by Tim Burton,

DreamWorks, 2007, disc 2. DVD.

● **42. Stand-alone audio segment**

"The Past Returns to Gdańsk." Written and narrated by Michael

Segalov, *BBC*, 26 Apr. 2021, www.bbc.co.uk/sounds/play

/m000vh4f.

● **43. Video from the web**   If the video emphasizes a single speaker or presenter, list that person as the author.

title of video / website title / upload information

"The Art of Single Stroke Painting in Japan." *Youtube*, uploaded

date / URL

by National Geographic, 13 July 2018, www.youtube.com

/watch?v=g7H8IhGZnpM.

author/speaker / title of video

Kundu, Anindya. "The 'Opportunity Gap' in US Public Education

website title / date / URL

— and How to Close It." *TED*, May 2019, www.ted.com

/talks/anindya_kundu_the_opportunity_gap_in_us_public

_education_and_how_to_close_it.

● **44. Video game**   List the developer or author of the game (if any); the title, italicized; the version, if there is one; and the distributor and date of publication. If the game can be played on the web, add information as for a work from a website (see item 36).

Gearbox Software. *Borderlands 3: Deluxe Edition*. 2K Games, 2019.

● **45. Computer software or app**

NYT Cooking. Version 4.36, The New York Times, 2021.

● **46. Television or radio episode or program**

title of episode / program title / contributor

"Umbrellas Down." *This American Life*, hosted by Ira Glass,

network / broadcast date

WBEZ, 10 July 2020.

title of episode   program title   episode

"Shock and Delight." *Bridgerton,* season 1, episode 2,
streaming service

distributor   date

Shondaland / Netflix, 2020. *Netflix,* www.netflix.com.

Hillary. Directed by Nanette Burstein, Propagate Content /
Hulu, 2020. *Hulu* app.

● 47. Transcript

Kundu, Anindya. "The 'Opportunity Gap' in US Public Education
— and How to Close It." *TED,* May 2019, www.ted.com
/talks/anindya_kundu_the_opportunity_gap_in_us_public
_education_and_how_to_close_it/transcript. Transcript.

● 48. Live performance

Schreck, Heidi. *What the Constitution Means to Me.* Directed
by Oliver Butler, 16 June 2019, Helen Hayes Theater, New
York City.

Beethoven, Ludwig van. *Piano Concerto No. 3.* Conducted by Andris
Nelsons, performed by Paul Lewis and Boston Symphony
Orchestra, 9 Oct. 2015, Symphony Hall, Boston.

● 49. Lecture or public address

Gay, Roxane. "Difficult Women, Bad Feminists and Unruly
Bodies." Beatty Lecture Series, 18 Oct. 2018, McGill
University.

Eugenides, Jeffrey. Lecture. Portland Arts and Lectures, 30 Sept.
2003, Arlene Schnitzer Concert Hall, Portland, Oregon.

● 50. Musical score

Beethoven, Ludwig van. *Symphony no. 5 in C Minor, Opus
67.* 1807. Center for Computer Assisted Research in the
Humanities, 2008, scores.ccarh.org/beethoven/sym
/beethoven-sym5-1.pdf.

● **51. Music recording**

Bach, Johann Sebastian. *Bach: Violin Concertos*. Performances
 by Itzhak Perlman, Pinchas Zukerman, and English
 Chamber Orchestra, EMI, 2002.

Bad Bunny. "Vete." *YHLQMDLG*, Rimas, 2020. *Apple Music* app.

● **52. Artwork, photograph, or other visual art**   If you
viewed the original work, give the date of composition
followed by a comma and the location. If you viewed
the work online, give the date of composition followed
by a period and the website title, publisher (if any),
and URL. If you viewed the work reproduced in a book,
cite as a work in an anthology or a collection (item 29),
giving the date of composition after the title.

Bradford, Mark. *Let's Walk to the Middle of the Ocean*. 2015,
 Museum of Modern Art, New York City.

Lange, Dorothea. *Migrant Mother, Nipomo, California*. Mar. 1936.
 MOMA, www.moma.org/collection/works/50989.

Kertész, André. *Meudon*. 1928. *Street Photography: From Atget
 to Cartier-Bresson*, by Clive Scott, Tauris, 2011, p. 61.

● **53. Visual such as a table, a chart, or another graphic**
Add a descriptive label at the end of the citation if the
type of visual is not clear from the title.

"New COVID-19 Cases Worldwide." *Coronavirus Resource Center*,
 Johns Hopkins U and Medicine, 3 May 2021, coronavirus
 .jhu.edu/data/new-cases. Chart.

"Number of Measles Cases Reported by Year 2010–2019." *Centers
 for Disease Control and Prevention*, 22 Feb. 2019, www
 .cdc.gov/measles/cases-outbreaks.html. Table.

● **54. Cartoon**

Munroe, Randall. "Heartbleed Explanation." *xkcd*, xkcd.com/1354/.
 Accessed 10 Oct. 2020.

Shiell, Mike. Cartoon. *The Saturday Evening Post*, Jan.–Feb.
 2021, p. 8.

55. Advertisement

Advertisement for Better World Club. *Mother Jones*, Mar.–Apr. 2021, p. 2.

"The Whole Working-from-Home Thing — Apple." *YouTube*, uploaded by Apple, 13 July 2020, www.youtube.com /watch?v=6_pru8U2RmM.

56. Map

"Map of Sudan." *Global Citizen*, Citizens for Global Solutions, 2011, globalsolutions.org/blog/bashir#.VthzNMfi_FI.

"Vote on Secession, 1861." *Perry-Castañeda Library Map Collection*, U of Texas at Austin, 1976, www.lib.utexas .edu/maps/atlas_texas/texas_vote_secession_1861.jpg. Map.

Government and legal documents

● **57. Government document** If you are using several government sources, you may want to standardize your list of works cited by listing the name of the government, followed by the name of any agencies and subagencies, as in the first example. Otherwise, give the name of the publishing agency as presented by the source, as in the second example.

government   department   agency (or agencies)

United States, Department of Transportation, Federal Highway

title of work

Administration. *Environmental Justice Analysis in Transportation*

date

Planning and Programming: State of the Practice. Feb. 2019,

URL

www.fhwa.dot.gov/environment/environmental_justice

/publications/tpp/fhwahep19022.pdf.

U.S. Bureau of Labor Statistics. "Consumer Expenditures Report 2019." *BLS Reports*, Dec. 2020, www.bls.gov/opub /reports/consumer-expenditures/2019/home.htm.

● **58. Historical document**   The titles of most historical documents, such as treaties and bills, are neither italicized nor put in quotation marks. When citing a constitution, use the title as it appears in the version you cited, in italics.

The Constitution of the United States: A Transcription. 2020.
    America's Founding Documents, US National Archives and
    Records Administration, www.archives.gov/founding-docs
    /constitution-transcript.

● **59. Legislative act (law)**   Begin with the name of the legislative body and the act's Public Law number.

United States, Congress. Public Law 116–136. *United States
    Statutes at Large*, vol. 134, 2019, pp. 281–615. *U.S.
    Government Publishing Office*, www.govinfo.gov/content
    /pkg/PLAW-116publ136/uslm/PLAW-116publ136.xml.

● **60. Court case**   List the name of the court. Then provide the title of the case, the date of the decision, and publication information.

United States, Supreme Court. *Utah v. Evans*. 20 June 2002.
    Legal Information Institute, Cornell Law School, www.law
    .cornell.edu/supremecourt/text/536/452.

Personal communication and social media

● **61. Personal letter**

Nadir, Abdul. Letter to the author. 6 May 2021. Typescript.

● **62. E-mail message**

Lewis-Truth, Antoine. E-mail to the Office of Student Financial
    Assistance. 30 Aug. 2020.

● **63. Text message**

Primak, Shoshana. Text message to the author. 6 May 2021.

● **64. Social media post**   Begin with the author (see item 11 for citing screen names). Use the caption or full text of the post as the title, if it is brief; if the post is long, use the first few words followed by an ellipsis.

If the post has no text, or if you focus on a visual element in your paper, provide a description of the post.

Abdurraqib, Hanif [@NifMuhammad]. "Tracy Chapman really one of the greatest Ohio writers." *Twitter*, 30 Mar. 2021, twitter.com/NifMuhammad/status/1377086355667320836.

ACLU. "Public officials have . . . ." *Facebook*, 10 May 2021, www.facebook.com/aclu /photos/a.74134381812/10157852911711813.

Rosa, Camila [camixvx]. Illustration of nurses in masks with fists raised. *Instagram*, 28 Apr. 2020, www.instagram .com/p/B_h62W9pJaQ/.

33c   MLA information notes (optional)

Researchers who use the MLA system of parenthetical documentation may also use information notes for one of two purposes:

1. to provide additional material that is important but might interrupt the flow of the paper
2. to refer to several sources that support a single point or to provide comments on sources

Information notes may be either footnotes or endnotes. Footnotes appear at the foot of the page; endnotes appear on a separate page at the end of the paper, just before the list of works cited. For either style, the notes are numbered consecutively throughout the paper. The text of the paper contains a raised arabic numeral that corresponds to the number of the note.

TEXT

In the past several years, employees have filed a number of lawsuits against employers because of online monitoring practices.[1]

NOTE

    [1] For a discussion of federal law applicable to electronic surveillance in the workplace, see Kesan 293.

34 MLA format; sample research paper

The following guidelines are consistent with advice given in the *MLA Handbook*, 9th edition (MLA, 2021), and with typical requirements for student papers. For a sample MLA research paper, see 34b.

34a MLA format

Formatting the paper   Papers written in MLA style should be formatted as follows.

Font   If your instructor does not require a specific font, choose one that is standard and easy to read (such as Times New Roman).

Title and identification   On the first page of your paper, place your name, your instructor's name, the course title, and the date on separate lines against the left margin. Then center your title. (See p. 179 for a sample first page.)

If you are writing a group project, create a separate cover page with all members' names, the professor's name, the course, and the date, all aligned left on separate double-spaced lines. Center the title on a new line a few spaces down.

Page numbers (running head)   Put the page number preceded by your last name in the upper right corner of each page, one-half inch below the top edge. For a group project, starting on the first text page, include all members' last names before the page number. If all last names will not fit on a single line, include only the page number.

Margins, line spacing, and paragraph indents   Leave margins of one inch on all sides of the page. Left-align the text. Double-space throughout the paper. Do not add extra space above or below the title of the paper or between paragraphs. Indent the first line of each paragraph one-half inch from the left margin.

Capitalization, italics, and quotation marks   In titles of works, capitalize all words except articles (*a, an, the*), prepositions (*to, from, between,* and so on), coordinating conjunctions (*and, but, or, nor, for, so, yet*), and the *to* in infinitives—unless the word is first or last in the title or subtitle. Follow these guidelines in your paper even if the title appears in all capital or all lowercase letters in the source.

In the text of an MLA paper, when a complete sentence follows a colon, lowercase the first word following the colon, except in certain situations (such as if the sentence following the colon is a question or a definition).

Italicize the titles of books, journals, magazines, and other long works, such as websites. Use quotation marks around the titles of articles, short stories, poems, and other short works.

Long quotations   When a quotation is longer than four typed lines of prose or three lines of poetry, set it off from the text by indenting the entire quotation one-half inch from the left margin. Do not use quotation marks when a quotation has been set off from the text by indenting. See page 184 for an example.

Headings   While headings are generally not needed for brief essays, readers may find them helpful for long or complex essays. Place each heading in the same style and size. If you need subheadings (level 2, level 3), be consistent in styling them. Place headings at the left margin without any indent. Capitalize headings as you would titles.

Visuals   MLA classifies visuals as tables and figures (figures include graphs, charts, maps, photographs, and drawings). Place visuals in your essay as near as possible to the relevant text. Label and number each table ("Table 1," "Table 2," and so on) and provide a clear title. Capitalize as you would the title of a work (see above). Place the table number and title on separate lines above the table, flush with the left margin.

For a table that you have borrowed or adapted, give the source below the table in a note like the following:

Source: Boris Groysberg and Michael Slind,
"Leadership Is a Conversation," *Harvard Business Review*, June 2012, p. 83.

All other visuals should be labeled "Figure" (abbreviated "Fig."), numbered, and captioned. The label and caption should appear on the same line, aligned left, underneath the visual. Include source information. If your caption includes full source information and you do not cite the source anywhere else in your essay, it is not necessary to include an entry in your list of works cited. Remember to refer to each visual in your text (*see table 1; as shown in figure 2*), indicating how it contributes to the point you are making. See page 180 for an example of a figure in a paper.

Preparing the list of works cited   Begin the list of works cited on a new page at the end of the paper. Center the title "Works Cited" about one inch from the top of the page. Double-space throughout. See pages 185–86 for a sample list of works cited.

Alphabetizing the list   Alphabetize the list by the last names of the authors (or editors); if a work has no author or editor, alphabetize by the first word of the title other than *A*, *An*, or *The*.

Indenting   Do not indent the first line of each works cited entry, but indent any additional lines one-half inch. This technique, called a hanging indent, highlights the names of the authors, making it easy for readers to scan the alphabetized list. See the works cited list on pages 185–86.

URLs and DOIs   Do not insert line breaks, spaces, or hyphens into URLs or DOIs in works cited entries. If the entire URL moves to another line, creating a short line, you may leave it that way.

34b   Sample MLA research paper

On the following pages is a research paper on the topic of the role of government in legislating food choices, written by Sophie Harba, a student in a composition class. Harba's paper is documented with in-text citations and a list of works cited in MLA style. Annotations in the margins of the paper draw your attention to Harba's use of MLA style and her effective writing.

Sophie Harba

Professor Baros-Moon

Engl 1101

9 November 2015

What's for Dinner? Personal Choices vs. Public Health **1**

Should the government enact laws to regulate healthy eating **2**

choices? Many Americans would answer an emphatic "No," arguing

that what and how much we eat should be left to individual choice

rather than unreasonable laws. Others might argue that it would be

unreasonable for the government not to enact legislation, given the rise

of chronic diseases that result from harmful diets. In this debate, both **3**

the definition of reasonable regulations and the role of government

to legislate food choices are at stake. In the name of public health **4**

and safety, state governments have the responsibility to shape health

policies and to regulate healthy eating choices, especially since doing

so offers a potentially large social benefit for a relatively small cost.

Debates surrounding the government's role in regulating

food have a long history in the United States. According to Lorine **5**

Goodwin, a food historian, nineteenth-century reformers who sought

to purify the food supply were called "fanatics" and "radicals" by

critics who argued that consumers should be free to buy and eat what

they want (77). Thanks to regulations, though, such as the 1906 **6**

federal Pure Food and Drug Act, food, beverages, and medicine are **7**

largely free from toxins. In addition, to prevent contamination and

the spread of disease, meat and dairy products are now inspected by

government agents to ensure that they meet health requirements.

Such regulations can be considered reasonable because they protect **8**

us from harm with little, if any, noticeable consumer cost. It is not

considered an unreasonable infringement on personal choice that

1 Title centered. **2** Opening question engages readers.
3 Writer highlights the research conversation. **4** Thesis
answers the question and presents main point. **5** Signal
phrase names the author. **6** Parenthetical citation gives page
number. **7** Harba provides historical background. **8** Harba
introduces key term, *reasonable*.

Harba 2

contaminated meat or arsenic-laced cough drops are unavailable at our local supermarket. Rather, it is an important government function to stop such harmful items from entering the marketplace.

❶ Even though our food meets current safety standards, there is a need for further regulation. Not all food dangers, for example, arise from obvious toxins like arsenic and *E. coli*. A diet that is low in nutritional value and high in sugars, fats, and refined grains — grains that have been processed to increase shelf life but that contain little fiber, iron, and B vitamins — can be damaging over time (United States, Department **❷** of Agriculture 36). A graph from the government's *Dietary Guidelines for Americans, 2010* shows that Americans consume about three times more fats and sugars and twice as many refined grains as is recommended but only half of the recommended foods (see fig. 1).

❸

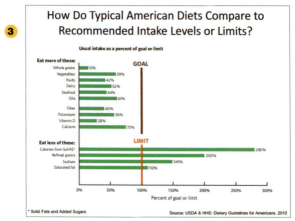

❹ Fig. 1. United States, Department of Agriculture, fig. 5-1.

❶ Transition helps readers move from one paragraph to the next. **❷** Parenthetical citation with shortened organization author name and page number. **❸** Harba uses a graph to illustrate Americans' poor nutritional choices. **❹** Figure number and citation provided under the visual. A full entry for this source appears in the works cited list.

Michael Pollan, who has written extensively about Americans' unhealthy eating habits, notes that "[t]he Centers for Disease Control estimates that fully three quarters of US health care spending goes to treat chronic diseases, most of which are preventable and linked to diet: heart disease, stroke, type 2 diabetes, and at least a third of all cancers." In fact, the amount of money the United States **(1)** spends to treat chronic illnesses is increasing so rapidly that the Centers for Disease Control has labeled chronic disease "the public health challenge of the 21st century" (United States, Department of Health 1). In fighting this epidemic, the primary challenge is not **(2)** the need to find a cure; the challenge is to prevent chronic diseases from striking in the first place.

Legislation, however, is not a popular solution when it comes **(3)** to most Americans and the food they eat. According to a nationwide poll, seventy-five percent of Americans are opposed to laws that restrict or put limitations on access to unhealthy foods (Neergaard and Agiesta). When New York mayor Michael Bloomberg proposed a regulation in 2012 banning the sale of soft drinks in servings greater than twelve ounces in restaurants and movie theaters, he was ridiculed as "Nanny Bloomberg." In California in 2011, legislators failed to pass a law that would impose a penny-per-ounce tax on soda, which would have funded obesity prevention programs. And in Mississippi, legislators passed "a ban on bans — a law that forbids . . . local restrictions on food or drink" (Conly). **(4)**

Why is the public largely resistant to laws that would limit unhealthy choices or penalize those choices with so-called fat taxes? Many consumers and civil rights advocates find such laws to be an **(5)** unreasonable restriction on individual freedom of choice. As health policy experts Mello and others point out, opposition to food and beverage regulation is similar to the opposition to early tobacco

(1) No page number available for web source. **(2)** Harba emphasizes the urgency of her argument. **(3)** Harba treats both sides fairly. **(4)** No page number provided for a one-page source. **(5)** Harba anticipates objections to her idea. She counters opposing views and supports her argument.

Harba 4

legislation: the public views the issue as one of personal responsibility rather than one requiring government intervention (2602). In other words, if people eat unhealthy food and become ill as a result, that is their choice. But those who favor legislation claim that freedom of choice is a myth because of the strong influence of food and beverage industry marketing on consumers' dietary habits. According to one nonprofit health advocacy group, food and beverage companies spend roughly two billion dollars per year marketing directly to children. As a result, kids see nearly four thousand ads per year encouraging

1 them to eat unhealthy food and drinks ("Facts"). As was the case with antismoking laws passed in recent decades, taxes and legal restrictions on junk food sales could help to counter the strong marketing messages that promote unhealthy products.

The United States has a history of state and local public health laws that have successfully promoted a particular behavior by punishing

2 an undesirable behavior. The decline in tobacco use as a result of antismoking taxes and laws is perhaps the most obvious example. Another example is legislation requiring the use of seat belts, which have significantly reduced fatalities in car crashes. One government agency reports that seat belt use saved an average of more than fourteen thousand lives per year in the United States between 2000 and 2010 (United States, Department of Transportation 231). Perhaps seat belt laws have public support because the cost of wearing a seat belt is small, especially when compared with the benefit of saving fourteen thousand lives per year.

Laws designed to prevent chronic disease by promoting healthier food and beverage consumption also have potentially

3 enormous benefits. To give just one example, Marion Nestle, New York University professor of nutrition and public health, notes that

---

1 Shortened title provided in parenthetical citation for source with no author. **2** An analogy extends Harba's argument. **3** Harba introduces a quotation with a signal phrase and shows readers why she chose to use the source.

Harba 5

"a 1% reduction in intake of saturated fat across the population would prevent more than 30,000 cases of coronary heart disease annually and save more than a billion dollars in health care costs" (7). Few would argue that saving lives and dollars is not an enormous benefit. But three-quarters of Americans say they would object to the costs needed to achieve this benefit — the regulations needed to reduce saturated fat intake.

Why do so many Americans believe there is a degree of ❶ personal choice lost when regulations such as taxes, bans, or portion limits on unhealthy foods are proposed? Some critics of anti-junk-food laws believe that even if state and local laws were successful in curbing chronic diseases, they would still be unacceptable. Bioethicist David Resnik emphasizes that such policies, despite their potential to make our society healthier, "open the door to excessive government control over food, which could restrict dietary choices, interfere with cultural, ethnic, and religious traditions, and exacerbate socioeconomic inequalities" (31). Resnik acknowledges that his argument relies on "slippery slope" thinking, but he insists that "social and political pressures" regarding food regulation make his concerns valid (31). Yet the social and political pressures that Resnik cites are really just the desire to improve public health, and limiting access to unhealthy, artificial ingredients seems a small price to pay. As legal scholars L. O. Gostin and K. G. Gostin explain, ❷ "[I]nterventions that do not pose a truly significant burden on individual liberty" are justified if they "go a long way towards safeguarding the health and well-being of the populace" (214).

To improve public health, advocates such as Bowdoin College philosophy professor Sarah Conly contend that it is the government's duty to prevent people from making harmful choices whenever feasible and whenever public benefits outweigh the costs.

❶ Harba acknowledges critics and counterarguments.
❷ Including the source's credentials makes Harba more credible.

In response to critics who claim that laws aimed at stopping us from eating whatever we want are an assault on our freedom of choice, Conly offers a persuasive counterargument:

> [L]aws aren't designed for each one of us individually. Some of us can drive safely at 90 miles per hour, but we're bound by the same laws as the people who can't, because individual speeding laws aren't practical. Giving up a little liberty is something we agree to when we agree to live in a democratic society that is governed by laws.

As Conly suggests, it's important to move from either/or thinking (either we have complete freedom of choice *or* we have government regulations and lose our freedom) to seeing health as a matter of public good, not individual liberty. Proposals such as Mayor Bloomberg's that seek to limit portions of unhealthy beverages aren't about giving up liberty; they are about asking individuals to choose substantial public health benefits at a very small cost.

Despite arguments in favor of regulating unhealthy food as a means to improve public health, public opposition has stood in the way of legislation. Americans freely eat as much unhealthy food as they want, and manufacturers and sellers of these foods have nearly unlimited freedom to promote such products and drive increased consumption, without any requirements to warn the public of potential hazards. Yet mounting scientific evidence points to unhealthy food as a significant contributing factor to chronic disease, which we know is straining our health care system, decreasing Americans' quality of life, and leading to unnecessary premature deaths. Americans must consider whether to allow the costly trend of rising chronic disease to continue in the name of personal choice or whether to support the regulatory changes and public health policies that will reverse that trend.

1 Signal phrase names the author. **2** Long quotation is set off from the text. Quotation marks are omitted. **3** Long quotation is followed with comments that connect the source to Harba's argument. **4** Conclusion sums up Harba's argument and provides closure.

Works Cited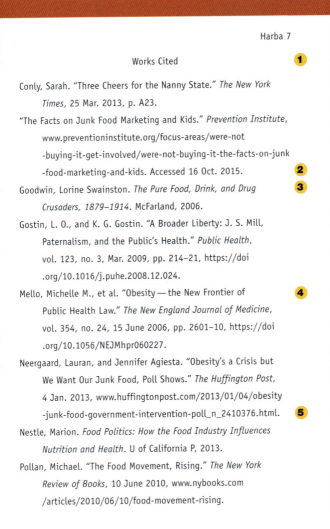

Conly, Sarah. "Three Cheers for the Nanny State." *The New York Times*, 25 Mar. 2013, p. A23.

"The Facts on Junk Food Marketing and Kids." *Prevention Institute*, www.preventioninstitute.org/focus-areas/were-not -buying-it-get-involved/were-not-buying-it-the-facts-on-junk -food-marketing-and-kids. Accessed 16 Oct. 2015.

Goodwin, Lorine Swainston. *The Pure Food, Drink, and Drug Crusaders, 1879–1914*. McFarland, 2006.

Gostin, L. O., and K. G. Gostin. "A Broader Liberty: J. S. Mill, Paternalism, and the Public's Health." *Public Health*, vol. 123, no. 3, Mar. 2009, pp. 214–21, https://doi .org/10.1016/j.puhe.2008.12.024.

Mello, Michelle M., et al. "Obesity — the New Frontier of Public Health Law." *The New England Journal of Medicine*, vol. 354, no. 24, 15 June 2006, pp. 2601–10, https://doi .org/10.1056/NEJMhpr060227.

Neergaard, Lauran, and Jennifer Agiesta. "Obesity's a Crisis but We Want Our Junk Food, Poll Shows." *The Huffington Post*, 4 Jan. 2013, www.huffingtonpost.com/2013/01/04/obesity -junk-food-government-intervention-poll_n_2410376.html.

Nestle, Marion. *Food Politics: How the Food Industry Influences Nutrition and Health*. U of California P, 2013.

Pollan, Michael. "The Food Movement, Rising." *The New York Review of Books*, 10 June 2010, www.nybooks.com /articles/2010/06/10/food-movement-rising.

1 Works Cited begins on new page. Heading is centered. **2** Access date used for undated online source. **3** List alphabetized by authors' last names (or by title if no author). **4** First line of each entry at the left margin; extra lines indented ½". **5** Double-spacing used throughout.

Harba 8

Resnik, David. "Trans Fat Bans and Human Freedom." *The American Journal of Bioethics*, vol. 10, no. 3, Mar. 2010, pp. 27–32.

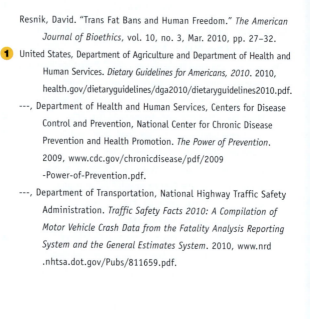 United States, Department of Agriculture and Department of Health and Human Services. *Dietary Guidelines for Americans, 2010*. 2010, health.gov/dietaryguidelines/dga2010/dietaryguidelines2010.pdf.

---, Department of Health and Human Services, Centers for Disease Control and Prevention, National Center for Chronic Disease Prevention and Health Promotion. *The Power of Prevention*. 2009, www.cdc.gov/chronicdisease/pdf/2009 -Power-of-Prevention.pdf.

---, Department of Transportation, National Highway Traffic Safety Administration. *Traffic Safety Facts 2010: A Compilation of Motor Vehicle Crash Data from the Fatality Analysis Reporting System and the General Estimates System*. 2010, www.nrd .nhtsa.dot.gov/Pubs/811659.pdf.

1 Author names are standardized for multiple government sources.

APA Papers

Instructors in the social sciences and other disciplines, such as business, education, and nursing, may ask you to document your sources with the American Psychological Association (APA) system of in-text citations and references described in section 38. When writing an APA-style paper that draws on sources, you will need to (1) support a thesis, (2) cite your sources accurately and avoid plagiarism, and (3) integrate source material effectively.

35   Supporting a thesis

▶   How to test your thesis   **109**

Most research assignments ask you to form a thesis, or main idea, and to support that thesis with well-organized evidence. A thesis, which usually appears at the end of the introduction, is a one-sentence (or occasionally a two-sentence) statement of your central idea. In a paper reviewing the literature on a topic, the thesis analyzes conclusions drawn by a variety of researchers.

35a   Forming a thesis statement

Once you have read a variety of sources, considered your issue from different perspectives, and chosen an entry point into a research conversation, you are ready to form a thesis. A thesis states your informed answer to your research question—an answer about which reasonable people might disagree. As your ideas develop, you'll revise your initial thesis (or *working thesis*) to make it more specific and focused. Notice how each of the thesis statements that follow takes a position on a debatable issue:

RESEARCH QUESTION

Can educational technology improve student learning and solve the problem of teacher shortages?

THESIS

In the face of mounting teacher shortages, public schools should embrace educational technology that promotes student-centered learning in order to help all students become successful learners.

RESEARCH QUESTION

Is medication the most effective treatment for the escalating problem of childhood obesity?

THESIS

Understanding the limitations of medical treatments for children highlights the complexity of the childhood obesity problem in the United States and underscores the need for physicians, advocacy groups, and policymakers to search for other solutions.

RESEARCH QUESTION

Why are boys diagnosed with ADHD more often than girls are diagnosed with the disorder?

THESIS

Recent studies have suggested that ADHD is diagnosed more often in boys than in girls because of personality differences between boys and girls as well as gender bias in referring adults, but an overlooked cause is that ADHD often coexists with other behavior disorders that exaggerate or mask gender differences.

For help with testing your thesis, see the guidelines on page 109.

35b Organizing your ideas

APA encourages the use of headings to help readers follow the organization of a paper. For an original research report, the major headings often follow a standard model: "Method," "Results," "Discussion." For a literature review, headings will vary, depending on the topic. Student writer April Wang used three questions to focus her research (see her final paper in 39b); the questions then became headings in her paper:

In what ways is student-centered learning effective?

Can educational technology help students drive their own learning?

How can public schools effectively combine teacher talent and educational technology?

35c Using sources to inform and support your argument

The source materials you have gathered will help you develop and support your argument. As you consider using a source, ask yourself what you learned from the source and how the source might function to help you answer your research question. Sources can play several different roles:

Providing background information or context Describe a study or offer a statistic to help readers grasp the significance of your topic or understand generalizations about it.

Explaining terms or concepts Explain words, phrases, or ideas that might be unfamiliar to your readers. Quoting or paraphrasing a source can help you define terms and concepts clearly and concisely.

Supporting your claims Back up your assertions with facts, examples, and other evidence from your research.

Lending authority to your argument Expert opinion can give weight to your argument. But don't rely on experts to make your argument for you. Construct your argument in your own words and cite authorities in the field to support your position.

Anticipating and countering objections Do not ignore sources that seem contrary to your position or that offer arguments different from your own. Instead, use them to state potential objections to your argument before you counter them.

36 Avoiding plagiarism

▶ How to be a responsible research writer **115**

In a research paper, you draw on the work of other researchers and writers. To be fair and responsible, you must document their contributions by citing your sources. When you acknowledge your sources, you avoid plagiarism, a form of academic dishonesty. Three different acts are considered plagiarism:

1. failing to cite quotations and borrowed ideas
2. failing to enclose borrowed language in quotation marks
3. failing to put summaries and paraphrases in your own words

36a Citing quotations and borrowed ideas

When you cite sources, you give credit to writers from whom you've borrowed words and ideas. You must cite anything you borrow from a source, including direct quotations; statistics and other specific facts; visuals such as tables, graphs, and diagrams; and any ideas you present in a summary or a paraphrase. Your citation guides readers quickly to the source of a quoted, paraphrased, or summarized idea so that they can find and read the original source.

The only exception is common knowledge—information your readers likely already know or could easily find in general sources. When you have seen certain information repeatedly in your reading, you don't need to cite it. However, when information has appeared in only a few sources, when it is highly specific (as with statistics), or when it is controversial, you should cite the source. If you're not sure whether you need to cite something, check with your instructor.

36b Using the APA citation system to lead readers to your sources

APA recommends an author-date style of citation. The date is important because disciplines that use APA style value current research. APA style also requires the use of the past tense or the present perfect tense when introducing cited material: Horn and Staker (2011) concluded . . . ; Bell (2010) has argued . . . Here, briefly, is how the author-date system usually works.

1. The source is introduced by a signal phrase that includes the last name of the author followed by the date of publication in parentheses.

2. The material being cited is followed by a locator (page number, paragraph number, or heading) in parentheses.
3. At the end of the paper, an alphabetized list of references gives publication information for each source.

IN-TEXT CITATION

Lanier (2018) argued that through the pervasiveness of social media, "what might once have been called advertising must now be understood as continuous behavior modification on a titanic scale" (p. 6).

ENTRY IN THE LIST OF REFERENCES

Lanier, J. (2018). *Ten arguments for deleting your social media accounts right now.* Henry Holt and Company.

NOTE: This basic APA format varies for different types of sources. For a detailed discussion and other models, see 38.

36c Using quotation marks around borrowed language

To indicate that you are using a source's exact phrases or sentences, you must enclose them in quotation marks. To omit the quotation marks is to claim—falsely—that the language is your own. Such an omission is plagiarism even if you have cited the source. In the example of plagiarism below, the student writer has cited the source, but has not used quotation marks around the words taken directly from the source (highlighted).

ORIGINAL SOURCE

Student-centered learning, or student centeredness, is a model which puts the student in the center of the learning process.

— Z. Çubukçu, "Teachers' Evaluation
of Student-Centered Learning
Environments" (2012), p. 50

PLAGIARISM

According to Çubukçu (2012), student-centered learning is a model which puts the student in the center of the learning process (p. 50).

BORROWED LANGUAGE IN QUOTATION MARKS

According to Çubukçu (2012), "student-centered learning . . . is a model which puts the student in the center of the learning process" (p. 50).

NOTE: Quotation marks are not used when quoted sentences are set off from the text by indenting (see pp. 196–97).

36d Putting summaries and paraphrases in your own words

A summary condenses information from a source; a paraphrase conveys the information using roughly the same number of words as the original source. When you summarize or paraphrase, it is not enough to name the source; you must present the source's meaning using your own words and sentence structure. You plagiarize if you patchwrite—half-copy the author's sentences, either by mixing the author's phrases with your own without using quotation marks or by plugging synonyms into the author's sentence structure. The following paraphrases are plagiarized—even though the source is cited—because their language or sentence structure is too close to that of the source.

> **ORIGINAL SOURCE**
>
> Student-centered teaching focuses on the student. Decision-making, organization and content are determined for most by taking individual students' needs and interests into consideration. Student-centered teaching provides opportunities to develop students' skills of transferring knowledge to other situations, triggering retention, and adapting a high motivation for learning.
> —Z. Çubukçu, "Teachers' Evaluation of Student-Centered Learning Environments" (2012), p. 52

PLAGIARISM: UNACCEPTABLE BORROWING OF PHRASES

According to Çubukçu (2012), student-centered teaching takes into account the needs and interests of each student, making it possible to foster students' skills of transferring knowledge to new situations and triggering retention (p. 52).

PLAGIARISM: UNACCEPTABLE BORROWING OF STRUCTURE

According to Çubukçu (2012), this new model of teaching centers on the student. The material and flow of the course are chosen by considering the students' individual requirements. Student-centered teaching gives a chance for students to develop useful, transferable skills, ensuring they'll remember material and stay motivated (p. 52).

NOTE: While a locator is not required after a paraphrase or summary, APA recommends using one when citing a long source to help readers locate the relevant section.

To avoid plagiarizing an author's language, don't look at the source while you are summarizing or paraphrasing. After you've restated the author's ideas in your own words, return to the source and check that you haven't used the author's language or sentence structure or misrepresented the author's ideas.

ACCEPTABLE PARAPHRASE

Çubukçu's (2012) research documents the numerous benefits of student-centered teaching in putting the student at the center of teaching and learning. When students are given the option of deciding what they learn and how they learn, they are motivated to apply their learning to new settings and to retain the content of their learning (p. 52).

See the box on page 115 for simple guidelines for being a responsible research writer.

37   Integrating sources

Quotations, summaries, paraphrases, and facts will help you develop your argument, but they cannot speak for you. Readers should always know who is speaking in your paper—you or one of your sources. You can use several strategies to integrate sources into your paper while maintaining your own voice.

37a Summarizing and paraphrasing effectively

When you summarize or paraphrase, you express an author's ideas in your own words. A summary condenses the author's key points and use fewer words than the original. You might summarize to compare arguments or ideas from various sources or to provide readers with an overview of a source before you discuss it.

A paraphrase uses approximately the same number of words and details as in the source. You might paraphrase to help readers understand complex ideas or data from a source.

Even though you're using your own words to summarize or paraphrase, the original ideas are the author's intellectual property, so you must include a citation. (For more advice on summarizing and paraphrasing, see 31a.)

37b Using quotations effectively

When you quote a source, you borrow some of the author's exact words and enclose them in quotation marks. Quotation marks show your readers that both the idea and the words belong to the author. You might quote a source when exact wording is needed for accuracy or when the original language is especially effective.

Limiting your use of quotations   Keep the emphasis on your own words and ideas. It is not always necessary to quote full sentences from a source. Often you can integrate language from a source into your own sentence structure.

Citing federal data, *The New York Times* reported a 30% drop in "people entering teacher preparation programs" between 2010 and 2014 (Rich, 2015, para. 10).

Using the ellipsis mark   To condense a quoted passage, you can use the an ellipsis — a series of three spaced periods — to indicate that you have omitted words. What remains must be grammatically complete.

Demski (2012) noted that "personalized learning . . . acknowledges and accommodates the range of abilities, prior experiences, needs, and interests of each student" (p. 33).

The writer has omitted the phrase *a student-centered teaching and learning model that* from the source.

If you want to leave out one or more full sentences, use a period before the ellipsis.

According to Demski (2012), "In any personalized learning model, the student — not the teacher — is the central figure. . . . Personalized learning may finally allow individualization and differentiation to actually happen in the classroom" (p. 34).

Ordinarily, do not use an ellipsis at the beginning or at the end of a quotation. Readers will understand that you have taken the quoted material from a longer passage. The only exception occurs when you feel it is necessary, for clarity, to indicate that your quotation begins or ends in the middle of a sentence.

USING SOURCES RESPONSIBLY: Make sure that omissions and ellipses do not distort the meaning of your source.

Using brackets   Brackets allow you to insert your own words into quoted material to clarify a confusing reference or to keep a sentence grammatical in the context of your writing.

Demski's (2012) research confirms that "implement[ing] a true personalized learning model on a national level" is difficult for a number of reasons (p. 36).

To indicate an error such as a misspelling in a quotation, insert [*sic*], italicized and with brackets around it, right after the error.

Setting off long quotations   When you quote forty or more words from a source, set off the quotation by indenting it one-half inch from the left margin.

Long quotations should be introduced by an informative sentence, usually followed by a colon. Quotation marks are unnecessary because the indented format tells readers that the passage is taken word-for-word from the source.

According to Svokos (2015), some educational technology resources entertain students while supporting student-centered learning:

> GlassLab, a nonprofit that was launched with grants from the Bill & Melinda Gates and MacArthur Foundations, creates educational games that are now being used in more than 6,000 classrooms across the country. Some of the company's games are education versions of existing ones — for example, its first release was SimCity EDU — while others are originals. Teachers get real-time updates on students' progress as well as suggestions on what subjects they need to spend more time perfecting. (5. Educational Games section)

The parenthetical citation with a locator goes outside the final mark of punctuation. (When a quotation is run into your text, the opposite is true. See the sample citations on the previous page.)

For more advice on how to punctuate quotations, see page 120.

37c Using signal phrases to integrate sources

Whenever you include a paraphrase, summary, or direct quotation of another writer's work in your paper, prepare readers for it with a *signal phrase*. A signal phrase usually names the author of the source, gives the publication year in parentheses, and often provides some context for the source. It is generally acceptable in APA style to call authors by their last name only, even on first mention. If your paper refers to two authors with the same last name, use their first initials as well.

When you write a signal phrase, choose a verb that fits the way you are using the source. For example, are you using the source to provide data, support a claim, or refute an argument? See the chart on page 199 for a list of verbs commonly used in signal phrases.

Marking boundaries   Readers need to move smoothly from your words to the words of a source. Avoid dropping a quotation into your text without warning. Instead, provide a clear signal phrase, including at least the author's name and the year of publication. A signal phrase marks the boundaries between the source material and your own words and can help readers understand why a source is worth quoting.

DROPPED QUOTATION

Many educators have been intrigued by the concept of blended learning but have been unsure how to define it. "Blended learning is a formal education program in which a student learns at least in part through online delivery of content and instruction with some element of student control over time, place, and pace" (Horn & Staker, 2011, p. 4).

QUOTATION WITH SIGNAL PHRASE

Many educators have been intrigued by the concept of blended learning but have been unsure how to define it. As Horn and Staker (2011) have argued, "Blended learning is a formal education program in which a student learns at least in part through online delivery of content and instruction with some element of student control over time, place, and pace" (p. 4).

Introducing summaries and paraphrases   Introduce most summaries and paraphrases with a signal phrase that names the author and the year and places the material in the context of your argument. Readers will then understand where the summary or paraphrase begins.

   Without the signal phrase (highlighted) in the following example, readers might think that only the last sentence is being cited, when in fact the whole paragraph is based on the source.

Watson (2008) reported that for American postsecondary students, technology is integral to their academic lives. Nearly three-quarters own their own laptops, and 83% have used a course management system for an online component of a class. Watson pointed out that online and blended learning models are even more widespread outside of the United States (p. 15).

Sometimes a summary or a paraphrase does not require a signal phrase. When the context makes clear where the cited material begins, you may omit the signal phrase and include the author's name and the year in parentheses.

A Stanford study came to a similar conclusion; researchers examined four schools that had moved from teacher-driven instruction to student-centered learning (Friedlaender et al., 2014).

6̃ Signal phrases at a glance APA

To avoid monotony, try to vary both the language and the placement of your signal phrases.

Model signal phrases

In the words of Mitra (2013), ". . ."

As Bell (2010) has noted, ". . ."

Donitsa-Schmidt and Zuzovsky (2014) pointed out that ". . ."

". . .," claimed Çubukçu (2012, Introduction section).

". . .," explained Demski (2012), ". . ."

Horn and Staker (2011) have offered a compelling argument for this view: ". . ."

In a recent study, Sharon et al. (2019) found that ". . ."

Verbs in signal phrases

admitted	contended	pointed out
agreed	declared	reasoned
argued	denied	refuted
asserted	emphasized	rejected
believed	explained	reported
claimed	insisted	responded
compared	noted	suggested
confirmed	observed	wrote

NOTE: In APA style, use the past tense or present perfect tense (*argued* or *has argued*) to introduce source material.

Integrating statistics and other facts   When you cite a statistic or another specific fact, a signal phrase is often not necessary. In most cases, readers will understand that the citation refers to the data (not the whole paragraph).

Of polled high school students, 43% said that they lacked confidence in their technological proficiency going into college and careers (Moeller & Reitzes, 2011).

There is nothing wrong, however, with using a signal phrase to introduce a statistic or another fact.

Putting source material in context   Readers should not have to guess why a source appears in your paper. You must put each source in context. A signal phrase can help you connect your own ideas with those of another writer by clarifying how the source will contribute to your paper. It's a good idea to sandwich a quotation between sentences of your own, introducing it with a signal phrase and following it with interpretive comments that link the quotation to your paper's argument. For guides on integrating source material with your own sentences, see the box on page 125.

QUOTATION WITH EFFECTIVE CONTEXT

According to the International Society for Technology in Education (2016), "Student-centered learning moves students from passive receivers of information to active participants in their own discovery process." The results of student-centered learning have been positive, not only for academic achievement but also for student self-esteem, because students actively participate in the process of learning.

37d Synthesizing sources

When you synthesize multiple sources in a research paper, you create a conversation about your research topic. You show readers that your argument is based on your analysis and integration of ideas and is not just a string of quotations and paraphrases. Your synthesis shows how your sources relate to one another; one source my support, extend, or counter the ideas of another. For an example of an effective synthesis, see 31d.

38 APA documentation style

The APA system for documenting sources is set forth in the *Publication Manual of the American Psychological Association,* 7th ed. (APA, 2020).

👓 APA documentation **at a glance**

The APA system of documentation requires an in-text citation and a reference list entry for each source you use in a paper. These parts work together to credit your sources and to help readers find the sources for themselves. For each source you use, you should have

- an **in-text citation**, made up of two elements: a *signal phrase* and a *parenthetical citation*. These elements introduce the source, provide the author and year, and (when relevant) give a locator for the information. (See 38a for how to use in-text citations in different situations.) The information in the in-text citation points readers to

- the **reference list entry** in your reference list at the end of the paper. Each entry includes the full bibliographic information for the source, such as the author, title, date, publisher, or URL or DOI. (See 38b to learn what information to include for different types of sources.)

In each example below — the first a quotation from a paginated journal article, the second a paraphrase from an online video — the information that connects the two parts is underlined.

IN-TEXT CITATION (within the body of your paper)
According to van der Vleuten and Schuwirth (2019), problem-based learning "focuses on promoting abilities such as clinical reasoning, team skills and metacognition" while "also aim[ing] to foster self-directed learning" (p. 903).

REFERENCE LIST ENTRY (in a list at the end of your paper)
van der Vleuten, C. P. M., & Schuwirth, L. W. R. (2019). Assessment in the context of problem-based learning. *Advances in Health Sciences Education,* 24(5), 903–914. https://doi.org/10.1007/s10459-019-09909-1

Continued ➜

IN-TEXT CITATION

The Scottish Prime Minister explained that the Scottish government created its National Performance Framework to measure the nation's success in the well-being of its people, not just in commerce or profit (Sturgeon, 2019).

REFERENCE LIST ENTRY

Sturgeon, N. (2019, July). *Why governments should prioritize well-being.* TED. https://www.ted.com /talks/nicola_sturgeon_why_governments_should _prioritize_well_being

List of APA in-text citation models

List of APA reference list models

Continued ➜

38a APA in-text citations

APA's in-text citations provide the author's last name and the year of publication, usually before the cited material, and a locator (page number, paragraph number, or section title) in parentheses directly after the cited material. In the following models, the elements of the in-text citation are highlighted.

NOTE: APA style requires the use of the past tense or the present perfect tense in signal phrases introducing cited material: Smith (2020) reported . . ., Smith (2020) has argued. . . .

● **1. Basic format for a quotation**   Ordinarily, introduce the quotation with a signal phrase that includes the author's last name followed by the year of publication in parentheses. Put the page number (preceded by "p.") in parentheses after the quotation. For sources without page numbers, see item 11a.

Çubukçu (2012) argued that for a student-centered approach to work, students must maintain "ownership for their goals and activities" (p. 64).

If the author is not named in the signal phrase, place the author's name, the year, and the page number in parentheses after the quotation: (Çubukçu, 2012, p. 64). (See items 5 and 11 for citing sources that lack authors; item 11 also explains how to handle sources without dates or page numbers.)

NOTE: Do not include a month in an in-text citation, even if the entry in the reference list includes the month.

● **2. Basic format for a summary or a paraphrase**   As for a quotation (see item 1), include the author's last name and the year either in a signal phrase introducing the material or in parentheses following it. Use a page number for long sources such as books. For sources without page numbers, see item 11a.

Watson (2008) offered a case study of the Cincinnati Public Schools Virtual High School, in which students were able to engage in highly individualized instruction according to their own needs, strengths, and learning styles, using 10 teachers as support (p. 7).

The Cincinnati Public Schools Virtual High School brought students together to engage in highly individualized instruction according to their own needs, strengths, and learning styles, using 10 teachers as support (Watson, 2008, p. 7).

● **3. Work with two authors**   Name both authors in the signal phrase or in parentheses each time you cite the work. In the signal phrase, use "and" between the authors' names as shown below; in the parentheses, use "&" as shown on the next page.

According to Donitsa-Schmidt and Zuzovsky (2014), "demographic growth in the school population" can lead to teacher shortages (p. 426).

● **3. Work with two authors (*cont.*)**

In the United States, most public school systems are struggling with teacher shortages, which are projected to worsen as the number of applicants to education schools decreases (Donitsa-Schmidt & Zuzovsky, 2014, p. 420).

● **4. Work with three or more authors**   Name the first author followed by "et al." in the signal phrase or in parentheses every time you cite the source.

Surprisingly, others have advised school administrators "not to jump into project-based pedagogy without training and feedback" (Harper et al., 2013, p. 797).

Hermann et al. (2012) tracked 42 students over a 3-year period to look closely at the performance of students in the laptop program (p. 49).

● **5. Work with unknown author**   If the author is unknown, mention the work's title in the signal phrase or give the first word or two of the title in the parentheses. Titles of short works such as articles are put in quotation marks; titles of long works such as books and reports are italicized.

Collaboration increases significantly among students who own or have regular access to a laptop ("Tech Seeds," 2015).

NOTE: In the rare case when "Anonymous" is specified as the author, treat it as if it were a real name: (Anonymous, 2011). In the list of references, also use Anonymous as the author's name.

● **6. Organization as author**   Name the organization in the signal phrase or in the parentheses the first time you cite the source.

According to the International Society for Technology in Education (2016), "Student-centered learning moves students from passive receivers of information to active participants in their own discovery process" (What Is It? section).

If the organization has a familiar abbreviation, you may include it in brackets the first time you cite the source and then use the abbreviation alone in later citations.

FIRST CITATION   (Texas Higher Education Coordinating Board [THECB], 2012)

LATER CITATIONS   (THECB, 2012)

● **7. Authors with the same last name**   If your reference list includes two or more authors with the same last name, use initials with the last names in your in-text citations.

Research by E. Smith (1989) revealed that . . .

One 2012 study contradicted . . . (R. Smith, p. 234).

● **8. Two or more works by the same author in the same year**   In the reference list, you will use lowercase letters ("a," "b," and so on) with the year to order the entries. (See item 8 in 38b.) Use those same letters with the year in the in-text citation.

Research by Durgin (2013b) has yielded new findings about the role of smartphones in the classroom.

● **9. Two or more works cited in the same parentheses** Put the works in the same order in which they appear in the reference list, separated with semicolons.

Researchers have indicated that studies of educational technology initiatives reveal the high cost of change (Nazer, 2015; Serrao et al., 2014).

● **10. Multiple citations to the same work in one paragraph**   If you give the author's name in the text of your paper and you mention that source again in the text of the same paragraph, give only the author's name, not the date, in the later citation. If any subsequent reference in the same paragraph is in parentheses, include both the author and the date (and a page number when appropriate) in the parentheses.

Bell (2010) has argued that the chief benefit of student-centered learning is that it can connect students with "real-world tasks," thus making learning more engaging as well as more comprehensive (p. 42). For example, Bell observed a group of middle-school students who wanted to build a social justice monument for their school. Students engaged in this kind of learning performed better on both project-based assessments and standardized tests (Bell, 2010).

● **11. Web source**   Cite sources from the web as you would cite any other source, giving the author and the year when they are available.

Atkinson (2011) found that children who spent at least 4 hours a day engaged in online activities in an academic environment were less likely to want to play video games or watch TV after school.

Usually a page number is not available; occasionally a web source will lack an author or a date.

a. No page numbers   When quoting a web source without stable numbered pages, include paragraph numbers, section headings, or both. Some sources have numbered paragraphs; if a source lacks headings or numbered paragraphs, count the paragraphs manually. When quoting audio and video sources, use a time stamp to indicate the start of the quotation.

Crush and Jayasingh (2015) pointed out that several other school districts in low-income areas had "jump-started their distance learning initiatives with available grant funds" (Funding Change section, para. 6).

You may also use shortened versions of long headings; place shortened headings in quotation marks: (Gregor, 2017, "What Happens When" section).

b. Unknown author   If no author is named in the source, mention the title of the source in a signal phrase or give the first word or two of the title in parentheses (see also item 5). (If an organization serves as the author, see item 6.)

A student's IEP may, in fact, recommend the use of mobile technology ("Considerations," 2012).

c. Unknown date   When the source does not give a date, use the abbreviation "n.d." (for "no date").

Administrators believe 1-to-1 programs boost learner engagement (Magnus, n.d.).

● **12. An entire website** If you mention an entire website from which you did not pull specific information, give the URL in the text of your paper but do not include it in the reference list.

The Berkeley Center for Teaching and Learning website (https:// teaching.berkeley.edu) shares ideas for using mobile technology in the classroom.

● **13. Personal communication** Interviews that you conduct, memos, letters, email messages, and similar communications that would be difficult for your readers to retrieve should be cited in the text only, not in the reference list. (Use the author's first initial as well as the last name in parentheses.)

One of Yim's colleagues, who has studied the effect of social media on children's academic progress, has contended that the benefits of this technology for children under 12 years old are few (F. Johnson, personal communication, October 20, 2013).

● **14. Course materials** Cite lecture notes from your instructor or your own class notes as personal communication (see item 13). If your instructor's material contains publication information, cite as you would the appropriate source. See also item 58 in 38b.

● **15. Part of a source (section, figure)** To cite a specific part of a source, such as a section of a web page or a figure or table, identify the element in parentheses. Don't abbreviate terms such as "Figure," "Chapter," and "Section"; "page" is abbreviated "p." (or "pp." for more than one page). Cite the work as a whole in your reference list.

The data support the finding that peer relationships are difficult to replicate in a completely online environment (Hanniman, 2010, Figure 8-3).

● **16. Indirect source (source quoted in another source)** When a published source is quoted in a source written by someone else, cite the original source first; include "as cited in" before the author and date of the source you read. In the example on the next page, Chow is the author of the source in the reference list; that source contains a quotation by Brailsford.

● **16. Indirect source (*cont.*)**

Brailsford (1990) commended the writer and educator's "sure understanding of the thoughts of young people" (as cited in Chow, 2019, para. 9).

● **17. Sacred or classical text** Identify the text (specifying the version or edition you used), the publication date(s), and the relevant part (book or chapter, verse, line).

Peace activists have long cited the biblical prophet's vision of a world without war: "And they shall beat their swords into plowshares, and their spears into pruning hooks; nation shall not lift up sword against nation, neither shall they learn war any more" (*Holy Bible Revised Standard Edition*, 1952/2004, Isaiah 2:4).

38b APA list of references

The information you will need for the reference list at the end of your paper will differ slightly for some sources, but the main principles apply to all sources: You should identify an author, a creator, or a producer whenever possible; give a title; and provide the date on which the source was produced. Some sources will require page numbers; some will require a publisher; and some will require retrieval information.

General guidelines for listing authors

The formatting of authors' names in items 1–11 applies to all sources in print and on the web — books, articles, websites, and so on. For more models of specific source types, see items 12–61.

● **1. Single author**

author: last | year
name + initial(s) | (book) | title (book)

Rosenberg, T. (2011). *Join the club: How peer pressure can*

publisher

transform the world. W. W. Norton & Company.

👓 The reference list **at a glance**

In the list of references, include only sources that you quote, summarize, or paraphrase in your paper.

Authors and dates

- Alphabetize entries by authors' last names; if a work has no author, alphabetize it by its title.

- For all authors' names, put the last name first, followed by a comma; use initials for the first and middle names.

- With two or more authors, separate the names with commas. Include names for up to 20 authors, with an ampersand (&) before the last author's name; if there are 21 or more authors, give the first 19 authors, followed by an ellipsis (three spaced periods) and the last author.

- If the author is a company or an organization, give the name in normal order.

- Put the date of publication in parentheses immediately after the first element of the citation.

- For books, give the year of publication. For magazines, newspapers, and newsletters, give the year and month or the year, month, and day. Use the season if a publication gives only a season, not a month. For web sources, give the date of posting, if available.

Titles

- Italicize the titles and subtitles of books, journals, and other stand-alone works. If a book title contains another book title or an article title, do not italicize the internal title and do not put quotation marks around it.

- Use no italics or quotation marks for the titles of articles. If an article title contains another article title or a term usually placed in quotation marks, use quotation marks around the internal title or the term.

- For books and articles, capitalize only the first word of the title and subtitle and all proper nouns.

- For the titles of journals, magazines, and newspapers, capitalize all words of four letters or more (and all nouns, pronouns, verbs, adjectives, and adverbs of any length).

Continued ➜

60 The reference list **at a glance** (Continued)

Publisher

- In publishers' names, omit business designations such as Inc. or Ltd. Otherwise, write the publisher's name exactly as it appears in the source.

- For online sources, list the name of the website in the publisher position (Twitter; YouTube; U.S. Census Bureau).

- If the publisher is the same as the author, do not repeat the name in the publisher position.

- Provide locations only for works associated with a single location (such as a conference presentation).

Volume, issue, and page numbers

- Include the volume and issue numbers for any journals, magazines, or other periodicals that have them.

- Italicize the volume number and put the issue number, not italicized, in parentheses.

- When an article appears on consecutive pages, provide the range of pages. When an article does not appear on consecutive pages, give all page numbers: A1, A17.

- Use "p." and "pp." before page numbers only with selections in edited books. Do not use "p." or "pp." with journals, magazines, and newspapers.

URLs, DOIs, and other retrieval information

- For articles and books from the web, use the DOI (digital object identifier) if the source has one. If a source from a website does not have a DOI, give the URL. Do not give URLs for sources from academic databases.

- Use a retrieval date for a web source only if the content is likely to change (such as the home page of a website or a social media profile).

- If a URL or DOI is long, you may use a permalink (if the website provides one) or create one using a shortening service (such as shortdoi.org or bitly.com).

● **2. Two to 20 authors** List up to 20 authors by last names followed by initials. Use an ampersand (&) before the name of the last author. (See items 3 and 4 in 38a for in-text citations.)

all authors:
last name + initial(s)   year (journal)

Kim, E. H., Hollon, S. D., & Olatunji, B. O. (2016). Clinical

title (article)   journal title   volume, issue

errors in cognitive-behavior therapy. *Psychotherapy, 53*(3),

page(s)   DOI

325–330. https://doi.org/10.1037/pst0000074

● **3. Twenty-one or more authors** List the first 19 authors followed by an ellipsis and the last author's name.

Sharon, G., Cruz, N. J., Kang, D.-W., Gandal, M. J., Wang, B.,
Kim, Y.-M., Zink, E. M., Casey, C. P., Taylor, B. C., Lane,
C. J., Bramer, L. M., Isern, N. G., Hoyt, D. W., Noecker,
C., Sweredoski, M. J., Moradian, A., Borenstein, E.,
Jansson, J. K., Knight, R., . . . Mazmanian, S. K. (2019).
Human gut microbiota from autism spectrum disorder
promote behavioral symptoms in mice. *Cell, 177*(6),
1600–1618. https://doi.org/10.1016/j.cell.2019.05.004

● **4. Organization as author**

author:
organization name   year   title (book)

American Psychiatric Association. (2013). *Diagnostic and statistical*

edition

manual of mental disorders (5th ed.).

● **5. Unknown author**

title (article)   year + month + day (weekly publication)   magazine title   volume, issue   page(s)

Pushed out. (2019, August 24). *The Economist, 432*(9157), 19–20.

● **6. Author using a pseudonym (pen name) or screen name** Use the author's real name, if known, and give the pseudonym or screen name in brackets exactly as it appears in the source. If only the screen name is known, begin with that name and do not use brackets, as in the example on the next page. (See also item 60.)

● **6. Author using a pseudonym (pen name) or screen name (*cont.*)**

screen name   year + month + day (online comment)   text of comment

dr.zachary.smith. (2019, October 30). What problem are they

label with original article title

trying to solve? [Comment on the article "Georgia is

title of publication   URL for comment

purging voter rolls again"]. *Slate*. https://fyre.it/sjSPFyza.4

● **7. Two or more works by the same author**   Use the author's name for all entries. List the entries by year, the earliest first.

Abdurraqib, H. (2017). *They can't kill us until they kill us*. Two
     Dollar Radio.

Abdurraqib, H. (2019). *Go ahead in the rain: Notes to A Tribe
     Called Quest*. University of Texas Press.

● **8. Two or more works by the same author in the same year**   List the works in chronological order (the earliest first), and add the letters "a," "b," and so on after the year. If the works have only a year or their exact dates are identical, arrange the entries alphabetically by title. (See also item 8 in 38a.)

Conover, E. (2019a, June 8). Gold's origins tied to collapsars.
     Science News, 195(10), 10.

Conover, E. (2019b, June 22). Space flames may hold secrets to
     soot-free fire. *Science News, 195*(11), 5.

● **9. Editor**   Use the abbreviation "Ed." for one editor, "Eds." for more than one editor.

editor   year   title (book)

Yeh, K.-H. (Ed.). (2019). *Asian indigenous psychologies in the*

publisher

global context. Palgrave Macmillan.

● **10. Author and editor**   After the title, in parentheses place the name of the editor(s) in normal order and the abbreviation "Ed." or "Eds."

author   year   title (book)   editor

Sontag, S. (2018). *Debriefing: Collected stories* (B. Taylor, Ed.).

publisher

Picador.

● **11. Translator** After the title, in parentheses place the name of the translator and the abbreviation "Trans." (for "Translator"). Add the original date of publication at the end of the entry.

author year   title (book)   translator
Calasso, P. (2019). *The unnamable present* (R. Dixon, Trans.).

             original publication
   publisher   information
Farrar, Straus and Giroux. (Original work published 2017)

Articles and other short works

▶ Citation at a glance: Online article in a journal or magazine **218**
▶ Citation at a glance: Article from a database **219**

● **12. Article in a journal** If an article from the web has no DOI, include the URL for the article. If an article from a database has no DOI, do not include a URL.

a. Print

  all authors: last
  name + initial(s)   year   article title
Ganegoda, D. B., & Bordia, P. (2019). I can be happy for you,

but not all the time: A contingency model of envy and
              journal title
positive empathy in the workplace. *Journal of Applied*

     volume,
     issue page(s)
Psychology, 104(6), 776–795.

b. Web

author year   article title
Bruns, A. (2019). The third shift: Multiple job holding and the
              journal title
incarceration of women's partners. *Social Science Research,*

volume,
issue page(s)   short DOI
80(1), 202–215. http://doi.org/dfgj

● **12. Article in a journal** (*cont.*)

b. Web (*cont.*)

author(s)   year   article title

Vicary, A. M., & Larsen, A. (2018). Potential factors influencing

attitudes toward veterans who commit crimes: An experimental

journal title

investigation of PTSD in the legal system. *Current Research*

volume,
issue   URL for article

in Social Psychology, *26*(2). https://www.uiowa.edu/crisp

/sites/uiowa.edu.crisp/files/crisp_vol_26_2.pdf

c. Database

author   year   article title

Maftsir, S. (2019). Emotional change: romantic love and the

journal title

university in postcolonial Egypt. *Journal of Social History*,

volume,
issue   page(s)   DOI

52(3), 831–859. https://doi.org/10.1093/jsh/shx155

● **13. Article in a magazine**   If an article from the web
has no DOI, include the URL for the article. If an article
from a database has no DOI, do not include a URL.

a. Print

year + month
(monthly
author   magazine)   article title

Andersen, R. (2019, April). The intention machine: A new

generation of brain-machine interface can deduce what a

volume,
magazine title   issue   page(s)

person wants. *Scientific American*, *320*(4), 24–31.

b. Web

author   date of posting   article title

Srinivasan, D. (2019, June 4). How digital advertising markets

magazine title   URL for article

really work. *The American Prospect*. https://prospect.org

/article/how-digital-advertising-markets-really-work

c. Database

author | year + month (monthly magazine) | article title

Greengard, S. (2019, August). The algorithm that changed

magazine title

quantum machine learning. *Communications of the ACM,*

volume, issue | page(s) | DOI

62(8), 15–17. http://doi.org/10.1145/3339458

● **14. Article in a newspaper**

a. Print

author | year + month + day | article title

Finucane, M. (2019, September 25). Americans still eating too

newspaper title | page(s)

many low-quality carbs. *The Boston Globe,* B2.

b. Web

author | year + month + day | article title

Daly, J. (2019, August 2). Duquesne's med school plan part

newspaper title

of national trend to train more doctors. *Pittsburgh*

shortened URL for article

Post-Gazette. http://bit.ly/2CbUZOX

● **15. Abstract** If you have only accessed the abstract of an article, place the label "Abstract" in brackets after the article title. If you have read the entire source, cite the article as a whole.

Brey, E., & Pauker, K. (2019). Teachers' nonverbal behaviors influence children's stereotypic beliefs [Abstract]. *Journal of Experimental Child Psychology, 188.* https://doi.org /10.1016/j.jecp.2019.104671

● **16. Supplemental material**

Blasi, D. E., Moran, S., Moisik, S. R., Widmer, P., Dediu, D., & Bickel, B. (2019). Human sound systems are shaped by post-Neolithic changes in bite configuration [Supplemental material]. *Science, 363*(6432). https://doi.org/10.1126/science.aav3218

6∂ Citation at a glance

Online article in a journal or magazine APA

To cite an online article in a journal or magazine in APA style, include the following elements:

1. Author(s)
2. Year of publication for journal; complete date for magazine
3. Title and subtitle of article
4. Name of journal or magazine
5. Volume and issue numbers
6. DOI if the article has one; otherwise, URL for article

ONLINE ARTICLE IN A JOURNAL

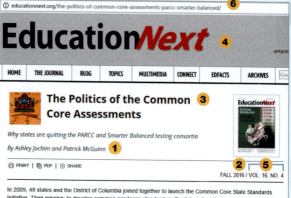

REFERENCE LIST ENTRY FOR AN ONLINE ARTICLE IN A JOURNAL OR MAGAZINE

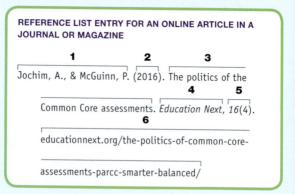

For more on citing articles in APA style, see items 12–14.

6∂ Citation at a glance

Article from a database APA

To cite an article from a database in APA style, include the following elements:

1. Author(s)
2. Year of publication for journal; complete date for magazine
3. Title and subtitle of article
4. Name of periodical
5. Volume and issue numbers
6. Page number(s)
7. DOI (digital object identifier), if available

DATABASE RECORD

Searching: OmniFile Full Text Select (H.W. Wilson) | Choose Databases
IN "American Journal of Economics & Sociology | in Select a Field (optional) | Search | Cl
AND | in Select a Field (optional)
AND | in Select a Field (optional) | Add Row

Basic Search | Advanced Search | Visual Search | Search History

‹Result List | Refine Search ◄ 3 of 11 ►

Detailed Record

3 Economics, Darwinism, and the Case of Disciplinary Impor

Check Article Linker for this item's availability. Check Article Linker for more information

Authors: Cojanu, Valentin

Source: American Journal of Economics & Sociology; Jan2013, Vol. 72

Document Type: Article

Subjects: Darwin, Charles, 1809-1882; Economic change; Interdisciplinary rese (Philosophy); Chance; Biology — Economic aspects; Causation — Eco aspects

Abstract: The problem of causality in economics is still contended by various e the received view of Darwinism in economics and examines the way ground in concepts and assumptions that reflect causal commonalti that the role the contingent pattern plays in understanding enclose

1 Authors: Cojanu, Valentin

2 5 6

4 Source: American Journal of Economics & Sociology; Jan2013, Vol. 72 Issue 1, p179-198, 20p, 1 Chart

may not be copied or emailed to multiple sites or posted to a listser written permission. However, users may print, download, or email a abridged. No warranty is given about the accuracy of the copy. Use of the material for the full abstract. (Copyright applies to all Abstrac

ISSN: 00029246

7 DOI: 10.1111/j.1536-7150.2012.00867.x

Accession Number: 84482931

REFERENCE LIST ENTRY FOR AN ARTICLE FROM A DATABASE

1 **2** **3**

Cojanu, V. (2013). Economics, Darwinism, and the case of

4

disciplinary imports. *American Journal of Economics*

5 6 7

& Sociology, 72(1), 179–198. https://doi.org/

10.1111/j.1536-7150.2012.00867.x

For more on citing articles from a database in APA style, see items 12c and 13c.

● **17. Letter to the editor**   If the letter has no title, use the bracketed label "Letter to the editor" as the title.

Stack, R. (2019, August 1). Popular opinion is shifting us away
     from capital punishment [Letter to the editor].
     The Washington Post. https://wapo.st/2WISxZh

● **18. Editorial or other unsigned article**

Gavin Newsom wants to stop rent gouging. Will lawmakers finally
     stand up for tenants? [Editorial]. (2019, September 4).
     Los Angeles Times. https://www.latimes.com/opinion
     /story/2019-09-03/gavin-newsom-rent-control-bill

● **19. Newsletter article**

Bond, G. (Fall, 2018). Celebrities as epidemiologists. *American
     College of Epidemiology Online Member Newsletter, 3.*
     https://www.acepidemiology.org/assets/ACE_
     Newsletter_Fall_2018%20FINAL.pdf

● **20. Review**   In brackets, give the type of work reviewed, the title, and the author for a book or the director for a film. If the review has no title, use the material in brackets as the title.

Douthat, R. (2019, October 14). A hustle gone wrong [Review
     of the film *Hustlers*, by L. Scafaria, Dir.]. *National Review,
     71*(18), 47.

Hall, W. (2019). [Review of the book *How to change your
     mind: The new science of psychedelics,* by M. Pollan].
     Addiction, 114(10), 1892–1893. https://doi.org
     /10.1111/add.14702

● **21. Published interview**   Cite the interviewer as the author. For a recorded (video or audio) interview, see item 48.

Remnick, D. (2019, July 1). Robert Caro reflects on Robert
     Moses, L.B.J., and his own career in nonfiction. *The New
     Yorker.* https://bit.ly/2Lukm3X

● **22. Article in a reference work (encyclopedia, dictionary, wiki)** When referencing an online, undated reference work entry, include the retrieval date. When referencing a work with archived versions, such as Wikipedia, use the date and URL of the archived version you read.

a. Print

Brue, A. W., & Wilmshurst, L. (2018). Adaptive behavior
   assessments. In B. B. Frey (Ed.), *The SAGE encyclopedia of*
   educational research, measurement, and evaluation. SAGE
   Publications.

b. Web

Behaviorism. (2019, September 13). In *Wikipedia*.
   https://en.wikipedia.org/w/index.php?title=
   Behaviorism&oldid=915544724

Merriam-Webster. (n.d.). Double-blind. In *Merriam-Webster.com*
   dictionary. Retrieved November 11, 2019, from https://
   www.merriam-webster.com/dictionary/double-blind

● **23. Comment on an online article** Include the first 20 words of the comment followed by the source in brackets.

lollyl2. (2019, September 25). My husband works in IT in a
   major city down South. He is a permanent employee now,
   but for years [Comment on the article "The Google
   workers who voted to unionize in Pittsburgh are part of
   tech's huge contractor workforce"]. *Slate*. https://fyre
   .it/0RT8HmeL.4

● **24. Paper or poster presented at a conference or meeting (unpublished)** Include the full dates of the conference or meeting.

Wood, M. (2019, January 3–6). *The effects of an adult*
   development course on students' perceptions of aging
   [Poster presentation]. National Institute on the Teaching
   of Psychology, St. Pete Beach, FL, United States.

Books and other long works

▶ Citation at a glance: Book **223**

● **25. Basic format for a book**

a. Print

author(s):
last name
+ initial(s)   year   book title

Treuer, D. (2019). *The heartbeat of Wounded Knee: Native*

                                          publisher

America from 1890 to the present. Riverhead Books.

b. Web (or online library)   Give the URL for the page where you accessed the book.

author   year   book title publisher

Obama, M. (2018). *Becoming.* Crown. https://books.google.

                              URL

com/books?id=YbtNDwAAQBAJ

c. E-book   Include the DOI or, if a DOI is not available, the URL for the page from which you downloaded the book.

Coates, T.-N. (2017). *We were eight years in power: An American*

tragedy. One World. https://www.amazon.com/dp/

B01MT7340D/

d. Database   If the book has a DOI, include it. If not, do not list a URL or database name.

Kilby, P. (2019). *The green revolution: Narratives of politics,*

technology and gender. Routledge. http://doi.org/dfgt

● **26. Edition other than the first**

Dessler, A. E., & Parson, E. A. (2019). *The science and politics*

of global climate change: A guide to the debate (3rd ed.).

Cambridge University Press.

● **27. Selection in an anthology or a collection**

a. Entire anthology

                                          title of
editor(s)   year   anthology

Lindert, J., & Marsoobian, A. T. (Eds.). (2018). *Multidisciplinary*

                              publisher

perspectives on genocide and memory. Springer.

6∂ Citation at a glance

Book APA

To cite a print book in APA style, include the following elements:

1 Author(s)
2 Year of publication
3 Title and subtitle
4 Publisher

TITLE PAGE

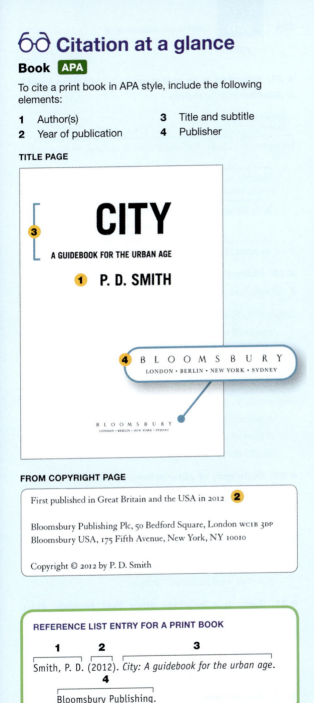

CITY

A GUIDEBOOK FOR THE URBAN AGE

1 P. D. SMITH

4 B L O O M S B U R Y
LONDON · BERLIN · NEW YORK · SYDNEY

B L O O M S B U R Y
LONDON · BERLIN · NEW YORK · SYDNEY

FROM COPYRIGHT PAGE

First published in Great Britain and the USA in 2012 **2**

Bloomsbury Publishing Plc, 50 Bedford Square, London WC1B 3DP
Bloomsbury USA, 175 Fifth Avenue, New York, NY 10010

Copyright © 2012 by P. D. Smith

REFERENCE LIST ENTRY FOR A PRINT BOOK

   1   **2**   **3**

Smith, P. D. (2012). *City: A guidebook for the urban age.*
          4

   Bloomsbury Publishing.

For more on citing books in APA style, see items 25–31.

● **27. Selection in an anthology or a collection (*cont.*)**

b. Selection in an anthology

author of selection ⌐ year ⌐ title of selection

Pettigrew, D. (2018). The suppression of cultural memory and

identity in Bosnia and Herzegovina. In J. Lindert &
editors of anthology — title of anthology

A. T. Marsoobian (Eds.), *Multidisciplinary perspectives*
page numbers
of selection — publisher

on genocide and memory (pp. 187–198). Springer.

● **28. Multivolume work**

a. All volumes

Zeigler-Hill, V., & Shackelford, T. K. (Eds.). (2018). *The SAGE
handbook of personality and individual differences*
(Vols. I–III). SAGE Publications.

b. One volume, with title

Zeigler-Hill, V., & Shackelford, T. K. (Eds.). (2018). *The SAGE
handbook of personality and individual differences: Vol. II.
Origins of personality and individual differences.* SAGE
Publications.

● **29. Dictionary or other reference work**

Leong, F. T. L. (Ed.). (2008). *Encyclopedia of counseling*
(Vols. 1–4). SAGE Publications.

● **30. Republished book**

Fremlin, C. (2017). *The hours before dawn.* Dover Publications.
(Original work published 1958)

● **31. Book in a language other than English** Place
the English translation of the title, not italicized, in
brackets.

Carminati, G. G., & Méndez, A. (2012). *Étapes de vie, étapes de
soins* [Stages of life, stages of care]. Médecine & Hygiène.

● **32. Dissertation** If you accessed a dissertation from
a specialized database, include the database title at the
end of the reference, as in the example on the next page.

Bacaksizlar, N. G. (2019). *Understanding social movements through simulations of anger contagion in social media* (Publication No. 13805848) [Doctoral dissertation, University of North Carolina at Charlotte]. ProQuest Dissertations & Theses.

● 33. Conference proceedings

Srujan Raju, K., Govardhan, A., Padmaja Rani, B., Sridevi, R., & Ramakrishna Murty, M. (Eds.) (2018). *Proceedings of the third international conference on computational intelligence and informatics.* Springer.

● 34. Government document
If the document has a report number, place the number in parentheses after the title.

Berchick, E. R., Barnett, J. C., & Upton, R. D. (2019, September 10). *Health insurance coverage in the United States: 2018* (Report No. P60-267). U.S. Census Bureau. https://www.census.gov/library/publications/2019/demo/p60-267.html

National Park Service. (2019, April 11). *Travel where women made history: Ordinary and extraordinary places of American women.* U.S. Department of the Interior. https://www.nps.gov/subjects/travelwomenshistory/index.htm

● 35. Report from a private organization

Ford Foundation International Fellowships Program. (2019). *Leveraging higher education to promote social justice: Evidence from the IFP alumni tracking study.* https://p.widencdn.net/kei61u/IFP-Alumni-Tracking-Study-Report-5

● 36. Legal source
The title of a court case is italicized in an in-text citation but not in the reference list.

Sweatt v. Painter, 339 U.S. 629 (1950). http://www.law.cornell.edu/supct/html/historics/USSC_CR_0339_0629_ZS.html

● 37. Sacred or classical text
Include the title, year, and editor/translator (if any) of the version you are using. If the original date is known, include it at the end of the citation. If a year is approximate, include "ca." (for "circa"); use "B.C.E." for ancient texts.

● **37. Sacred or classical text (*cont.*)**

The Holy Bible 1611 edition King James version. (2006).
    Hendrickson Publishers. (Original work published 1611)

Homer. (2018). *The odyssey* (E. Wilson, Trans.). W. W. Norton &
    Company. (Original work published ca. 675–725 B.C.E.)

Websites and parts of websites

▶ Citation at a glance: Page from a website **227**

● **38. Entire website** If you retrieved specific information from the home page of a website, include the
website name, retrieval date, and URL in your reference
list entry. If you only mention the website in the body
of your paper, do not include it in your reference list.
(See item 12 in 38a.)

● **39. Page from a website** If the names of the author
and the website are not the same, include the website's
name after the page title.

National Institute of Mental Health. (2016, March). *Seasonal
    affective disorder.* National Institutes of Health.
    https://www.nimh.nih.gov/health/topics/seasonal
    -affective-disorder/index.shtml

6∂ Citing online sources **at a glance**

Sometimes an online source does not include one or
more pieces of publication information. In such cases,
use the following guidelines:

- **Unknown author.** If known, list the name of the
  organization as the author. If not, list the title of
  the article (or the name of the web page if there
  is no title) first. Then list the date of publication, if
  known. Finally, include the source URL. (See also
  item 5 in section 38a.)

- **Unknown publication date.** After the author's
  name — or after the title, if the author is
  unknown — write "(n.d.)."

- **No title.** List the name of the web page or the
  heading under which the information appears.
  Otherwise, include a description of the work
  in brackets in place of a title: [Map of Europe
  showing population in 1950].

6∂ Citation at a glance

Page from a website APA

To cite a page from a website in APA style, include the following elements:

1. Author(s)
2. Date of publication or most recent update ("n.d." if there is no date)
3. Title of web page
4. Name of website (if not named as author)
5. URL of web page

PAGE FROM A WEBSITE

REFERENCE LIST ENTRY FOR A PAGE FROM A WEBSITE

```
            1                       2           3
Minnesota Department of Health. (n.d.). 2010 Minnesota
                                            4
health statistics annual summary. http://www
.health.state.mn.us/divs/chs/annsum/10annsum
/index.html
```

For more on citing sources from websites in APA style, see items 39 and 40.

● **40. Document from a website** Most documents published on websites fall into other categories, such as a government document or a report from an organization (see items 34 and 35).

Tahseen, M., Ahmed, S., & Ahmed, S. (2018). *Bullying of Muslim youth: A review of research and recommendations.* The Family and Youth Institute. http://www.thefyi.org /wp-content/uploads/2018/10/FYI-Bullying-Report.pdf

● **41. Blog post** Cite a blog post as you would an article in a periodical.

Fister, B. (2019, February 14). Information literacy's third wave. *Library Babel Fish.* https://www.insidehighered .com/blogs/library-babel-fish/information-literacy %E2%80%99s-third-wave

Audio, visual, and multimedia sources

● **42. Podcast series or episode**

Abumrad, J., & Krulwich, R. (Hosts). (2002–present). *Radiolab* [Audio podcast]. WNYC Studios. https://www.wnycstudios .org/podcasts/radiolab/podcasts

Longoria, J. (Host & Producer). (2019, April 19). Americanish [Audio podcast episode]. In J. Abumrad & R. Krulwich (Hosts), *Radiolab.* WNYC Studios. https://www.wnycstudios .org/podcasts/radiolab/articles/americanish

● **43. Video or audio on the web**

The New York Times. (2018, January 9). *Taking a knee and taking down a monument* [Video]. YouTube. https://www .youtube.com/watch?v=qY34DQCdUvQ

Wray, B. (2019, May). *How climate change affects your mental health* [Video]. TED Conferences. https://www.ted.com/ talks/britt_wray_how_climate_change_affects_your_ mental_health

● **44. Transcript of an audio or a video file**

Gopnik, A. (2019, July 10). *A separate kind of intelligence* [Video transcript]. Edge. https://www.edge.org/ conversation/alison_gopnik-a-separate- kind-of-intelligence

● **45. Film** If the film is a special version, like an extended cut, include that information in brackets after the title.

Peele, J. (Director). (2017). *Get out* [Film]. Universal Pictures.

Hitchcock, A. (Director). (1959). *The essentials collection: North by northwest* [Film; special ed. on DVD]. Metro-Goldwyn-Mayer; Universal Pictures Home Entertainment.

● **46. Television or radio program or episode**

Waller-Bridge, P., Williams, H., & Williams, J. (Executive Producers). (2016–2019). *Fleabag* [TV series]. Two Brothers Pictures; BBC.

Waller-Bridge, P. (Writer), & Bradbeer, H. (Director). (2019, March 18). The provocative request (Season 2, Episode 3) [TV series episode]. In P. Waller-Bridge, H. Williams, & J. Williams (Executive Producers), *Fleabag*. Two Brothers Pictures; BBC.

● **47. Music recording** For classical works, put the composer in the author position and the performer in brackets with the source type.

Nielsen, C. (2014). *Carl Nielsen: Symphonies 1 & 4* [Album recorded by New York Philharmonic Orchestra]. Dacapo Records. (Original work published 1892–1916)

Carlile, B. (2018). The mother [Song]. On *By the way, I forgive you*. Low Country Sound; Elektra.

● **48. Recorded lecture, speech, address, or interview** Cite the speaker or interviewee as the author. For a published (print) interview, see item 21.

Warren, E. (2019, September 16). *Senator Elizabeth Warren speech in Washington Square Park* [Speech video recording]. C-SPAN. https://www.c-span.org/video/?464314-1/senator-elizabeth-warren-campaigns-york-city

● **49. Data set or graphic representation of data (graph, chart, table)** If the item is numbered in the source, indicate the number in parentheses after the title.

Reid, L. (2019). *Smarter homes: Experiences of living in low carbon homes 2013–2018* [Data set]. UK Data Service. http://doi.org/10.5255/UKDA-SN-853485

● **49. Data set or graphic representation of data (*cont.*)**

Pew Research Center. (2018, November 15). *U.S. public is closely divided about overall health risk from food additives* [Chart]. https://www.pewresearch.org /science/2018/11/19/public-perspectives-on-food-risks/

● **50. Mobile app**   Begin with the developer of the app, if known.

Google. (2019). *Google Earth* (Version 9.3.3) [Mobile app]. App Store. https://apps.apple.com/us/app/google-earth /id293622097

● **51. Video game**

ConcernedApe. (2016). *Stardew Valley* [Video game]. Chucklefish.

● **52. Map**

Desjardins, J. (2017, November 17). *Walmart nation: Mapping the largest employers in the U.S.* [Map]. Visual Capitalist. https://www.visualcapitalist.com /walmart-nation-mapping-largest-employers-u-s/

● **53. Advertisement**

America's Biopharmaceutical Companies [Advertisement]. (2018, September). *The Atlantic, 322*(2), 2.

● **54. Work of art or photograph**

O'Keeffe, G. (1931). *Cow's skull: Red, white, and blue* [Painting]. Metropolitan Museum of Art, New York, NY, United States. https://www.metmuseum.org/art/collection /search/488694

Helmet mask (kakaparaga) [Artifact]. (ca. late 19th century). Museum of Fine Arts, Boston, MA, United States.

Liittschwager, D. (2019). [Photograph series of octopuses]. National Geographic. https://on.natgeo.com/34stlZw

● **55. Brochure or fact sheet**

National Council of State Boards of Nursing. (2018). *A nurse manager's guide to substance use disorder in nursing* [Brochure].

World Health Organization. (2019, July 15). *Immunization coverage* [Fact sheet]. https://www.who.int/news-room/fact-sheets/detail/immunization-coverage

● **56. Press release**

New York University. (2019, September 5). *NYU Oral Cancer Center awarded $2.5 million NIH grant to study cancer pain* [Press release]. http://bit.ly/32j6EFN

● **57. Presentation slides**

Centers for Disease Control and Prevention. (2019, April 16). *Building local response capacity to protect families from emerging health threats* [Presentation slides]. CDC Stacks. https://stacks.cdc.gov/view/cdc/77687

● **58. Lecture notes or other course materials** Cite material from your instructor that is not available to others as personal communication in the text of your paper (see items 13 and 14 in 38a).

Chatterjee, S., Constenla, D., Kinghorn, A., & Mayora, C. (2018). *Teaching vaccine economics everywhere: Costing in vaccine planning and programming* [Lecture notes and slides]. Department of Population, Family, and Reproductive Health, Johns Hopkins University. http://ocw.jhsph.edu/index.cfm/go/viewCourse/course/TeachVaccEconCosting/coursePage/lectureNotes/

Social media

● **59. Email** Email messages, letters, and other personal communication are not included in the list of references. (See item 13 in 38a for citing these sources in the text of your paper.)

● **60. Social media post** Begin with the author (see item 6 for citing screen names). For the title, include up to 20 words (including hashtags or emojis) of the post or caption. List any attachments (such as a photo or a link) and the type of post in separate brackets. List the website or app in the publisher position, followed by the post's URL. See the examples on the next page. Cite personal media posts that are not accessible to all readers as personal communication in the text of your paper (see item 13 in 38a).

● **60. Social media post (*cont.*)**

National Science Foundation [@NSF]. (2019, October 13).
Understanding how forest structure drives carbon sequestra-
tion is important for ecologists, climate modelers and forest
managers, who are working on [Thumbnail with
link attached] [Tweet]. Twitter. https://twitter.com/NSF
/status/1183388649263652864

Georgia Aquarium. (2019, June 25). *True love [two hearts emoji]*
Charlie and Lizzy are a bonded pair of African penguins
who have been together for more than [Image attached]
[Status update]. Facebook. https://www.facebook.com
/GeorgiaAquarium/photos/a.163898398123
/10156900637543124/?type=3&theater

Smithsonian [@smithsonian]. (2019, October 7). *You're*
looking at a ureilite meteorite under a microscope. When
illuminated with polarized light, they appear in dazzling
colors, influenced [Photograph]. Instagram. https://www
.instagram.com/p/B3VI27yHLQG/

● **61. Social media profile or highlight**   Because profiles are designed to change over time, include the date
you viewed the web page.

National Science Foundation [@NSF]. (n.d.). *Tweets* [Twitter
profile]. Twitter. Retrieved October 15, 2019, from
https://twitter.com/NSF

Smithsonian [@smithsonian]. (n.d.). *#Apollo50*
[Highlight]. Instagram. Retrieved October 15, 2019,
from https://www.instagram.com/stories/highlig
hts/17902787752343364/

39   **APA format; sample research
paper**

The guidelines in this section are consistent with
advice given in the *Publication Manual of the American
Psychological Association*, 7th ed. (2020) and with typical requirements for student papers. Differences in

requirements for professional papers (papers prepared for publication) are noted in this section. If you are unsure what is required for your assignment, check with your instructor.

39a APA format

Formatting the paper   Student papers in APA style should be formatted as follows. Additional elements for professional papers (papers submitted for publication) are also described where relevant.

Font   If your instructor does not require a specific font, choose one that is standard and easy to read (such as 12-point Times New Roman).

Title page   Put the page number 1 flush with the right margin. A few lines down the page, center the full title of your paper in bold. After a blank line, include your name, then the following assignment details on separate lines: the department and the school, the course code and name, your instructor's name, and the due date. Professional papers typically require an author note at the bottom of the page, which begins with the heading "Author Note," centered and in bold, followed by acknowledgments, disclosures of conflicts of interest, and other additional information. See page 238 for a sample title page.

Page numbers and running head   Number all pages with arabic numerals (1, 2, 3, and so on) in the upper right corner one-half inch from the top of the page, including the title page. For professional papers, on every page, use a running head consisting of the title (shortened to no more than 50 characters in all capitals) flush left, on the same line as the page number. See page 250 for an example of a professional running head.

Margins, line spacing, and paragraph indents   Use margins of one inch on all sides of the page. Left-align the text. Double-space throughout the paper. Indent the first line of each paragraph and footnote one-half inch.

Capitalization, italics, and quotation marks   In titles of works in the text of the paper, capitalize all words of four letters or more (and all nouns, pronouns, verbs, adjectives, and adverbs of any length). Capitalize the first word following a colon in a title or a heading. In the body of your paper, capitalize the first word after a colon only if the word begins a complete sentence.

Italicize the titles of books, periodicals, and other long works, including websites. Use quotation marks for titles of periodical articles, short stories, and other short works named in the body of your paper.

NOTE: APA has different requirements for titles in the reference list. See page 236.

Long quotations When a quotation is 40 or more words, indent it one-half inch from the left margin. Double-space the quotation. Do not use quotation marks around it. (See page 243 for an example.)

Footnotes Insert footnotes using the footnote function of your word processing program. The number in the text should immediately follow a word or any mark of punctuation except a dash. The text of the footnote should begin with a paragraph indent and be single-spaced.

Abstract Professional papers require an abstract, an overview of the content of the paper, consisting of no more than 250 words. If your assignment requires one, include the abstract on a new page after the title page. Center the word "Abstract" (in bold) one inch from the top of the page. Double-space the abstract and do not indent the first line.

A list of keywords follows the abstract; keywords help readers search for a published paper on the web or in a database. On the line below the abstract, type the word "Keywords," indented and italicized, followed by a colon. Then list important words related to your paper. For an example of an abstract page, see page 250.

Introduction On a new page following the title page (or following the abstract page if one is required), center the complete title of the paper one inch below the top of the page in bold. Begin the first paragraph of the introduction with a one-half-inch indent immediately after the paper title. The introduction does not have a heading.

Headings Major (first-level) headings are centered and in bold. In research papers and laboratory reports, typical major headings are "Method," "Results," and "Discussion." In other types of papers, headings should be informative and concise, conveying the structure of the paper. Treat the capitalization of all headings the way you'd treat titles in your text. Most student papers require only one or two levels of headings.

First-Level Heading Centered

Second-Level Heading Flush Left

Third-Level Heading Flush Left

Visuals APA classifies visuals as tables and figures (figures include graphs, charts, drawings, and photographs). Place each visual after the paragraph in which it is called out or on the following page if it does not fit on the same page as the callout.

Label each table or figure with an arabic numeral (Table 1, Figure 2) and provide a clear title. The label and title should appear on separate lines above the visual, flush left and double-spaced. Type the number in bold font; italicize the title.

Table 2

Effect of Nifedipine (Procardia) on Blood Pressure in Women

If you have used data from an outside source or have taken or adapted the visual from a source, give the source information in a note below the visual. Begin with the word "Note," italicized and followed by a period. Use either "From" or "Adapted from" before the source information. Notes can also include additional information or context for the visual.

Preparing the list of references Begin your list of references on a new page at the end of the paper. Center the title "References" in bold one inch from the top of the page. Double-space throughout. For a sample reference list, see page 248.

Indenting entries Type the first line of each entry flush left and indent any additional lines one-half inch.

Alphabetizing the list   Alphabetize the reference list by the last names of the authors (or the full name of the organization, if the author is an organization); when a work has no author or editor, alphabetize by the first word of the title other than "A," "An," or "The."

If you list two or more works by the same author, arrange the entries by year, the earliest first. If you include two or more works by the same author in the same year, arrange them alphabetically by title. Add the letters "a," "b," and so on after the year in the parentheses. For books and journal articles, use only the year and the letter: (2015a). For articles in magazines and newspapers, use the full date and the letter in the reference list: (2015a, July 17); use only the year and the letter in in-text citations.

Authors' names   Invert all authors' names and use initials instead of first and middle names. Separate the names with commas. For two to 20 authors, use an ampersand (&) before the last author's name (see item 2 in section 38b). For 21 or more authors, give the first 19 authors, followed by an ellipsis mark and the last author (see item 3 in section 38b). If the author is an organization, do not invert the name.

Titles of books and articles   Italicize the titles and subtitles of books and other stand-alone works. Do not italicize or use quotation marks around the titles of articles. Capitalize only the first word of the title and subtitle (and all proper nouns). Capitalize names of periodicals as you would capitalize them normally (see page 233–34).

Abbreviations for page numbers   Abbreviations for "page" and "pages" ("p." and "pp.") are used before page numbers of selections from an anthology or a collection (see item 27b in section 38b) but not before page numbers of articles in periodicals (see items 12–14 in section 38b).

Breaking a URL or DOI   Do not insert any line breaks into URLs or DOIs (digital object identifiers). Any line breaks that your word processor makes automatically are acceptable. Do not add a period at the end of the URL or DOI.

39b Sample APA research paper

April Bo Wang, a student in an education course, wrote a research paper reviewing the literature on student-centered learning. Wang's paper, which begins on the next page, is documented with in-text citations and a list of references in APA style. Annotations draw your attention to Wang's use of APA style and her effective writing. Following Wang's paper is a sample professional abstract page.

**Technology and the Shift From Teacher-Delivered to
Student-Centered Learning: A Review of the Literature**

April Bo Wang

Department of Education, Glen County Community College

EDU 107: Education, Technology, and Media

Dr. Julien Gomez

October 29, XXXX

1. Page number flush right on all pages, including title page.
2. Paper title boldface, centered, followed by blank line.
3. Writer's name, department and school, course, instructor, and assignment due date, centered.

2

Technology and the Shift From Teacher-Delivered to **1**
Student-Centered Learning: A Review of the Literature

In the United States, most public school systems are struggling
with teacher shortages, which are projected to worsen as the number of
applicants to education schools decreases (Donitsa-Schmidt & Zuzovsky,
2014, p. 420). Citing federal data, *The New York Times* reported a 30% **2**
drop in "people entering teacher preparation programs" between 2010
and 2014 (Rich, 2015, para. 10). Especially in science and math fields, **3**
the teacher shortage is projected to escalate in the next 10 years
(Hutchison, 2012). In recent decades, instructors and administrators
have viewed the practice of student-centered learning as one promising
solution. Unlike traditional teacher-delivered (also called "transmissive")
instruction, student-centered learning allows students to help direct
their own education by setting their own goals and selecting appropriate
resources for achieving those goals. Though student-centered
learning might once have been viewed as an experimental solution in
understaffed schools, it is gaining credibility as an effective pedagogical
practice. What is also gaining momentum is the idea that technology
might play a significant role in fostering student-centered learning. This
literature review will examine three key questions:

1. In what ways is student-centered learning effective? **4**
2. Can educational technology help students drive their
   own learning?
3. How can public schools effectively combine teacher
   talent and educational technology?

In the face of mounting teacher shortages, public schools **5**
should embrace educational technology that promotes student-
centered learning in order to help all students become engaged and
successful learners.

1 Paper title, boldface and centered. **2** Source provides
background information and context. **3** In-text citation
includes locator (paragraph number) for a quotation from
an unpaginated source. **4** Wang sets up her organization by
positing three questions. **5** Wang states her thesis.

In What Ways Is Student-Centered Learning Effective?

According to the International Society for Technology in Education (2016), "Student-centered learning moves students from passive receivers of information to active participants in their own discovery process. What students learn, how they learn it, and how their learning is assessed are all driven by each individual student's needs and abilities" (What Is It? section). The results of student-centered learning have been positive, not only for academic achievement but also for student self-esteem. In this model of instruction, the teacher acts as a facilitator, and the students actively participate in the process of learning and teaching. With guidance, students decide on the learning goals most pertinent to themselves, they devise a learning plan that will most likely help them achieve those goals, they direct themselves in carrying out that learning plan, and they assess how much they learned (Çubukçu, 2012, Introduction section). The major differences between student-centered learning and instructor-centered learning are summarized in Table 1.

Bell (2010) has argued that the chief benefit of student-centered learning is that it can connect students with "real-world tasks," thus making learning more engaging as well as more comprehensive (p. 42). For example, Bell observed a group of middle-school students who wanted to build a social justice monument for their school. They researched social justice issues, selected several to focus on, and then designed a three-dimensional playground to represent those issues. In doing so, they achieved learning goals in the areas of social studies, physics, and mathematics and practiced research and teamwork. Students engaged in this kind of learning performed better on both project-based assessments and standardized tests (Bell, 2010).

① First-level heading, boldface and centered. **②** Wang uses a source to define a key term, "student-centered learning." **③** Locator (heading) provided for a paraphrase from a long unpaginated article. **④** Page number or other locator is not necessary for a paraphrase from a short article.

4

Table 1

Comparison of Two Approaches to Teaching and Learning ❷

Teaching and learning period	Instructor-centered approach	Student-centered approach
Before class	• Instructor prepares lecture/instruction on new topic. • Students complete homework on previous topic.	• Students read and view new material, practice new concepts, and prepare questions ahead of class. • Instructor views student practice and questions, identifies learning opportunities.
During class	• Instructor delivers new material in a lecture or prepared discussion. • Students — unprepared — listen, watch, take notes, and try to follow along with the new material.	• Students lead discussions of the new material or practice applying the concepts or skills in an active environment. • Instructor answers student questions and provides immediate feedback.
After class	• Instructor grades homework and gives feedback about the previous lesson. • Students work independently to practice or apply the new concepts.	• Students apply concepts/skills to more complex tasks, some of their own choosing, individually and in groups. • Instructor posts additional resources to help students.

Note. Adapted from *The Flipped Class Demystified*, by New York University, ❸
n.d. (https://www.nyu.edu/faculty/teaching-and-learning-resources
/instructional-technology-support/instructional-design-assessment
/flipped-classes/the-flipped-class-demystified.html).

❶ Table number (boldface) and heading (italic) flush left.
❷ Wang uses a table to compare and contrast two concepts for readers. ❸ Table note provides source information.

5

A Stanford study came to a similar conclusion; researchers examined four schools that had moved from teacher-driven instruction **(1)** to student-centered learning (Friedlaender et al., 2014). The study focused on students from a mix of racial, cultural, and socioeconomic backgrounds, with varying levels of English-language proficiency. The researchers predicted that this mix of students, representing differing levels of academic ability, would benefit from a student-centered approach. Through interviews, surveys, and classroom observations, the researchers identified key characteristics of the new student-centered learning environments at the four schools:

- teachers who prioritized building relationships with students
- support structures for teachers to improve and collaborate on instruction
- a shift in classroom activity from lectures and tests to **(2)** projects and performance-based assessments (pp. 5–7)

After the schools designed their curriculum to be personalized to individual students rather than standardized across a diverse student body and to be inclusive of skills such as persistence as well as traditional academic skills, students outperformed peers on state tests and increased their rates of high school and college graduation (Friedlaender et al., 2014, p. 3).

Can Educational Technology Help Students Drive Their Own Learning?

When students engage in self-directed learning, they rely less on teachers to deliver information and require less face-to-face time with teachers. For content delivery, many school districts have begun to use educational technology resources that, in recent years, have become more available, more affordable, and easier to use. For the purposes of this paper, the term "educational technology resources" encompasses

(1) For a source with three or more authors, only the first author's name is given followed by "et al." **(2)** Authors and year are given earlier in the paragraph, so only page numbers are provided at the end of the paraphrase.

the following: distance learning, by which students learn from a remote instructor online; other online education programming such as slide shows and video or audio lectures; interactive online activities, such as quizzing or games; and the use of computers, tablets, smartphones, SMART Boards, or other such devices for coursework.

Much like student-centered learning, the use of educational **①** technology began in many places as a temporary measure to keep classes running despite teacher shortages. A Horn and Staker (2011) study **②** examined the major patterns over time for students who subscribed to distance learning, for example. A decade ago, students who enrolled in distance learning often fell into one of the following categories: They lived in a rural community that had no alternative for learning; they attended a school where there were not enough qualified teachers to teach certain subjects; or they were homeschooled or homebound. But faced with tighter budgets, teacher shortages, increasingly diverse student populations, and rigorous state standards, schools recognized the need and the potential for distance learning across the board.

As the teacher shortage has intensified, educational technology resources have become more tailored to student needs and more affordable. Pens that convert handwritten notes to digital text and organize them, backpacks that charge electronic devices, and apps that create audiovisual flash cards are just a few of the more recent innovations. According to Svokos (2015), some educational technology resources entertain students while supporting student-centered learning:

> GlassLab, a nonprofit that was launched with grants **③**
> from the Bill & Melinda Gates and MacArthur
> Foundations, creates educational games that are now being
> used in more than 6,000 classrooms across the country.
> Some of the company's games are education versions of

① Wang develops her thesis. **②** For a source with two authors, "and" links the authors' names in a signal phrase; date is given in parentheses. **③** Quotation of more than forty words is indented without quotation marks.

existing ones — for example, its first release was SimCity
EDU — while others are originals. Teachers get real-time
updates on students' progress as well as suggestions on
what subjects they need to spend more time perfecting.

(1)　　　　(5. Educational Games section)

Many of the companies behind these products offer institutional
discounts to schools where such devices are used widely by students
and teachers.

Horn and Staker (2011) concluded that the chief benefit of
technological learning was that it could adapt to the individual student
in a way that whole-class delivery by a single teacher could not. Their
study examined various schools where technology enabled student-
centered learning. For example, Carpe Diem High School in Yuma,
Arizona, hired only six certified subject teachers and then outfitted its
classrooms with 280 computers connected to online learning programs.
The programs included software that offered "continual feedback,
assessment, and incremental victory in a way that a face-to-face teacher
with a class of 30 students never could. After each win, students
continue to move forward at their own pace" (p. 9). Students alternated
between personalized 55-minute courses online and 55-minute courses
with one of the six teachers. The academic outcomes were promising.
Carpe Diem ranked first in its county for student math and reading
scores. Similarly, Rocketship Education, a charter network that serves
low-income, predominantly Latino students, created a digital learning
lab, reducing the need to hire more teachers. Rocketship's academic
scores ranked in the top 15 of all California low-income public schools.

(2)　　　　It is clear that educational technology will continue to play
a role in student and school performance. Horn and Staker (2011)
acknowledged that they focused on programs in which integration of

---

(1) Locator (heading) is used for a direct quotation of an
unpaginated online source. Parenthetical citation is placed
after final punctuation mark in block quotation. **(2)** Wang
uses her own analysis to shape the conversation among her
sources in this synthesis paragraph.

8

educational technology led to improved student performance. In other schools, technological learning is simply distance learning — watching a remote teacher — and not student-centered learning that allows students to partner with teachers to develop enriching learning experiences. That said, many educators seem convinced that educational technology has the potential to help them transition from traditional teacher-driven learning to student-centered learning. All four schools in the Stanford study heavily relied on technology (Friedlaender et al., 2014). And indeed, Demski (2012) argued that technology is not supplemental but instead is "central" to student-centered learning (p. 33). Rather than turning to a teacher as the source of information, students are sent to investigate solutions to problems by searching online, emailing experts, collaborating with one another in a wiki space, or completing online practice. Rather than turning to a teacher for the answer to a question, students are driven to perform — driven to use technology to find those answers themselves.

How Can Public Schools Effectively Combine Teacher Talent and Educational Technology?

Some researchers have expressed doubt that schools are ready for student-centered learning — or any type of instruction — that is driven by technology. In a recent survey conducted by the Nellie Mae Education Foundation, Moeller and Reitzes (2011) reported not only that many teachers lacked confidence in their ability to incorporate technology in the classroom but that 43% of polled high school students said that they lacked confidence in their technological proficiency going into college and careers. The study concluded that technology alone would not improve learning environments. Yet others argued that students adapt quickly to even unfamiliar technology and use it to further their own learning. For example, Mitra (2013)

 Wang uses a source to introduce a counterargument.

caught the attention of the education world with his study of how to educate students in the slums of India. He installed an Internet-accessible computer in a wall in a New Delhi urban slum and left it there with no instructions. Over a few months, many of the children had learned how to use the computer, how to access information over the Internet, how to interpret information, and how to communicate this information to one another. Mitra's experiment was "not about making learning happen. [It was] about letting it happen" (16:31). He concluded that in the absence of teachers, even in developing countries less inundated by technology, a tool that allowed access to an organized database of knowledge (such as a search engine) was sufficient to provide students with a rewarding learning experience.

According to the Stanford study, however, the presence of teachers is still crucial (Friedlaender et al., 2014). Their roles will simply change from distributors of knowledge to facilitators and supporters of self-directed student-centered learning. The researchers asserted that teacher education and professional development programs can no longer prepare teachers in a single instructional mode, such as teacher-delivered learning; they must instead equip teachers with a wide repertoire of skills to support a wide variety of student learning experiences. The Stanford study argued that since teachers would be partnering with students to shape the learning experience, rather than designing and delivering a curriculum on their own, the main job of a teacher would become relationship building. The teacher would establish a relationship with each student so that the teacher could support whatever learning the student pursues.

Many schools have already effectively paired a reduced faculty with educational technology to support successful student-centered

① Brackets indicate Wang's change in the quoted material. A time stamp indicates the start of the direct quotation from a video.

10

learning. For example, Watson (2008) offered a case study of
the Cincinnati Public Schools Virtual High School, which brought
students together in a physical school building to work with an
assortment of online learning programs. Although there were only
10 certified teachers in the building, students were able to engage
in highly individualized instruction according to their own needs,
strengths, and learning styles, using the 10 teachers as support
(p. 7). Commonwealth Connections Academy (CCA), a public school
in Pennsylvania, also brings students into a physical school building
to engage in digital curriculum. However, rather than having
students identify their own learning goals and design their own
curriculum around those goals, CCA uses educational technology as
an assessment tool to identify areas of student weakness. It then
partners students with teachers to address those areas (pp. 8–9).

Conclusion

Public education faces the opportunity for a shift from the model **1**
of teacher-delivered instruction that has characterized American public
schools since their foundation to a student-centered learning model.
Not only has student-centered learning proved effective in improving
student academic and developmental outcomes, it can also synchronize
with technological learning for widespread adaptability across schools.
Because it relies on student direction rather than an established
curriculum, student-centered learning supported by educational
technology can adapt to the different needs of individual students
and a variety of learning environments — urban and rural, well funded
and underfunded. Similarly, when student-centered learning relies on
technology rather than a corps of uniformly trained teachers, it holds
promise for schools that would otherwise suffer from a lack of human
or financial resources.

1 Conclusion's tone is objective and presents answers to
Wang's three organizational questions.

11

1 **References**

Bell, S. (2010). Project-based learning for the 21st century: Skills
for the future. *The Clearing House, 83*(2), 39–43.

2 Çubukçu, Z. (2012). Teachers' evaluation of student-centered
learning environments. *Education, 133*(1).

Demski, J. (2012, January). This time it's personal. *THE Journal
(Technological Horizons in Education), 39*(1), 32–36.

3 Donitsa-Schmidt, S., & Zuzovsky, R. (2014). Teacher supply and
demand: The school level perspective. *American Journal
of Educational Research, 2*(6), 420–429. https://doi.
org/10.12691/education-2-6-14

4 Friedlaender, D., Burns, D., Lewis-Charp, H., Cook-Harvey, C. M.,
& Darling-Hammond, L. (2014). *Student-centered schools:
Closing the opportunity gap* [Research brief]. Stanford Center
for Opportunity Policy in Education. https://edpolicy.stanford.
edu/sites/default/files/scope-pub-student-centered-research-
brief.pdf

5 Horn, M. B., & Staker, H. (2011). *The rise of K-12 blended learning.*
Innosight Institute. http://www.christenseninstitute.org/
wp-content/uploads/2013/04/The-rise-of-K-12-blended-
learning.pdf

Hutchison, L. F. (2012). Addressing the STEM teacher shortage in
American schools: Ways to recruit and retain effective STEM
teachers. *Action in Teacher Education, 34*(5/6), 541–550.
https://doi.org/10.1080/01626620.2012.729483

6 International Society for Technology in Education. (2016). *Student-
centered learning.* http://www.id/iste.org/connected/
standards/essential-conditions/student-centered-learning

1 List of references begins on new page. Heading is
boldface and centered. **2** List is alphabetized by authors'
last names. Authors' names are inverted. **3** First line of each
entry is at the left margin; subsequent lines indent one-half
inch. **4** All authors' names are listed for sources with up to
twenty authors. **5** Double-spacing is used throughout.
6 Organization listed as author; name is presented in normal
order.

12

Mitra, S. (2013, February). *Build a school in the cloud*
[Video]. TED. https://www.ted.com/talks/
sugata_mitra_build_a_school_in_the_cloud?language=en

Moeller, B., & Reitzes, T. (2011, July). *Integrating technology with
student-centered learning.* Nellie Mae Education Foundation.
http://www.nmefoundation.org/research/personalization/
integrating-technology-with-student-centered-learn

Rich, M. (2015, August 9). Teacher shortages spur a nationwide
hiring scramble (credentials optional). *The New York Times.*
https://nyti.ms/1WaaV7a

Svokos, A. (2015, May 7). 5 innovations from the past decade
that aim to change the American classroom. *Huffpost.*
https://www.huffpost.com/entry/technology-changes-
classrooms_n_7190910

Watson, J. (2008, January). *Blended learning: The convergence of
online and face-to-face education.* North American Council
for Online Learning. http://www.inacol.org/wp-content/
uploads/2015/02/NACOL_PP-BlendedLearning-lr.pdf

Professional paper: Abstract and running head

1 TECHNOLOGY AND STUDENT-CENTERED LEARNING 2

2 **Abstract**

In recent decades, instructors and administrators have viewed student-centered learning as a promising pedagogical practice that **3** offers both the hope of increasing academic performance and a solution for teacher shortages. Differing from the traditional model of instruction in which a teacher delivers content from the front of a classroom, student-centered learning puts the students at the center of teaching and learning. Students set their own learning goals, select appropriate resources, and progress at their own pace. Student-centered learning has produced both positive results and increases in students' self-esteem. Given the recent proliferation of technology in classrooms, school districts are poised for success in making the shift to student-centered learning. The question for district leaders, however, is how to effectively balance existing teacher talent with educational technology.

4 *Keywords:* digital learning, student-centered learning, personalized learning, education technology, transmissive, blended

1 Running head, made up of short title (50 characters or less) in all capital letters, flush left on all pages. **2** Abstract appears on new page after title page. Heading boldface and centered. **3** Abstract is a fewer than 250-word overview of paper. **4** Keywords help readers search for a paper on the web or in databases.

Chicago
Papers

Most history instructors and some humanities instructors will ask you to document sources with footnotes or endnotes based on the *Chicago Manual of Style* system explained in section 43. When you write a *Chicago*-style paper using sources, you need to (1) support a thesis, (2) cite your sources and avoid plagiarism, and (3) integrate source material effectively.

40 Supporting a thesis

▶ How to test your thesis **109**

Most assignments based on reading or research ask you to form a thesis, or main idea, and to support that thesis with well-organized evidence. A thesis is a one-sentence (or occasionally a two-sentence) statement of your central idea. Usually your thesis will appear at the end of the first paragraph (see the example on p. 289).

40a Forming a thesis statement

A thesis expresses your informed, reasoned answer to your research question—an answer about which reasonable people might disagree. Here are some examples:

RESEARCH QUESTION

To what extent was Confederate Major General Nathan Bedford Forrest responsible for the massacre of Union troops at Fort Pillow?

THESIS

By encouraging racism among his troops, Nathan Bedford Forrest was directly responsible for the massacre of Union troops at Fort Pillow.

RESEARCH QUESTION

How did the 365-day combat tour affect soldiers' experiences of the Vietnam War?

THESIS

Letters and diaries written by combat soldiers in Vietnam reveal that when soldiers' tours of duty were shortened, their investment in the war shifted from fighting for victory to fighting for survival.

Each of these thesis statements expresses a view on a debatable issue—an issue about which intelligent, well-meaning people might disagree. The writer's job is to convince such readers that this view is worth taking seriously. For help with testing your thesis, see the guidelines on page 109.

40b Organizing your ideas

The body of your paper will consist of evidence in support of your thesis. To get started, sketch an informal plan to focus and organize your evidence. Ned Bishop, the student who wrote about Fort Pillow, used a simple list of questions to structure his ideas. These questions became headings that helped readers follow his line of argument.

What happened at Fort Pillow?

Did Forrest order the massacre?

Can Forrest be held responsible for the massacre?

40c Using sources to inform and support your argument

Sources can support your thesis by playing several different roles. They might provide background information on your topic, explain important concepts, support or lend authority to your argument, or acknowledge objections to your claims. For detailed advice on how to use your sources to inform and support your argument, see page 111.

41 Avoiding plagiarism

▶ How to be a responsible research writer **115**
▶ How to paraphrase effectively **118**

In a research paper, you draw on the work of other researchers, and must document their contributions by citing your sources. When you acknowledge and document your sources, you avoid plagiarism, a form of academic dishonesty. Three different acts are considered plagiarism:

1. failing to cite quotations and borrowed ideas
2. failing to enclose borrowed language in quotation marks
3. failing to put summaries and paraphrases in your own words

41a Citing quotations and borrowed ideas

When you cite sources, you give credit to writers from whom you've borrowed words and ideas. You must cite anything you borrow from a source, including direct quotations; statistics and other specific facts; visuals such as maps, graphs, and diagrams; and any ideas you present in a summary or a paraphrase. Your citation guides readers quickly to the source of a quoted, paraphrased, or summarized idea so that they can find and read that original source.

The only exception is common knowledge — information your readers likely already know or could easily find in general sources. When you have seen certain information repeatedly in your reading, you don't need to cite it. However, when information has appeared in only a few sources, when it is highly specific (as with statistics), or when it is controversial, you should cite the source. If you're not sure whether you need to cite something, check with your instructor.

41b Using the *Chicago* citation system to lead readers to your sources

Chicago citations consist of superscript numbers in the text of the paper that refer readers to notes with corresponding numbers either at the foot of the page (footnotes) or at the end of the paper (endnotes).

TEXT

Governor John Andrew was not allowed to recruit black soldiers from out of state. "Ostensibly," writes Peter Burchard, "no recruiting was done outside Massachusetts, but it was an open secret that Andrew's agents were working far and wide."[1]

NOTE

1. Peter Burchard, *One Gallant Rush: Robert Gould Shaw and His Brave Black Regiment* (New York: St. Martin's, 1965), 85.

For detailed advice on using *Chicago* notes, see 43a. When you use footnotes or endnotes, you will usually need to provide a bibliography as well (see 43b).

41c Using quotation marks around borrwed language

To indicate that you are using a source's exact phrases or sentences, you must enclose them in quotation marks. To omit the quotation marks is to claim — falsely — that the language is your own. Such an omission is plagiarism even if you have cited the source. In the example of plagiarism below, the student writer has cited the source, but has not used quotation marks around the words taken directly from the source.

ORIGINAL SOURCE

For many Southerners it was psychologically impossible to see a black man bearing arms as anything but an incipient slave uprising complete with arson, murder, pillage, and rapine.

> —Dudley Taylor Cornish, *The Sable Arm: Negro Troops in the Union Army, 1861–1865*, p. 158

PLAGIARISM

According to Civil War historian Dudley Taylor Cornish, for many Southerners it was psychologically impossible to see a black man bearing arms as anything but an incipient slave uprising complete with arson, murder, pillage, and rapine.[2]

BORROWED LANGUAGE IN QUOTATION MARKS

According to Civil War historian Dudley Taylor Cornish, "For many Southerners it was psychologically impossible to see a black man bearing arms as anything but an incipient slave uprising complete with arson, murder, pillage, and rapine."[2]

NOTE: Long quotations are set off from the text by indenting and do not need quotation marks (see p. 259).

41d Putting summaries and paraphrases in your own words

A summary condenses information from a source; a paraphrase conveys the information using roughly the same number of words as the original source. When you summarize or paraphrase, you must name the source and restate the source's meaning in your own words and sentence structure. Half-copying the author's sentences either by using the author's phrases in your own sentences without quotation marks or by plugging synonyms into the author's sentence structure is a form of plagiarism.

In the following example, the paraphrase is plagiarized—even though the source is cited—because too much of its language is borrowed from the original. The highlighted strings of words have been copied exactly (without quotation marks). In addition, the writer has closely followed the sentence structure of the original source, merely making a few substitutions (underlined).

ORIGINAL SOURCE

Half of the force holding Fort Pillow were Negroes, former slaves now enrolled in the Union Army. Toward them Forrest's troops had the fierce, bitter animosity of men who had been educated to regard the colored race as inferior and who for the first time had encountered that race armed and fighting against white men. The sight enraged and perhaps terrified many of the Confederates and aroused in them the ugly spirit of a lynching mob.

—Albert Castel, "The Fort Pillow Massacre," pp. 46–47

PLAGIARISM: UNACCEPTABLE BORROWING

Albert Castel suggests that much of the brutality at Fort Pillow can be traced to racial attitudes. Fifty percent of the troops holding Fort Pillow were Negroes, former slaves who had joined the Union Army. Toward them Forrest's soldiers displayed the savage hatred of men who had been taught the inferiority of blacks and who for the first time had confronted them armed and fighting against white men. The vision angered and perhaps frightened the Confederates and aroused in them the ugly spirit of a lynching mob.[3]

To avoid plagiarizing an author's language, resist the temptation to look at the source while you are summarizing or paraphrasing. In your own words, state your understanding of the author's ideas. Then return to the source to check that you haven't used the author's language or sentence structure or misrepresented the author's ideas. See the box on page 115 for more guidance on being a responsible research writer.

ACCEPTABLE PARAPHRASE

Albert Castel suggests that much of the brutality at Fort Pillow can be traced to racial attitudes. Nearly half of the Union troops were blacks, men whom the Confederates had been raised to consider their inferiors. The shock and perhaps fear of facing armed ex-slaves in battle for the first time may well have unleashed the fury that led to the massacre.[3]

See section 31a for more advice on when to summarize and paraphrase. For specific guidelines on paraphrasing effectively, see page 118.

42 Integrating sources

▶ Using sentence guides at a glance **125**
▶ Signal phrases at a glance *Chicago* **261**

Facts and ideas from other sources will help you develop your argument, but they cannot speak for you. You can use several strategies to integrate information from sources into your paper while maintaining your own voice.

42a Using quotations effectively

When you quote a source, you borrow some of the author's exact words and enclose them in quotation marks. Quotation marks show your readers that both the idea and the words belong to the author. You might quote a source when exact wording is needed for accuracy or when the original language is especially effective. Using the words of an authority can also lend weight to your argument. For more advice on when to use quotations, see 31b.

Limiting your use of quotations   Keep the emphasis on your own words and ideas. It is not always necessary to quote full sentences from a source. Often you can integrate words or phrases from a source into your own sentence structure.

As Hurst has pointed out, until "an outcry erupted in the Northern press," even the Confederates did not deny that there had been a massacre at Fort Pillow.[4]

Using the ellipsis mark   To condense a quoted passage, you can use an ellipsis—a series of three spaced periods—to indicate that you have omitted words. What remains must be grammatically complete.

Union surgeon Fitch's testimony that all women and children had been evacuated from Fort Pillow before the attack conflicts with Forrest's report: "We captured . . . about 40 negro women and children."[5]

The writer has omitted several words not relevant to the issue at hand: *164 Federals, 75 negro troops, and.*

When you want to leave out one or more full sentences, use a period before the ellipsis. For an example, see the long quotation on page 259.

You do not need an ellipsis at the beginning or at the end of a quotation. Readers will understand that you have taken the quoted material from a longer passage.

USING SOURCES RESPONSIBLY: Make sure that omissions and ellipsis marks do not distort the meaning of your source.

Using brackets   Brackets allow you to insert your own words into quoted material to clarify a confusing reference or to keep a sentence grammatical in the context of your writing.

According to Albert Castel, "It can be reasonably argued that he [Forrest] was justified in believing that the approaching steamships intended to aid the garrison [at Fort Pillow]."[6]

To indicate an error in a quotation, such as a misspelling, insert [*sic*], italicized and with brackets around it, right after the error.

Setting off long quotations   *Chicago* style allows you flexibility in deciding whether to set off a long quotation or run it into your text. For emphasis, you may want to set off a quotation of more than five lines of text; you should always set off quotations of ten lines or more. To set off a quotation, indent it one-half inch from the left margin.

Long quotations should be introduced by an informative sentence, usually ending in a colon. Quotation marks are unnecessary because the indented format tells readers that the passage is taken word-for-word from the source.

In a letter home, Confederate officer Achilles V. Clark recounted what happened at Fort Pillow:

> Words cannot describe the scene. The poor deluded negroes would run up to our men fall upon their knees and with uplifted hands scream for mercy but they were ordered to their feet and then shot down. The whitte [*sic*] men fared but little better. . . . I with several others tried to stop the butchery and at one time had partially succeeded, but Gen. Forrest ordered them shot down like dogs, and the carnage continued.[7]

42b Using signal phrases to integrate sources

Whenever you include a paraphrase, summary, or direct quotation of another writer's work in your paper, prepare readers for it with a *signal phrase*. A signal phrase names the author of the source, points out the author's credentials, and often provides some context for the source material. The first time you mention an author, use the full name: *Shelby Foote argues. . . .* When you refer to the author again, you may use the last name only: *Foote raises an important question.*

When you write a signal phrase, choose a verb that is appropriate for the way you are using the source. Are you providing background, explaining a concept, supporting a claim, lending authority, or refuting an argument? See the chart on page 261 for a list of verbs commonly used in signal phrases.

Marking boundaries Avoid dropping a quotation into your text without warning. Provide a clear signal phrase, including at least the author's name, to indicate the boundary between your words and the source's words.

DROPPED QUOTATION

Unionists claimed that their troops had abandoned their arms and were in full retreat. "The Confederates, however, all agreed that the Union troops retreated to the river with arms in their hands."[8]

QUOTATION WITH SIGNAL PHRASE

Unionists claimed that their troops had abandoned their arms and were in full retreat. "The Confederates, however," writes historian Albert Castel, "all agreed that the Union troops retreated to the river with arms in their hands."[8]

Introducing summaries and paraphrases Introduce most summaries and paraphrases with a signal phrase that mentions the author and places the material in the context of your own writing. Readers will then understand where the summary or paraphrase begins.

Without the signal phrase (highlighted) in the following example, readers might think that only the last sentence is being cited, when in fact the whole paragraph is based on the source.

According to Jack Hurst, official Confederate policy was that black soldiers were to be treated as runaway slaves; in addition, the Confederate Congress decreed that white Union officers commanding black troops be killed. Confederate Lieutenant General Kirby Smith went one step further, declaring that he would kill all captured black troops. Smith's policy never met with strong opposition from the Richmond government.[9]

Integrating statistics and other facts When you cite a statistic or another specific fact, a signal phrase is often not necessary. In most cases, readers will understand that the citation refers to the statistic or fact (not the whole paragraph).

Of 295 white troops garrisoned at Fort Pillow, 168 were taken prisoner. Black troops fared worse, with only 58 of 262 captured and most of the rest presumably killed or wounded.[10]

There is nothing wrong, however, with using a signal phrase to introduce a statistic or another specific fact.

Putting source material in context   Readers should not have to guess why source material appears in your paper. A signal phrase can help you connect your own ideas with those of another writer by clarifying how the source will contribute to your paper. It's a good idea to embed a quotation between sentences of your own, introducing it with a signal phrase and following it with interpretive comments that link the source material to your paper's argument. See the next page for an example.

6⌒ Signal phrases **at a glance** `Chicago`

To avoid monotony, try to vary both the language and the placement of your signal phrases.

Model signal phrases

In the words of historian James M. McPherson, ". . ."[1]

As Dudley Taylor Cornish has argued, ". . ."[2]

In a letter to his wife, a Confederate soldier who witnessed the massacre wrote that ". . ."[3]

". . .," claims Benjamin Quarles.[4]

". . .," writes Albert Castel, ". . ."[5]

Shelby Foote offers an intriguing interpretation: ". . ."[6]

Verbs in signal phrases

admits	contends	reasons
agrees	declares	refutes
argues	denies	rejects
asserts	emphasizes	reports
believes	insists	responds
claims	notes	suggests
compares	observes	thinks
confirms	points out	writes

NOTE: In *Chicago* style, use the present tense or present perfect tense (*argues* or *has argued*) to introduce quotations or other material from nonfiction sources. Use the past tense (*argued*) only if you include a date or another marker that specifies the time of the original author's writing.

QUOTATION WITH EFFECTIVE CONTEXT

In a respected biography of Nathan Bedford Forrest, Hurst suggests that the temperamental Forrest "may have ragingly ordered a massacre and even intended to carry it out — until he rode inside the fort and viewed the horrifying result" and ordered it stopped.[12] While this is an intriguing interpretation of events, even Hurst would probably admit that it is merely speculation.

For some sentences starters to guide you in integrating sources, see page 125.

42c Synthesizing sources

When you synthesize multiple sources in a research paper, you create a conversation about your research topic. You show readers that your argument is based on your analysis and integration of ideas and is not just a string of quotations and paraphrases. Your synthesis shows how your sources relate to one another; one source my support, extend, or counter the ideas of another. For an example of an effective synthesis, see 31d.

43   *Chicago* documentation style

In history and some other humanities courses, you may be asked to use the documentation system of *The Chicago Manual of Style*, 17th ed. (Chicago: University of Chicago Press, 2017).

43a First and later notes for a source

The first time you cite a source, the note should include publication information for that work as well as the page number for the passage you are citing.

1. Peter Burchard, *One Gallant Rush: Robert Gould Shaw and His Brave Black Regiment* (New York: St. Martin's, 1965), 85.

For later references to a source you have already cited, you may simply give the author's last name, a short form of the title, and the page or pages cited. A short form of the title of a book or another long work is italicized; a short form of the title of an article or another short work is put in quotation marks.

4. Burchard, *One Gallant Rush*, 31.

👓 *Chicago* documentation **at a glance**

The *Chicago* documentation system requires numbered notes and specific information to credit your sources and to help readers find the sources for themselves. Every time you reference a source in your paper, you should have

- a **superscript number** (like this:[1]) after the material you've cited. This number corresponds to

- a **note** either at the bottom of the page (*footnote*) or at the end of the paper (*endnote*). Each note begins with the number to which it is referring in the text. The note provides publication information for the source and the page on which the quoted or paraphrased material appears.

- A **bibliography entry** for each source is often required as well. The bibliography appears at the end of the paper and gives publication information for all the works cited in the notes.

In the example below, the number which connects the quotation to the note is underlined.

TEXT

Evictions in American cities were once a rare occurrence, and when they did occur, "they drew crowds. . . . Sometimes neighbors confronted the marshals directly, sitting on the evicted family's furniture to prevent its removal or moving the family back in."[1]

FOOTNOTE (at the bottom of the page) OR ENDNOTE (at the end of the paper)

1. Matthew Desmond, *Evicted: Poverty and Profit in the American City* (New York: Crown, 2016), 3.

BIBLIOGRAPHY ENTRY (in a list at the end of the paper)

Desmond, Matthew. *Evicted: Poverty and Profit in the American City*. New York: Crown, 2016.

When you have two notes in a row from the same source, give the author's last name and the page or pages cited.

5. Jack Hurst, *Nathan Bedford Forrest: A Biography* (New York: Knopf, 1993), 8.

6. Hurst, 174.

43b *Chicago*-style bibliography

A bibliography at the end of your paper lists the works you have cited in your notes; it may also include works you consulted but did not cite. See page 287 for formatting; see page 291 for a sample bibliography.

NOTE: If you include a bibliography, you may shorten all notes, including the first reference to a source (see 43a). Check with your instructor, however, to see whether using an abbreviated note for a first reference to a source is acceptable.

43c Model notes and bibliography entries

The following models are consistent with guidelines in *The Chicago Manual of Style*, 17th ed. For each type of source, a model note appears first, followed by a model bibliography entry. The note shows the format you should use when citing a source for the first time. For subsequent citations of a source, use shortened notes.

Some sources from the web, typically periodical articles, use a permanent locator called a digital object identifier (DOI). Use the DOI, when it is available, in place of a URL. (For guidelines about breaking a URL or DOI across lines, see p. 286.)

General guidelines for listing authors

● **1. One author**

1. Salman Rushdie, *Joseph Anton: A Memoir* (New York: Random House, 2012), 135.

Rushdie, Salman. *Joseph Anton: A Memoir*. New York: Random House, 2012.

List of *Chicago*-style notes and bibliography entries

Continued ➜

● **2. Two or three authors**   Give all authors' names in both the note and the bibliography entry.

2. Bill O'Reilly and Martin Dugard, *Killing Lincoln: The Shocking Assassination That Changed America Forever* (New York: Holt, 2012), 33.

O'Reilly, Bill, and Martin Dugard. *Killing Lincoln: The Shocking Assassination That Changed America Forever.* New York: Holt, 2012.

● **3. Four or more authors**   In the note, give the first author's name followed by "et al." (Latin for "and others"); in the bibliography entry, list all authors' names.

3. Lynn Hunt et al., *The Making of the West: Peoples and Cultures*, 5th ed. (Boston: Bedford/St. Martin's, 2015), 541.

Hunt, Lynn, Thomas R. Martin, Barbara H. Rosenwein, and Bonnie G. Smith. *The Making of the West: Peoples and Cultures.* 5th ed. Boston: Bedford/St. Martin's, 2015.

● **4. Organization as author**

4. Johnson Historical Society, *Images of America: Johnson* (Charleston, SC: Arcadia Publishing, 2011), 24.

Johnson Historical Society. *Images of America: Johnson.* Charleston, SC: Arcadia Publishing, 2011.

● **5. Unknown author**

5. *The Men's League Handbook on Women's Suffrage* (London, 1912), 23.

The Men's League Handbook on Women's Suffrage. London, 1912.

● **6. Multiple works by the same author** In the bibliography, arrange the entries alphabetically by title. Use six hyphens in place of the author's name in the second and subsequent entries.

Winchester, Simon. *The Alice behind Wonderland*. New York: Oxford University Press, 2011.

------. *Atlantic: Great Sea Battles, Heroic Discoveries, Titanic Storms, and a Vast Ocean of a Million Stories*. New York: HarperCollins, 2010.

● **7. Editor**

7. Teresa Carpenter, ed., *New York Diaries: 1609–2009* (New York: Modern Library, 2012), 316.

Carpenter, Teresa, ed. *New York Diaries: 1609–2009*. New York: Modern Library, 2012.

● **8. Editor with author**

8. Susan Sontag, *As Consciousness Is Harnessed to Flesh: Journals and Notebooks, 1964–1980*, ed. David Rieff (New York: Farrar, Straus and Giroux, 2012), 265.

Sontag, Susan. *As Consciousness Is Harnessed to Flesh: Journals and Notebooks, 1964–1980*. Edited by David Rieff. New York: Farrar, Straus and Giroux, 2012.

● **9. Translator with author**

9. Richard Bidlack and Nikita Lomagin, *The Leningrad Blockade, 1941–1944: A New Documentary from the Soviet Archives*, trans. Marian Schwartz (New Haven: Yale University Press, 2012), 26.

Bidlack, Richard, and Nikita Lomagin. *The Leningrad Blockade, 1941–1944: A New Documentary from the Soviet Archives*. Translated by Marian Schwartz. New Haven: Yale University Press, 2012.

Books and other long works

▶ Citation at a glance: Book **268**

● **10. Basic format for a book**

a. Print

10. Mary N. Woods, *Beyond the Architect's Eye: Photographs and the American Built Environment* (Philadelphia: University of Pennsylvania Press, 2009), 45.

6ə Citation at a glance

Book *Chicago*

To cite a print book in *Chicago* style, include the following elements:

1 Author(s)
2 Title and subtitle
3 City of publication

4 Publisher
5 Year of publication
6 Page number(s) cited (for notes)

TITLE PAGE

THE PENGUIN PRESS
New York
2012

THE
TWILIGHT WAR

The Secret History of America's Thirty-Year Conflict with Iran

DAVID CRIST

The Penguin Press
New York
2012

FROM COPYRIGHT PAGE

First published in 2012 by The Penguin Press, a member of Penguin Group (USA) Inc.

The Penguin Press, New York, 2012.

NOTE

1. David Crist, *The Twilight War: The Secret History of America's Thirty-Year Conflict with Iran* (New York: Penguin Press, 2012), 354.

BIBLIOGRAPHY

Crist, David. *The Twilight War: The Secret History of America's Thirty-Year Conflict with Iran.* New York: Penguin Press, 2012.

For more on citing books in *Chicago* style, see items 10–17.

● **10. Basic format for a book (*cont.*)**

a. Print (cont.)

Woods, Mary N. *Beyond the Architect's Eye: Photographs and the American Built Environment*. Philadelphia: University of Pennsylvania Press, 2009.

b. E-book

10. Drew Gilpin Faust, *This Republic of Suffering: Death and the American Civil War* (New York: Knopf, 2008), chap. 4, NOOK.

Faust, Drew Gilpin. *This Republic of Suffering: Death and the American Civil War*. New York: Knopf, 2008. NOOK.

c. Web (or online library)

10. Charles Hursthouse, *New Zealand, or Zealandia, the Britain of the South* (1857; HathiTrust Digital Library, n.d.), 2:356, http://hdl.handle.net/2027/uc1.b304920.

Hursthouse, Charles. *New Zealand, or Zealandia, the Britain of the South*. 2 vols. 1857. HathiTrust Digital Library, n.d. http://hdl.handle.net/2027/uc1.b304920.

● **11. Edition other than the first**

11. Josephine Donovan, *Feminist Theory: The Intellectual Traditions*, 4th ed. (New York: Continuum, 2012), 86.

Donovan, Josephine. *Feminist Theory: The Intellectual Traditions*. 4th ed. New York: Continuum, 2012.

● **12. Volume in a multivolume work**   If the volumes do not have individual titles, give the volume and page number in the note (for example, 2:356) and the total number of volumes in the bibliography entry (see item 10c).

12. Robert A. Caro, *The Passage of Power*, vol. 4 of *The Years of Lyndon Johnson* (New York: Knopf, 2012), 198.

Caro, Robert A. *The Passage of Power*. Vol. 4 of *The Years of Lyndon Johnson*. New York: Knopf, 2012.

● **13. Work in an anthology or a collection**

13. Janet Walsh, "Unequal in Africa: How Property Rights Can Empower Women," in *The Unfinished Revolution: Voices from the Global Fight for Women's Rights*, ed. Minky Worden (New York: Seven Stories Press, 2012), 161.

● **13. Work in an anthology or a collection (*cont.*)**

Walsh, Janet. "Unequal in Africa: How Property Rights Can
Empower Women." In *The Unfinished Revolution: Voices
from the Global Fight for Women's Rights,* edited by Minky
Worden, 159–66. New York: Seven Stories Press, 2012.

● **14. Introduction, preface, foreword, or afterword**

14. Alice Walker, afterword to *The Indispensable Zinn: The
Essential Writings of the "People's Historian,"* by Howard Zinn,
ed. Timothy Patrick McCarthy (New York: Free Press, 2012), 373.

Walker, Alice. Afterword to *The Indispensable Zinn: The Essential
Writings of the "People's Historian,"* by Howard Zinn,
371–76. Edited by Timothy Patrick McCarthy. New York:
Free Press, 2012.

● **15. Republished book**

15. W. S. Blatchley, *A Nature Wooing at Ormond by the Sea*
(1902; repr., Stockbridge, MA: Hard Press, 2012), 26.

Blatchley, W. S. *A Nature Wooing at Ormond by the Sea*. 1902.
Reprint, Stockbridge, MA: Hard Press, 2012.

● **16. Book with a title in its title**   Use quotation marks
around any title within an italicized title.

16. Claudia Durst Johnson, ed., *Race in Mark Twain's
"Adventures of Huckleberry Finn"* (Detroit: Greenhaven Press, 2009).

Johnson, Claudia Durst, ed. *Race in Mark Twain's "Adventures of
Huckleberry Finn."* Detroit: Greenhaven Press, 2009.

● **17. Sacred text**   Sacred texts are usually not included
in the bibliography.

17. Matt. 20:4–9 (Revised Standard Version).

● **18. Government document**

18. United States Senate, Committee on Foreign Relations,
*Implications of the Kyoto Protocol on Climate Change: Hearing
before the Committee on Foreign Relations, United States Senate*,
105th Cong., 2nd sess. (Washington, DC: GPO, 1998).

United States Senate. Committee on Foreign Relations.
*Implications of the Kyoto Protocol on Climate Change:
Hearing before the Committee on Foreign Relations, United
States Senate*, 105th Cong., 2nd sess. Washington, DC:
GPO, 1998.

● **19. Published proceedings of a conference**   Cite as a book, adding the location and dates of the conference after the title.

19. Stacey K. Sowards et al., eds., *Across Borders and Environments: Communication and Environmental Justice in International Contexts*, University of Texas at El Paso, June 25–28, 2011 (Cincinnati, OH: International Environmental Communication Association, 2012), 114.

Sowards, Stacey K., Kyle Alvarado, Diana Arrieta, and Jacob Barde, eds. *Across Borders and Environments: Communication and Environmental Justice in International Contexts*. University of Texas at El Paso, June 25–28, 2011. Cincinnati, OH: International Environmental Communication Association, 2012.

● **20. Source quoted in another source (a secondary source)**

20. Thomas Wentworth Higginson, *Margaret Fuller Ossoli* (Boston: Houghton Mifflin, 1890), 11, quoted in John Matteson, *The Lives of Margaret Fuller* (New York: Norton, 2012), 7.

Higginson, Thomas Wentworth. *Margaret Fuller Ossoli*. Boston: Houghton Mifflin, 1890, 11. Quoted in John Matteson, *The Lives of Margaret Fuller* (New York: Norton, 2012), 7.

Articles and other short works

▶ Citation at a glance: Article in an online journal **272**
▶ Citation at a glance: Article from a database **274**

● **21. Article in a journal**   If an article in a database or on the web shows only a beginning page, use a plus sign after the page number in the bibliography: 212+.

a. Print

21. Catherine Foisy, "Preparing the Quebec Church for Vatican II: Missionary Lessons from Asia, Africa, and Latin America, 1945–1962," *Historical Studies* 78 (2012): 8.

Foisy, Catherine. "Preparing the Quebec Church for Vatican II: Missionary Lessons from Asia, Africa, and Latin America, 1945–1962." *Historical Studies* 78 (2012): 7–26.

b. Web   If no DOI is available, give the URL for the article.

21. Anne-Lise François, "Flower Fisting," *Postmodern Culture* 22, no. 1 (2011), https://doi.org/10.1353/pmc.2012.0004.

6ᵈ Citation at a glance

Article in an online journal `Chicago`

To cite an article in an online journal in *Chicago* style, include the following elements:

1. Author(s)
2. Title and subtitle of article
3. Title of journal
4. Volume and issue numbers
5. Year of publication
6. Page number(s) cited (for notes); page range of article (for bibliography), if available
7. DOI, if article has one; otherwise, URL for article

ISSUE CONTENTS PAGE

ARTICLE HOME PAGE (top) AND FULL TEXT (bottom)

NOTE

       1   **2**

1. Kwadwo Adusei-Asante, "A Community-Based

                   3

Program in a Non-Existent Community," *African Studies*

     4   **5**   **6**   **7**

Quarterly 15, no. 2 (2015): 72, http://asq.africa.ufl.edu

/files/Volume-15-Issue-2-Adusei-Asante.pdf.

BIBLIOGRAPHY

      1   **2**

Adusei-Asante, Kwadwo. "A Community-Based Program in

                 3

a Non-Existent Community." *African Studies Quarterly*

 4   **5**   **6**   **7**

15, no. 2 (2015): 69–84. http://asq.africa.ufl.edu

/files/Volume-15-Issue-2-Adusei-Asante.pdf.

For more on citing articles in *Chicago* style, see items 21–23.

● **21. Article in a journal (*cont.*)**

b. Web (cont.)

François, Anne-Lise. "Flower Fisting." *Postmodern Culture* 22,
no. 1 (2011). https://doi.org/10.1353/pmc.2012.0004.

c. Database   Give one of the following pieces of information from the database listing, in this order of preference: a DOI for the article; or the name of the database; or a "stable" or "persistent" URL for the article. (The DOI consists of the prefix https://doi.org/ followed by the DOI identifier.)

   21. Patrick Zuk, "Nikolay Myaskovsky and the Events of 1948," *Music and Letters* 93, no. 1 (2012): 61, Project Muse.

Zuk, Patrick. "Nikolay Myaskovsky and the Events of 1948."
Music and Letters 93, no. 1 (2012): 61. Project Muse.

6ᗥ Citation at a glance

Article from a database [Chicago]

To cite an article from a database in *Chicago* style, include the following elements:

1. Author(s)
2. Title and subtitle of article
3. Title of journal
4. Volume and issue numbers
5. Year of publication
6. Page number(s) cited (for notes); page range of article (for bibliography), if available
7. DOI; *or* database name; *or* stable URL for article

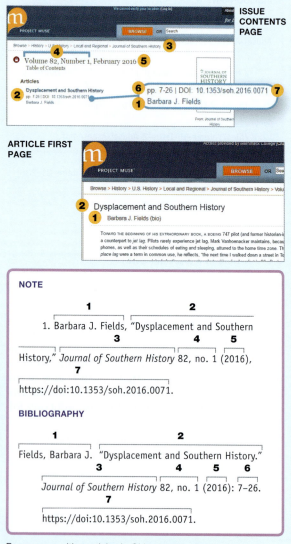

ISSUE CONTENTS PAGE

ARTICLE FIRST PAGE

NOTE

    1   2
1. Barbara J. Fields, "Dysplacement and Southern
        3   4   5
History," *Journal of Southern History* 82, no. 1 (2016),
    7
https://doi:10.1353/soh.2016.0071.

BIBLIOGRAPHY

    1   2
Fields, Barbara J. "Dysplacement and Southern History."
        3   4   5   6
Journal of Southern History 82, no. 1 (2016): 7–26.
        7
https://doi:10.1353/soh.2016.0071.

For more on citing articles in *Chicago* style, see items 21–23.

● **22. Article in a magazine** Give the month and year for a monthly publication; give the month, day, and year for a weekly publication. If an article in a database or on the web shows only a beginning page, use a plus sign after the page number in the bibliography: 212+.

a. Print

22. Alan Lightman, "Our Place in the Universe: Face to Face with the Infinite," *Harper's*, December 2012, 34.

Lightman, Alan. "Our Place in the Universe: Face to Face with the Infinite." *Harper's*, December 2012, 33–38.

b. Web If no DOI is available, include the URL for the article.

22. James Verini, "The Tunnels of Gaza," *National Geographic*, December 2012, http://ngm.nationalgeographic .com/2012/12/gaza-tunnels/verini-text.

Verini, James. "The Tunnels of Gaza." *National Geographic*, December 2012. http://ngm.nationalgeographic .com/2012/12/gaza-tunnels/verini-text.

c. Database Give one of the following from the database listing, in this order of preference: a DOI for the article; or the name of the database; or a "stable" or "persistent" URL for the article.

22. Ron Rosenbaum, "The Last Renaissance Man," *Smithsonian*, November 2012, 40, OmniFile Full Text Select.

Rosenbaum, Ron. "The Last Renaissance Man." *Smithsonian*, November 2012, 39–44. OmniFile Full Text Select.

● **23. Article in a newspaper** Page numbers are not necessary; a section letter or number, if available, is sufficient.

a. Print

23. Alissa J. Rubin, "A Pristine Afghan Prison Faces a Murky Future," *New York Times*, December 18, 2012, sec. A.

Rubin, Alissa J. "A Pristine Afghan Prison Faces a Murky Future." *New York Times*, December 18, 2012, sec. A.

● **23. Article in a newspaper (*cont.*)**

b. Web   Include the complete URL for the article.

23. David Brown, "New Burden of Disease Study Shows World's People Living Longer but with More Disability," *Washington Post*, December 13, 2012, https://www.washingtonpost.com /national/health-science/burden-of-disease-study-shows-a-world -living-longer-and-with-more-disability/2012/12/13/9d1e5278 -4320-11e2-8061-253bccfc7532_story.html.

Brown, David. "New Burden of Disease Study Shows World's People Living Longer but with More Disability." *Washington Post*, December 13, 2012. https://www .washingtonpost.com/national/health-science /burden-of-disease-study-shows-a-world-living-longer -and-with-more-disability/2012/12/13/9d1e5278-4320 -11e2-8061-253bccfc7532_story.html.

c. Database   Give one of the following from the database listing, in this order of preference: a DOI for the article; or the name of the database; or a "stable" or "persistent" URL for the article.

23. "Safe in Sioux City at Last: Union Pacific Succeeds in Securing Trackage from the St. Paul Road," *Omaha Daily Herald*, May 16, 1889, America's Historical Newspapers.

"Safe in Sioux City at Last: Union Pacific Succeeds in Securing Trackage from the St. Paul Road." *Omaha Daily Herald*, May 16, 1889. America's Historical Newspapers.

● **24. Unsigned newspaper article**

24. "Next President Better Be a Climate Change Believer," *Chicago Sun-Times*, June 24, 2016, https://chicago.suntimes .com/opinion/editorial-next-president-better-be-a-climate -change-believer/.

Chicago Sun-Times. "Next President Better Be a Climate Change Believer." June 24, 2016. https://chicago.suntimes.com /opinion/editorial-next-president-better-be-a-climate -change-believer/.

● **25. Article with a title in its title**   Use italics for titles of long works such as books and for terms that are normally italicized. Use single quotation marks for titles of short works and terms that would otherwise be placed in double quotation marks.

25. Karen Garner, "Global Gender Policy in the 1990s: Incorporating the 'Vital Voices' of Women," *Journal of Women's History* 24, no. 4 (2012): 130.

Garner, Karen. "Global Gender Policy in the 1990s: Incorporating the 'Vital Voices' of Women." *Journal of Women's History* 24, no. 4 (2012): 121–48.

● **26. Review**

26. David Eggleton, review of *Stalking Nabokov*, by Brian Boyd, *New Zealand Listener*, December 13, 2012, http://www .listener.co.nz/culture/books/stalking-nabokov-by-brian-boyd -review/.

Eggleton, David. Review of *Stalking Nabokov*, by Brian Boyd. *New Zealand Listener*, December 13, 2012. http://www .listener.co.nz/culture/books/stalking-nabokov-by-brian -boyd-review/.

● **27. Letter to the editor**   Do not use the letter's title, even if the publication gives one.

27. Andy Bush, letter to the editor, *Economist*, December 15, 2012, http://www.economist.com/.

Bush, Andy. Letter to the editor. *Economist*, December 15, 2012. http://www.economist.com/.

● **28. Article in a reference work (encyclopedia, dictionary, wiki)**   Reference works such as encyclopedias do not require publication information and are usually not included in the bibliography. The abbreviation "s.v." is for the Latin phrase *sub verbo* ("under the word").

28. *Encyclopaedia Britannica*, 15th ed. (2010), s.v. "Monroe Doctrine."

28. Wikipedia, s.v. "James Monroe," last modified December 19, 2012, http://en.wikipedia.org/wiki/James_Monroe.

28. Bryan A. Garner, *Garner's Modern American Usage*, 3rd ed. (Oxford: Oxford University Press, 2009), s.v. "brideprice."

Garner, Bryan A. *Garner's Modern American Usage*. 3rd ed. Oxford: Oxford University Press, 2009.

● **29. Letter in a published collection**   Use the day-month-year form for the date of the letter. If the letter writer's name is part of the book title, begin the note with only the last name but begin the bibliography entry with the full name.

▶   Citation at a glance: Letter in a published collection **278**

6⊘ Citation at a glance

Letter in a published collection `Chicago`

To cite a letter in a published collection in *Chicago* style, include the following elements:

1 Author of letter
2 Recipient of letter
3 Date of letter
4 Title of collection
5 Editor of collection
6 City of publication
7 Publisher
8 Year of publication
9 Page number(s) cited (for notes)

TITLE PAGE OF BOOK

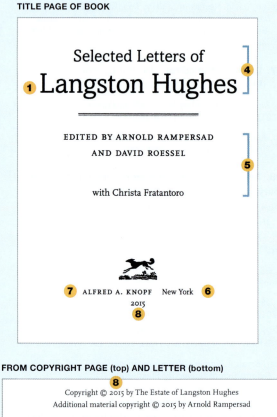

Selected Letters of

1 **Langston Hughes** **4**

EDITED BY ARNOLD RAMPERSAD
AND DAVID ROESSEL

5

with Christa Fratantoro

7 ALFRED A. KNOPF New York **6**
2015
8

FROM COPYRIGHT PAGE (top) AND LETTER (bottom)

8
Copyright © 2015 by The Estate of Langston Hughes
Additional material copyright © 2015 by Arnold Rampersad

All rights reserved. Published in the United States by Alfred A. Knopf, a division of Random House LLC, New York, and distributed in Canada by Random House of

9 344 SELECTED LETTERS OF LANGSTON HUGHES

2 TO RICHARD WRIGHT [TLS]

August 11, 1957 **3**

Dear Dick:
Sometime ago, Knopf forwarded to me your request to use the last four lines of LET AMERICA BE AMERICA AGAIN in your book of four lectures.* I am

278

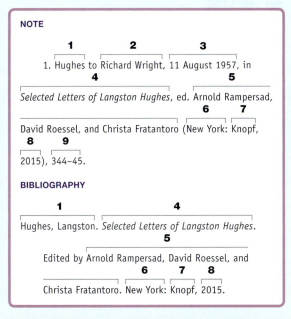

NOTE

1. Hughes to Richard Wright, 11 August 1957, in *Selected Letters of Langston Hughes*, ed. Arnold Rampersad, David Roessel, and Christa Fratantoro (New York: Knopf, 2015), 344–45.

BIBLIOGRAPHY

Hughes, Langston. *Selected Letters of Langston Hughes*. Edited by Arnold Rampersad, David Roessel, and Christa Fratantoro. New York: Knopf, 2015.

For another citation of a letter in *Chicago* style, see item 29.

● **29. Letter in a published collection (*cont.*)**

29. Dickens to Thomas Beard, 1 June 1840, in *The Selected Letters of Charles Dickens*, ed. Jenny Hartley (New York: Oxford University Press, 2012), 65.

Dickens, Charles. *The Selected Letters of Charles Dickens*. Edited by Jenny Hartley. New York: Oxford University Press, 2012.

Web sources For most websites, include an author if a site has one, the title of the site, the sponsor, the date of publication or the modified (update) date, and the site's complete URL. Do not italicize a website title unless the site is an online book or periodical. Use quotation marks for the titles of sections or pages in a website. If a site does not have a date of publication or a modified date, give the date you accessed the site ("accessed January 3, 2016").

● **30. An entire website**

30. Chesapeake and Ohio Canal National Historical Park (website), National Park Service, last modified November 25, 2012, http://www.nps.gov/choh/index.htm.

National Park Service. Chesapeake and Ohio Canal National Historical Park (website). Last modified November 25, 2012. http://www.nps.gov/choh/index.htm.

● **31. Work from a website**

▶ Citation at a glance: Primary source from a website **282**

31. Dan Archer, "Using Illustrated Reportage to Cover Human Trafficking in Nepal's Brick Kilns," Poynter, last modified December 18, 2012, https://www.poynter.org/news/using-illustrated-reportage-cover-human-trafficking-nepals-brick-kilns.

Archer, Dan. "Using Illustrated Reportage to Cover Human Trafficking in Nepal's Brick Kilns." Poynter, last modified December 18, 2012. https://www.poynter.org/news /using-illustrated-reportage-cover-human-trafficking -nepals-brick-kilns.

● **32. Blog post**   Italicize the name of the blog. Insert "blog" in parentheses after the name if the word *blog* is not part of the name. If the blog is part of a larger site, add the title of the site after the blog title (see item 33).

32. Gregory LeFever, "Skull Fraud 'Created' the Brontosaurus," *Ancient Tides* (blog), December 16, 2012, http://ancient-tides .blogspot.com/2012/12/skull-fraud-created-brontosaurus.html.

LeFever, Gregory. "Skull Fraud 'Created' the Brontosaurus." *Ancient Tides* (blog), December 16, 2012. http:// ancient-tides.blogspot.com/2012/12/skull-fraud-created -brontosaurus.html.

● **33. Comment on a blog post**

33. Didomyk, December 18, 2012, comment on B.C., "A New Spokesman," *Pomegranate: The Middle East* (blog), *Economist,* https://www.economist.com/blogs/pomegranate/2012 /12/christians-middle-east.

Didomyk. December 18, 2012. Comment on B.C., "A New Spokesman." *Pomegranate: The Middle East* (blog). *Economist.* https://www.economist.com/blogs /pomegranate/2012/12/christians-middle-east.

Audio, visual, and multimedia sources

● **34. Podcast**

34. Peter Limb, "Economic and Cultural History of the Slave Trade in Western Africa," Episode 69, December 12, 2012, in *Africa Past and Present*, African Online Digital Library, podcast, MP3 audio, 25:32, http://afripod.aodl.org/2012/12 /afripod-69/.

Limb, Peter. "Economic and Cultural History of the Slave Trade in Western Africa." Episode 69, December 12, 2012. *Africa Past and Present*. African Online Digital Library. Podcast, MP3 audio, 25:32. http://afripod.aodl.org/2012/12/afripod-69/.

● **35. Online audio or video**   If the source is a downloadable file, identify the file format or medium before the URL.

35. Tom Brokaw, "Global Warming: What You Need to Know," Discovery Channel, January 23, 2012, http://www.youtube.com/watch?v=xcVwLrAavyA.

Brokaw, Tom. "Global Warming: What You Need to Know." Discovery Channel, January 23, 2012. http://www.youtube.com/watch?v=xcVwLrAavyA.

● **36. Published or broadcast interview**

36. Jane Goodall, interview by Suza Scalora, *Origin*, n.d., http://www.originmagazine.com/2012/12/07/dr-jane-goodall-interview-with-suza-scalora.

Goodall, Jane. Interview by Suza Scalora. *Origin*, n.d. http://www.originmagazine.com/2012/12/07/dr-jane-goodall-interview-with-suza-scalora.

36. Julian Castro and Joaquin Castro, interview by Charlie Rose, *Charlie Rose Show*, WGBH, Boston, December 17, 2012.

Castro, Julian, and Joaquin Castro. Interview by Charlie Rose. *Charlie Rose Show*. WGBH, Boston, December 17, 2012.

● **37. Film**   Include both the date of original release and the date of release for the format being cited.

37. *Argo*, directed by Ben Affleck (2012; Burbank, CA: Warner Bros. Pictures, 2013), DVD.

Affleck, Ben, dir. *Argo*. 2012; Burbank, CA: Warner Bros. Pictures, 2013. DVD.

● **38. Sound recording**

38. Gustav Holst, *The Planets*, Royal Philharmonic Orchestra, conducted by André Previn, recorded April 14–15, 1986, Telarc 80133, compact disc.

Holst, Gustav. *The Planets*. Royal Philharmonic Orchestra. Recorded April 14–15, 1986. Conducted by André Previn. Telarc 80133, compact disc.

● **39. Musical score or composition**

39. Antonio Vivaldi, *L'Estro armonico*, op. 3, ed. Eleanor Selfridge-Field (Mineola, NY: Dover, 1999).

Vivaldi, Antonio. *L'Estro armonico*, op. 3. Edited by Eleanor Selfridge-Field. Mineola, NY: Dover, 1999.

6∂ Citation at a glance

Primary source from a website   Chicago

To cite a primary source (or any other document) from a website in *Chicago* style, include as many of the following elements as are available:

1 Author(s)
2 Title of document
3 Title of site
4 Sponsor of site

5 Publication date or modified date; date of access (if no publication date)
6 URL of document page

WEBSITE HOME PAGE

FIRST PAGE OF DOCUMENT

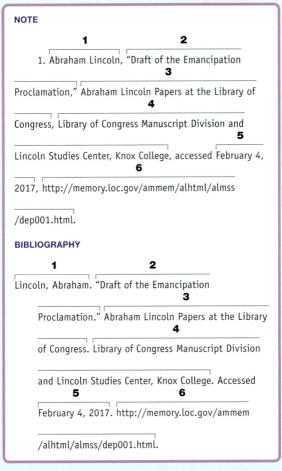

For more on citing documents from websites in *Chicago* style, see item 31.

● **40. Work of art**

    40. Aaron Siskind, *Untitled (The Most Crowded Block)*, 1939, gelatin silver print, Kemper Museum of Contemporary Art, Kansas City, MO.

Siskind, Aaron. *Untitled (The Most Crowded Block)*. 1939. Gelatin silver print. Kemper Museum of Contemporary Art, Kansas City, MO.

● **41. Performance**

    41. Jackie Sibblies Drury, *Social Creatures*, directed by Curt Columbus, Trinity Repertory Company, Providence, RI, March 15, 2013.

Drury, Jackie Sibblies. *Social Creatures*. Directed by Curt Columbus. Trinity Repertory Company, Providence, RI, March 15, 2013.

Personal communication and social media

● **42. Personal communication**   Personal communications are not included in the bibliography.

    42. Sara Lehman, email message to author, August 13, 2012.

● **43. Online posting or email**   If an online posting has been archived, include a URL. Emails that are not part of an online discussion are treated as personal communication (see item 42). Online postings and emails are not included in the bibliography.

    43. Bart Dale, reply to "Which country made best science/ technology contribution?," Historum General History Forums, December 15, 2015, http://historum.com/general-history /46089-country-made-best-science-technology-contribution-16 .html.

● **44. Social media post**

    44. NASA (@nasa), "This galaxy is a whirl of color," Instagram photo, September 23, 2017, https://www.instagram .com/p/BZY8adnnZQJ/.

NASA. "This galaxy is a whirl of color." Instagram photo, September 23, 2017. https://www.instagram.com /p/BZY8adnnZQJ/.

44   *Chicago* format; sample pages

44a *Chicago* format

The following guidelines for formatting a *Chicago*-style paper and preparing its endnotes and bibliography are based on advice given in *The Chicago Manual of Style*, 17th ed. (Chicago: University of Chicago Press, 2017). For pages from a sample paper, see 44b.

Formatting the paper

Font If your instructor does not require a specific font, choose one that is standard and easy to read (such as Times New Roman).

Title page   Include the full title of your paper, your name, the course title, the instructor's name, and the date. See page 288 for a sample title page.

Pagination   Using arabic numerals (1, 2, 3, and so on), number the pages in the upper right corner. Do not number the title page but count it in the manuscript numbering; that is, the first page of the text is numbered 2. Depending on your instructor's preference, you may also use a short title or your last name before the page numbers to help identify pages.

Margins, line spacing, and paragraph indents   Leave margins of at least one inch at the top, bottom, and sides of the page. Double-space the body of the paper, including long quotations that have been set off from the text. (For line spacing in notes and the bibliography, see p. 287.) Left-align the text.

Indent the first line of each paragraph one-half inch from the left margin.

Capitalization, italics, and quotation marks   In titles of works, capitalize all words except articles (*a, an, the*), prepositions (*at, from, between*, and so on), coordinating conjunctions (*and, but, or, nor, for, so, yet*), and *to* and *as*—unless the word is first or last in the title or subtitle. Follow these guidelines in your paper even if the title is styled differently in the source.

In your text, lowercase the first word following a colon even if the word begins a complete sentence. When the colon introduces a series of sentences or questions, capitalize the first word in all sentences in the series, including the first.

Italicize the titles of books and other long works. Use quotation marks around the titles of periodical articles, short stories, poems, and other short works.

Long quotations   You can choose to set off a long quotation of five to ten typed lines by indenting the entire quotation one-half inch from the left margin. (Always set off quotations of ten or more lines.) Double-space the quotation; do not use quotation marks and do not add extra space above or below it. (See also pp. 258–59.)

Visuals   *Chicago* classifies visuals as tables and figures (graphs, drawings, photographs, maps, and charts). Keep visuals as simple as possible.

Label each table with an arabic numeral (Table 1, Table 2, and so on) and provide a clear title that identifies the table's subject. The label and the title should appear on separate lines above the table, left-aligned. For a table that you have borrowed or adapted, give its source in a note like this one, below the table:

Source: Edna Bonacich and Richard P. Appelbaum, *Behind the Label* (Berkeley: University of California Press, 2000), 145.

For each figure, place a label and a caption below the figure, left-aligned. The label and caption need not appear on separate lines. The word "Figure" may be abbreviated to "Fig."

In the text of your paper, discuss the most significant features of each visual. Place visuals as close as possible to the sentences that relate to them unless your instructor prefers that visuals appear in an appendix.

URLs and DOIs   When a URL or a DOI (digital object identifier) must break across lines, do not insert a hyphen or break at a hyphen. Instead, break after a colon or a double slash or before any other mark of punctuation. If you will post your project online or submit it electronically and you want to include live URLs for readers to click on, do not insert any line breaks.

Headings   *Chicago* does not provide guidelines for the use of headings in student papers. If you would like to insert headings in a long essay or research paper, check first with your instructor. See page 289 for typical placement and formatting of headings in a *Chicago*-style paper.

Preparing the endnotes   Begin the endnotes on a new page at the end of the paper. Center the title "Notes" about one inch from the top of the page, and number the pages consecutively with the rest of the paper. See page 290 for an example.

Indenting and numbering   Indent the first line of each note one-half inch from the left margin; do not indent additional lines in the note. Begin the note with the arabic numeral that corresponds to the number in the text. Put a period after the number.

Line spacing   Single-space each note and double-space between notes (unless your instructor prefers double-spacing throughout).

Preparing the bibliography   Typically, the notes in *Chicago*-style papers are followed by a bibliography, an alphabetically arranged list of all the works cited or consulted. Begin the bibliography on a new page, and center the title "Bibliography" about one inch from the top of the page. Number bibliography pages consecutively with the rest of the paper. See page 291 for a sample bibliography.

Alphabetizing the list   Alphabetize the bibliography by the last names of the authors (or editors); when a work has no author or editor, alphabetize it by the first word of the title other than *A*, *An*, or *The*.

If your list includes two or more works by the same author, arrange the entries alphabetically by title. Then use six hyphens instead of the author's name in all entries after the first. (See item 6 in 43c.)

Indenting and line spacing   Begin each entry at the left margin, and indent any additional lines one-half inch. Single-space each entry and double-space between entries (unless your instructor prefers double-spacing throughout).

44b   Sample pages from a *Chicago* research paper

Following are pages from a research paper by Ned Bishop, a student in a history class. Bishop used *Chicago*-style endnotes, bibliography, and manuscript format. The annotations point out *Chicago*-style formatting and effective writing.

(1)

The Massacre at Fort Pillow:
Holding Nathan Bedford Forrest Accountable

(2)

Ned Bishop

(3)

History 214
Professor Citro
March 22, 2012

(1) Paper title, centered. (2) Writer's name. (3) Course title, instructor's name, date.

Sample *Chicago* first text page

Bishop 2

Although Northern newspapers of the time no doubt exaggerated some of the Confederate atrocities at Fort Pillow, most modern sources agree that a massacre of Union troops took place there on April 12, 1864. It seems clear that Union soldiers, particularly black soldiers, were killed after they had stopped fighting or had surrendered or were being held prisoner. Less clear is the role played by Major General Nathan Bedford Forrest in leading his troops. Although we will never know whether Forrest directly ordered the massacre, evidence **①** suggests that he was responsible for it.

What happened at Fort Pillow? **②**

Fort Pillow, Tennessee, which sat on a bluff overlooking the Mississippi River, had been held by the Union for two years. It was garrisoned by 580 men, 292 of them from United States Colored Heavy and Light Artillery regiments, 285 from the white Thirteenth Tennessee Cavalry. Nathan Bedford Forrest commanded about 1,500 troops.[1]

The Confederates attacked Fort Pillow on April 12, 1864, and had virtually surrounded the fort by the time Forrest arrived on the battlefield. At 3:30 p.m., Forrest demanded the surrender of the Union forces: "The conduct of the officers and men garrisoning Fort Pillow has been such as to entitle them to being treated as prisoners of war. . . . Should my demand be refused, I cannot be responsible for the fate of your command."[2] Union Major **③** William Bradford, who had replaced Major Booth, killed earlier by sharpshooters, asked for an hour to consider the demand. Forrest, worried that vessels in the river were bringing in more Union troops, "shortened the time to twenty minutes."[3] Bradford refused to surrender, and Forrest quickly ordered the attack.

The Confederates charged to the fort, scaled the parapet, and fired on the forces within. Victory came quickly, with the Union

① Writer's thesis. **②** Headings (centered) guide readers.
③ Quotation cited with endnote.

Sample *Chicago* endnotes

Notes

(1) 1. John Cimprich and Robert C. Mainfort Jr., eds., "Fort Pillow Revisited: New Evidence about an Old Controversy," *Civil War History* 28, no. 4 (1982): 293–94.

(2) 2. Quoted in Brian Steel Wills, *A Battle from the Start: The Life of Nathan Bedford Forrest* (New York: HarperCollins, 1992), 182.

3. Quoted in Wills, 183.

4. Shelby Foote, *The Civil War, a Narrative: Red River to Appomattox* (New York: Vintage, 1986), 110.

5. Nathan Bedford Forrest, "Report of Maj. Gen. Nathan B. Forrest, C. S. Army, Commanding Cavalry, of the Capture of Fort Pillow," Shotgun's Home of the American Civil War, accessed March 6, 2012, http://www.civilwarhome.com /forrest.htm.

(3) 6. Jack Hurst, *Nathan Bedford Forrest: A Biography* (New York: Knopf, 1993), 174.

7. Foote, *Civil War*, 111.

(4) 8. Cimprich and Mainfort, "Fort Pillow," 295.

9. Cimprich and Mainfort, 305.

10. Cimprich and Mainfort, 299.

11. Foote, *Civil War*, 110.

12. Quoted in Wills, *Battle from the Start*, 187.

(5) 13. Albert Castel, "The Fort Pillow Massacre: A Fresh Examination of the Evidence," *Civil War History* 4, no. 1 (1958): 44–45.

14. Cimprich and Mainfort, "Fort Pillow," 300.

(1) First line of note indented one-half inch. **(2)** Note number not raised, followed by period. **(3)** Authors' names not inverted. **(4)** Last names and shortened title refer to earlier note by same authors. **(5)** Notes single-spaced; double-spacing between notes.

Sample *Chicago* bibliography

Bibliography

Castel, Albert. "The Fort Pillow Massacre: A Fresh Examination of the Evidence." *Civil War History* 4, no. 1 (1958): 37–50. **1**

Cimprich, John, and Robert C. Mainfort Jr., eds. "Fort Pillow Revisited: New Evidence about an Old Controversy." *Civil War History* 28, no. 4 (1982): 293–306.

Cornish, Dudley Taylor. *The Sable Arm: Black Troops in the Union Army, 1861–1865.* Lawrence: University Press of Kansas, 1987. **2**

Foote, Shelby. *The Civil War, a Narrative: Red River to Appomattox.* New York: Vintage, 1986.

Forrest, Nathan Bedford. "Report of Maj. Gen. Nathan B. Forrest, C. S. Army, Commanding Cavalry, of the Capture of Fort Pillow." Shotgun's Home of the American Civil War. Accessed March 6, 2012. http://www.civilwarhome.com/forrest.htm.

Hurst, Jack. *Nathan Bedford Forrest: A Biography.* New York: Knopf, 1993. **3**

McPherson, James M. *Battle Cry of Freedom: The Civil War Era.* New York: Oxford University Press, 1988.

Wills, Brian Steel. *A Battle from the Start: The Life of Nathan Bedford Forrest.* New York: HarperCollins, 1992.

1 Alphabetized by authors' last names. **2** First line of each entry at left margin; additional lines indented one-half inch. **3** Entries single-spaced; double-spacing between entries.

CSE Papers

45 CSE documentation style

In science classes, you may be asked to use one of three systems of documentation recommended by the Council of Science Editors (CSE) in *Scientific Style and Format: The CSE Manual for Authors, Editors, and Publishers*, 8th ed. (Chicago: Council of Science Editors, 2014).

45a CSE documentation systems

The three CSE documentation systems specify the ways that sources are cited in the text of the paper and documented in the reference list at the end of the paper.

In the *citation-sequence system*, each source is given a superscript number the first time it appears in the paper. Any subsequent references to that source are marked with the same number. At the end of the paper, a list of references provides full publication information for each numbered source. Entries in the reference list are numbered in the order in which they are mentioned in the paper.

In the *citation-name system*, the list of references is created first, with entries alphabetized by authors' last names. The entries are numbered according to their alphabetical order, and the numbers are used in the text to cite the sources from the list.

In the *name-year system*, the author of the source is named in the text or in parentheses, and the date is given in parentheses. The reference list at the end of the paper is arranged alphabetically by authors' last names.

Sections 45b and 45c describe formatting of in-text citations and the reference list, respectively, in all three systems.

45b CSE in-text citations

In-text citations in all three CSE systems refer readers to the reference list at the end of the paper. The reference list is organized differently in the three systems (see 45c).

● 1. Basic format

Citation-sequence or citation-name

Scientists are beginning to question the validity of linking genes to a number of human traits and disorders.[1]

Name-year

Scientists are beginning to question the validity of linking genes to a number of human traits and disorders (Allen 2009).

● 2. Author named in the text

Citation-sequence or citation-name

Smith,[2] studying 3 species of tree frogs, identified variations in coloring over a small geographic area.

Name-year

Smith (2010), studying 3 species of tree frogs, identified variations in coloring over a small geographic area.

● 3. Specific part of source

Citation-sequence or citation-name

Our data differed markedly from Markam's study[3(Figs. 2,7)] on the same species in North Dakota.

Researchers observed an immune response in "19 of 20 people who ate a potato vaccine aimed at the Norwalk virus," according to Langridge.[4(p. 68)]

Name-year

Our data differed markedly from Markam's study (2010, Figs. 2, 7) on the same species in North Dakota.

Researchers observed an immune response in "19 of 20 people who ate a potato vaccine aimed at the Norwalk virus," according to Langridge (2009, p. 68).

● **4. Work by two authors**   See item 2 in 45c for a work with multiple authors in the reference list.

Citation-sequence or citation-name

Follow item 1, 2, or 3 in 45b, depending on how you use the source in your paper. Use "and" between the two authors' names.

Name-year

Use "and" between the two authors' names in parentheses or in the text.

Self-organization plays a complex role in the evolution of biological systems (Johnson and Lam 2010).

Johnson and Lam (2010) explored the complex role of self-organization in evolution.

● **5. Work by three or more authors**   See item 2 in 45c for a work with multiple authors in the reference list.

Citation-sequence or citation-name

Follow item 1, 2, or 3 in 45b, depending on how you use the source in your paper.

Name-year

Give the first author's name followed by "et al." in parentheses or in the text.

Orchid seed banking is a promising method of conservation to preserve species in situ (Seaton et al. 2010).

Seaton et al. (2010) provided a range of in situ techniques for orchid seed banking as a method of conservation of species.

● **6. Multiple works by one author**

Citation-sequence or citation-name

Gawande's work[4,5,6] deals not just with the practice of modern medicine but more broadly with the way we rely on human expertise in every aspect of society.

Name-year: works in different years

Gawande's work (2003, 2007, 2009) deals not just with the practice of modern medicine but more broadly with the way we rely on human expertise in every aspect of society.

Name-year: works in the same year

The works are arranged in the reference list in chronological order (the earliest first). The letters "a," "b," and so on are added after the year, in both the reference list and the in-text citation. (See also item 5 in 45c.)

Scientists have investigated the role of follicle-stimulating hormone (FSH) in the growth of cancer cells beyond the ovaries and testes (Seppa 2010a).

● **7. Organization as author**

Citation-sequence or citation-name

Follow item 1, 2, or 3 in 45b, depending on how you use the source in your paper.

Name-year

The reference list entry gives the abbreviation for the organization's name, followed by the full name of the organization (Office of Biorepositories and Biospecimen Research); only the abbreviation is used in the in-text citation. (See item 3 in 45c.)

Developing standards for handling and processing biospecimens is essential to ensure the validity of cancer research and, ultimately, treatment (OBBR 2010).

45c CSE reference list

In the citation-sequence system, entries in the reference list are numbered in the order in which they appear in the text of the paper. In the citation-name system, entries in the reference list are put into alphabetical order and then numbered in that order. In the name-year system, entries are listed alphabetically in the reference list; they are not numbered. See 45b for examples of in-text citations using all three systems. See 46b for details about formatting the reference list.

General guidelines for listing authors

● **1. Single author**

Citation-sequence or citation-name

1. Bliss M. The making of modern medicine: turning points in the treatment of disease. Chicago (IL): University of Chicago Press; 2011.

Name-year

Bliss M. 2011. The making of modern medicine: turning points in the treatment of disease. Chicago (IL): University of Chicago Press.

● **2. Two or more authors**   For a source with two to ten authors, list all authors' names; for a source with more than ten authors, list the first ten authors followed by a comma and "et al."

Citation-sequence or citation-name

2. Seaton PT, Hong H, Perner H, Pritchard HW. Ex situ conservation of orchids in a warming world. Bot Rev. 2010;76(2):193–203.

Name-year

Seaton PT, Hong H, Perner H, Pritchard HW. 2010. Ex situ conservation of orchids in a warming world. Bot Rev. 76(2):193–203.

● **3. Organization as author**

Citation-sequence or citation-name

3. American Cancer Society. Cancer facts and figures for African Americans 2005-2006. Atlanta (GA): The Society; 2005.

Name-year

Give the abbreviation of the organization name in brackets at the beginning of the entry; alphabetize the entry by the first word of the full name. (For an in-text citation, see the name-year model in item 7 in 45b.)

[ACS] American Cancer Society. 2005. Cancer facts and figures for African Americans 2005-2006. Atlanta (GA): The Society.

● **4. Two or more works by the same author**

Citation-sequence or citation-name

In the citation-sequence system, list the works in the order in which they appear in the paper. In the citation-name system, order the works alphabetically by title. (The following examples are presented in the citation-name system.)

4. Gawande A. Better: a surgeon's notes on performance. New York (NY): Metropolitan; 2007.

5. Gawande A. The checklist manifesto: how to get things right. New York (NY): Metropolitan; 2009.

6. Gawande A. Complications: a surgeon's notes on an imperfect science. New York (NY): Picador; 2003.

Name-year

List the works chronologically (the earliest first).

Gawande A. 2003. Complications: a surgeon's notes on an imperfect science. New York (NY): Picador.

Gawande A. 2007. Better: a surgeon's notes on performance. New York (NY): Metropolitan.

Gawande A. 2009. The checklist manifesto: how to get things right. New York (NY): Metropolitan.

● **5. Two or more works by the same author in the same year**

Citation-sequence or citation-name

In the citation-sequence system, list the works in the order in which they appear in the paper. In the citation-name system, order the works alphabetically by title. (The following examples are presented in the citation-sequence system.)

5. Seppa N. Protein implicated in many cancers. Sci News. 2010 Oct 20 [accessed 2011 Jan 22]. http://www.sciencenews.org /view/generic/id/64426.

8. Seppa N. Anticancer protein might combat HIV. Sci News. 2010 Nov 20:9.

● **5. Two or more works by the same author in the same year (*cont.*)**

Name-year

List the works in chronological order (the earliest first), and add the letters "a," "b," and so on after the year. If the works have only a year but not exact dates, arrange the entries alphabetically by title.

Seppa N. 2010a Jul 31. Fish oil may fend off breast cancer: other
   supplements studied show no signs of protection. Sci News. 13.

Seppa N. 2010b Sep 25. Ovary removal boosts survival: procedure
   shown to benefit women with BRCA mutations. Sci News. 12.

Articles and other short works

Use the basic format for an article in print publications when citing articles or other short works in most other media. See also "Online sources" on pages 303–05.

● **6. Article in a print journal**

Citation-sequence or citation-name

6. Wasserman EA, Blumberg MS. Designing minds: how
   should we explain the origins of novel behaviors? Am Sci.
   2010;98(3):183–185.

Name-year

Wasserman EA, Blumberg MS. 2010. Designing minds: how
   should we explain the origins of novel behaviors? Am Sci.
   98(3):183–185.

● **7. Article in a print magazine**

Citation-sequence or citation-name

7. Quammen D. Great migrations. Natl Geogr. 2010 Nov:31–51.

Name-year

Quammen D. 2010 Nov. Great migrations. Natl Geogr. 31–51.

● **8. Article in a print newspaper**

Citation-sequence or citation-name

8. Wald M. Scientists call for new sources of critical elements. New
   York Times (New York Ed.). 2011 Feb 19;Sect. B:5 (col. 1).

Name-year

Wald M. 2011 Feb 19. Scientists call for new sources of critical
elements. New York Times (New York Ed.). Sect. B:5
(col. 1).

● **9. Selection or chapter in an edited book**

Citation-sequence or citation-name

9. Underwood AJ, Chapman MG. Intertidal ecosystems. In: Levin
SA, editor. Encyclopedia of biodiversity. Vol. 3. San Diego (CA):
Academic Press; 2000. p. 485–499.

Name-year

Underwood AJ, Chapman MG. 2000. Intertidal ecosystems. In:
Levin SA, editor. Encyclopedia of biodiversity. Vol. 3. San
Diego (CA): Academic Press; p. 485–499.

Books and other long works

Use the basic format for a print book when citing
books and other long works in most other media. See
also "Online sources" on pages 303–05.

● **10. Print book**

Citation-sequence or citation-name

10. Tobin M. Endangered: biodiversity on the brink. Golden
(CO): Fulcrum; 2010.

Name-year

Tobin M. 2010. Endangered: biodiversity on the brink. Golden
(CO): Fulcrum.

● **11. Book with an editor**

Citation-sequence or citation-name

11. Kurimoto N, Fielding D, Musani A, editors. Endobronchial
ultrasonography. New York (NY): Wiley-Blackwell; 2011.

Name-year

Kurimoto N, Fielding D, Musani A, editors. 2011. Endobronchial
ultrasonography. New York (NY): Wiley-Blackwell.

● **12. Edition other than the first**

Citation-sequence or citation-name

12. Mai J, Paxinos G, Assheuer J. Atlas of the human brain. 2nd
    ed. Burlington (MA): Elsevier; 2004.

Name-year

Mai J, Paxinos G, Assheuer J. 2004. Atlas of the human brain.
    2nd ed. Burlington (MA): Elsevier.

● **13. Report from an organization or a government agency**

Citation-sequence or citation-name

13. National Institute on Drug Abuse (US). Inhalant abuse.
    Bethesda (MD): National Institutes of Health (US); 2010 Jul.
    NIH Pub. No.: 10–3818. Available from: National Clearinghouse
    on Alcohol and Drug Information, Rockville, MD 20852.

13. National Institute on Drug Abuse (US). Inhalant abuse.
    Bethesda (MD): National Institutes of Health (US); [accessed
    2011 Jan 23]. NIH Pub. No.: 10–3818. http://www
    .drugabuse.gov/ResearchReports/Inhalants/inhalants.html.

Name-year

[NIDA] National Institute on Drug Abuse (US). 2010 Jul. Inhalant
    abuse. Bethesda (MD): National Institutes of Health (US). NIH
    Pub. No.: 10–3818. Available from: National Clearinghouse on
    Alcohol and Drug Information, Rockville, MD 20852.

[NIDA] National Institute on Drug Abuse (US). 2010 Jul.
    Inhalant abuse. Bethesda (MD): National Institutes of
    Health (US); [accessed 2010 Jan 23]. NIH Pub. No.:
    10–3818. http://www.drugabuse.gov/ResearchReports
    /Inhalants/inhalants.html.

● **14. Conference proceedings**   Cite a paper or presentation from the conference proceedings as you
would a selection in an edited book (see item 9).

Citation-sequence or citation-name

14. Proceedings of the 2004 National Beaches Conference; 2004
    Oct 13–15; San Diego, CA. Washington (DC): Environmental
    Protection Agency (US); 2005 Mar. Document
    No.: EPA-823-R-05-001.

Name-year

Proceedings of the 2004 National Beaches Conference. 2005
    Mar. 2004 Oct 13–15; San Diego, CA. Washington (DC):
    Environmental Protection Agency (US). Document No.:
    EPA-823-R-05-001.

Online sources

● 15. Entire website

Citation-sequence or citation-name

15. American Society of Gene and Cell Therapy. Milwaukee (WI):
    The Society; c2000–2011 [accessed 2011 Jan 16]. http://
    www.asgt.org/.

Name-year

[ASGCT] American Society of Gene and Cell Therapy. c2000–
    2011. Milwaukee (WI): The Society; [accessed 2011 Jan 16].
    Available from: http://www.asgt.org/.

● 16. Short work from a website   Begin with the author
of the short work, if there is one, and include the date of
the short work in brackets as an "updated" or "modified"
date. Include the title of the website and publishing information for the website.

Citation-sequence or citation-name

16. Butler R. The year in review for rain forests. Mongabay
    .com. Menlo Park (CA): Mongabay; c2011 [updated 2011
    Dec 28; accessed 2012 Jan 11]. http://news.mongabay
    .com/2011/1228-year_in_rainforests_2011.html.

Name-year

Butler R. c2011. The year in review for rain forests. Mongabay
    .com. Menlo Park (CA): Mongabay; [updated 2011 Dec 28;
    accessed 2012 Jan 11]. http://news.mongabay
    .com/2011/1228-year_in_rainforests_2011.html.

● **17. Online book**

Citation-sequence or citation-name

17. Wilson DE, Reeder DM, editors. Mammal species of the
    world. Washington (DC): Smithsonian Institution; c2011
    [accessed 2012 Oct 14]. http://vertebrates.si.edu/msw
    /mswcfapp/msw/index.cfm.

Name-year

Wilson DE, Reeder DM, editors. c2011. Mammal species of
    the world. Washington (DC): Smithsonian Institution;
    [accessed 2012 Oct 14]. http://vertebrates.si.edu/msw
    /mswcfapp/msw/index/cfm.

● **18. Article in an online journal or magazine** Give
whatever publication information is available as for a
print source. End with the URL and DOI (if any).

Citation-sequence or citation-name

18. Leslie M. The power of one. Science. 2011 [accessed 2011
    Feb 3];331(6013):24–26. http://www.sciencemag.org/content
    /331/6013/24.1.summary. doi:10.1126/science.331.6013.24-a.

18. Matson J. Twisted light could enable black hole detection.
    Sci Am. 2011 Feb 14 [accessed 2011 Feb 28]. http://www
    .scientificamerican.com/article.cfm?id=twisting-light-oam.

Name-year

Leslie M. 2011. The power of one. Science. [accessed 2011
    Feb 3];331(6013):24–26. http://www.sciencemag.org
    /content/331/6013/24.1.summary. doi:10.1126
    /science.331.6013.24-a.

Matson J. 2011 Feb 14. Twisted light could enable black hole
    detection. Sci Am. [accessed 2011 Feb 28]. http://www
    .scientificamerican.com/article.cfm?id=twisting-light-oam.

● **19 Article from a database**

Citation-sequence or citation-name

19. Logan CA. A review of ocean acidification and America's
    response. BioScience. 2010 [accessed 2011 Jun 17];
    60(10):819–828. General OneFile. http://find.galegroup
    .com.ezproxy.bpl.org/. Document No.: A241952492.

Name-year

Logan CA. 2010. A review of ocean acidification and America's
    response. BioScience. [accessed 2011 Jun 17];60(10):
    819–828. General OneFile. http://find.galegroup.com
    .ezproxy.bpl.org/. Document No.: A241952492.

● **20. Blog post**

Citation-sequence or citation-name

20. Salopek P. The river door [blog post]. Out of Eden walk:
    dispatches from the field from Paul Salopek. 2014 Apr 17
    [accessed 2014 May 19]. http://outofedenwalk
    .nationalgeographic.com/.

Name-year

Salopek P. 2014 Apr 17. The river door [blog post]. Out of
    Eden walk: dispatches from the field from Paul Salopek.
    [accessed 2014 May 19]. http://outofedenwalk
    .nationalgeographic.com/.

● **21. Social media**

Citation-sequence or citation-name

21. National Science Foundation. Facebook [organization page].
    2013 Jan 21, 10:31 a.m. [accessed 2013 Jan 22].
    https://www.facebook.com/US.NSF.

Name-year

National Science Foundation. 2013 Jan 21, 10:31 a.m. Facebook
    [organization page]. [accessed 2013 Jan 22]. https://
    www.facebook.com/US.NSF.

● **22. Email or other personal communication**   CSE
recommends not including personal communications
such as e-mail and personal letters in the reference list.
A parenthetical note in the text usually suffices: (2010
email to me; unreferenced).

Audio, visual, and multimedia sources

● 23. CD, DVD, or BD

Citation-sequence or citation-name

23. NOVA: secrets beneath the ice [DVD]. Seifferlein B, editor;
    Hochman G, producer. Boston (MA): WGBH Educational
    Foundation; 2010. 1 DVD: 52 min.

Name-year

NOVA: secrets beneath the ice [DVD]. 2010. Seifferlein B, editor;
    Hochman G, producer. Boston (MA): WGBH Educational
    Foundation. 1 DVD: 52 min.

● 24. Online video

Citation-sequence or citation-name

24. Life: creatures of the deep: nemertean worms and sea stars
    [video]. Gunton M, executive producer; Holmes M, series
    producer. 2010 Mar 21, 2:55 min. [accessed 2011 Feb 4].
    http://dsc.discovery.com/videos/life-the-series-videos
    /?bcid=73073289001.

Name-year

Life: creatures of the deep: nemertean worms and sea stars [video].
    2010 Mar 21, 2:55 min. Gunton M, executive producer; Holmes
    M, series producer. [accessed 2011 Feb 4]. http://dsc.discovery
    .com/videos/life-the-series-videos/?bcid=73073289001.

● 25. Podcast

Citation-sequence or citation-name

25. Mirsky S, host; Conrad N, interviewee. The spirit of
    innovation: from high school to the moon [podcast]. Sci
    Am. 2011 Feb 17, 19:26 min. [accessed 2011 Feb 27].
    http://www.scientificamerican.com/podcast/episode
    .cfm?id=from-high-school-innovation-to-the-11-02-17.

Name-year

Mirsky, S, host; Conrad N, interviewee. 2011 Feb 17, 19:26 min.
    The spirit of innovation: from high school to the moon
    [podcast]. Sci Am. [accessed 2011 Feb 27]. http://www
    .scientificamerican.com/podcast/episode.cfm?id=from
    -high-school-innovation-to-the-11-02-17.

46 CSE format

The guidelines in this section are adapted from advice given in *Scientific Style and Format: The CSE Manual for Authors, Editors, and Publishers*, 8th ed. (Chicago: Council of Science Editors, 2014). When in doubt about the formatting required in your course, check with your instructor.

46a Formatting the paper

Font If your instructor does not require a specific font, choose one that is standard and easy to read (such as Times New Roman).

Title page Center all information on the title page: the title of your paper, your name, the course name, and the date.

Pagination The title page is counted as page 1, although a number does not appear. Number the first page of the text of the paper as page 2. Type a shortened form of the title followed by the page number in the top right corner of each page.

Margins, spacing, and indentation Leave margins of at least one inch on all sides of the page. Double-space throughout the paper. Indent the first line of each paragraph one-half inch. When a quotation is set off from the text, indent the entire quotation one-half inch from the left margin. (See page 120 for an example.)

Abstract An abstract is a single paragraph at the beginning of the paper that summarizes the paper and might include your research methods, findings, and conclusions. Do not include citations in the abstract.

Headings CSE encourages the use of headings to help readers follow the organization of a paper. Common headings for papers reporting research are "Introduction," "Methods," "Results," and "Discussion."

Visuals A visual, such as a table, figure, or chart, should be placed as closely as possible to the text that discusses it. In general, try to place visuals at the top of a page.

Appendixes Appendixes may be used for relevant information that is too long to include in the body of the paper. Label each appendix and give it a title (for example, "Appendix 1: Methodologies of Previous Researchers").

Acknowledgments An acknowledgments section is common in scientific writing because research is often conducted with help from others. Place the acknowledgments at the end of the paper, before the reference list.

46b Formatting the reference list

Basic format Begin on a new page. Center the title "References" and then list the works you have cited in the paper. Double-space throughout.

Organization of the list In the citation-sequence system, number the entries in the order in which they appear in the text.

In the citation-name system, first alphabetize all the entries by authors' last names (or by organization name or by title for works with no author, ignoring any initial *A, An,* or *The*); for two or more works by the same author, arrange the entries alphabetically by title.

In both systems, number the entries in the order in which they appear in the list. Left-align the first line of each entry, and indent subsequent lines one-quarter inch. In both systems, use the number from the reference list whenever you refer to the source in the text of the paper.

In the name-year system, alphabetize the entries by authors' last names (or by organization name or by title for works with no author, ignoring any initial *A, An,* or *The*). Place the year after the last author's name, followed by a period. For two or more works by the same author, arrange the entries by year, the earliest first. For two or more works by the same author in the same year, see item 5 in 45a. Left-align the first line of each entry, and indent any additional lines one-quarter inch.

Authors' names Give the last name first; use initials for first and middle names, with no periods after the initials and no space between them. Do not use a comma between the last name and the initials. For a work with up to ten authors, use all authors' names; for a work with eleven or more authors, list the first ten names followed by a comma and "et al." (for "and others").

Titles of books and articles   Capitalize only the first word and all proper nouns in the title and subtitle of a book or an article. Do not underline or italicize titles of books; do not place titles of articles in quotation marks.

Titles of journals   Abbreviate titles of journals that consist of more than one word. Omit the words *the* and *of* and apostrophes. Capitalize all the words or abbreviated words in the title; do not underline or italicize the title: Science, Sci Am, N Engl J Med, Womens Health.

Page ranges   Do not abbreviate page ranges for articles in journals or periodicals or for chapters in edited works. When an article does not appear on consecutive pages, list all pages or page ranges, separated by commas: 145–149, 162–174. For chapters in edited volumes, use the abbreviation "p." before the numbers: p. 63–90.

Breaking a URL or DOI   When a URL or a DOI (digital object identifier) must be divided, break it before or after a double slash, a slash, or any other mark of punctuation. Do not insert a hyphen. If you will post your project online or submit it electronically and you want to include live URLs for readers to click on, do not insert any line breaks.

Glossaries

Glossary of usage

This glossary includes words commonly confused, words commonly misused, and words that are nonstandard. It also lists colloquialisms that may be appropriate in informal speech but are inappropriate in formal writing.

a, an   Use *an* before a vowel sound, *a* before a consonant sound: *an apple, a peach.* Problems sometimes arise with words beginning with *h* or *u.* If the *h* is silent, the word begins with a vowel sound, so use *an: an hour, an heir, an honest senator.* If the *h* is pronounced, the word begins with a consonant sound, so use *a: a hospital, a historian, a hotel.* Words such as *university* and *union* begin with a consonant sound, so use *a: a union.* Words such as *uncle* and *umbrella* begin with a vowel sound, so use *an: an underground well.* When an abbreviation or acronym begins with a vowel sound, use *an: an EKG, an MRI.*

accept, except   *Accept* is a verb meaning "to receive." *Except* is usually a preposition meaning "excluding." *I will accept all the packages except that one. Except* is also a verb meaning "to exclude." *Please except that item from the list.*

adapt, adopt   *Adapt* means "to adjust or become accustomed"; it is usually followed by *to. Adopt* means "to take as one's own." *Our family adopted a Vietnamese child, who quickly adapted to his new life.*

adverse, averse   *Adverse* means "unfavorable." *Averse* means "opposed" or "reluctant"; it is usually followed by *to. I am averse to your proposal because it could have an adverse impact on the economy.*

advice, advise   *Advice* is a noun, *advise* a verb. *We advise you to follow John's advice.*

affect, effect   *Affect* is usually a verb meaning "to influence." *Effect* is usually a noun meaning "result." *The drug did not affect the disease, and it had adverse side effects. Effect* can also be a verb meaning "to bring about." *Only the president can effect such a change.*

all ready, already   *All ready* means "completely prepared." *Already* means "previously." *Susan was all ready for the concert, but her friends had already left.*

all right   *All right,* written as two words, is correct. *Alright* is nonstandard.

all together, altogether   *All together* means "everyone gathered." *Altogether* means "entirely." *We were not altogether sure that we could bring the family all together for the reunion.*

allusion, illusion   An *allusion* is an indirect reference; an *illusion* is a misconception or false impression. *Did you* *catch my allusion to Shakespeare? Mirrors give the room an illusion of depth.*

a lot   *A lot* is two words. Do not write *alot*.

among, between   Ordinarily, use *among* with three or more entities, *between* with two. *The prize was divided among several contestants. You have a choice between carrots and beans.*

amoral, immoral   *Amoral* means "neither moral nor immoral"; it also means "not caring about moral judgments." *Immoral* means "morally wrong." *Many business courses are taught from an amoral perspective. Theft is immoral.*

amount, number   Use *amount* with quantities that cannot be counted; use *number* with those that can. *This recipe calls for a large amount of sugar. We have a large number of toads in our garden.*

an   See *a, an*.

and/or   Avoid *and/or* except in technical or legal documents.

anxious   *Anxious* means "worried" or "apprehensive." In formal writing, avoid using *anxious* to mean "eager." *We are eager* (not *anxious*) *to see your new house.*

anybody, anyone   See sections 10d and 12a.

anyone, any one   *Anyone,* an indefinite pronoun, means "any person at all." *Any one* refers to a particular person or thing in a group. *Anyone in the class may choose any one of the books to read.*

anyways, anywheres   *Anyways* and *anywheres* are nonstandard for *anyway* and *anywhere*.

as   *As* is sometimes used to mean "because." But do not use it if there is any chance of ambiguity. *We canceled the picnic because* (not *as*) *it began raining. As here could mean "because" or "when."*

as, like   See *like, as*.

averse   See *adverse, averse*.

awhile, a while   *Awhile* is an adverb; it can modify a verb, but it cannot be the object of a preposition such as *for*. The two-word form *a while* is a noun preceded by an article and therefore can be the object of a preposition. *Stay awhile. Stay for a while.*

back up, backup   *Back up* is a verb phrase. *Back up the car carefully. Be sure to back up your hard drive. Backup* is a noun often meaning "duplicate of electronically stored data." *Keep your backup in a safe place. Backup* can also be used as an adjective. *I regularly create backup disks.*

bad, badly *Bad* is an adjective, *badly* an adverb. *They felt bad about being early and ruining the surprise. Her arm hurt badly after she slid into second.* See section 13.

being as, being that *Being as* and *being that* are nonstandard expressions. Write *because* instead.

beside, besides *Beside* is a preposition meaning "at the side of" or "next to." *Annie sleeps with a flashlight beside her bed. Besides* is a preposition meaning "except" or "in addition to." *No one besides Terrie can have that ice cream. Besides* is also an adverb meaning "in addition." *I'm not hungry; besides, I don't like ice cream.*

between See *among, between.*

bring, take Use *bring* when an object is being transported toward you, *take* when it is being moved away. *Please bring me a glass of water. Please take these magazines to Mr. Scott.*

can, may *Can* is traditionally reserved for ability, *may* for permission. *Can you speak French? May I help you?*

capital, capitol *Capital* refers to a city, *capitol* to a building where lawmakers meet. *The residents of the state capital protested the development plans. The capitol has undergone extensive renovations. Capital* also refers to wealth or resources.

censor, censure *Censor* means "to remove or suppress material considered objectionable." *Censure* means "to criticize severely." *The school's policy of censoring books has been censured by the media.*

cite, site *Cite* means "to quote as an authority or example." *Site* is usually a noun meaning "a particular place." *He cited the zoning law in his argument against the proposed site of the gas station.* Locations on the Internet are usually referred to as *sites*.

complement, compliment *Complement* is a verb meaning "to go with or complete" or a noun meaning "something that completes." As a verb, *compliment* means "to flatter"; as a noun, it means "flattering remark." *Her skill at rushing the net complements his skill at volleying. Sheiying's music arrangements receive many compliments.*

conscience, conscious *Conscience* is a noun meaning "moral principles"; *conscious* is an adjective meaning "aware or alert." *Let your conscience be your guide. Were you conscious of his love for you?*

continual, continuous *Continual* means "repeated regularly and frequently." *She grew weary of the continual telephone calls. Continuous* means "extended or prolonged without interruption." *The broken siren made a continuous wail.*

could care less Write *couldn't care less* when referring to someone who does not care about something. (*Could care* *less* is nonstandard and means that the person described does care.)

could of *Could of* is nonstandard for *could have*.

council, counsel A *council* is a deliberative body, and a *councilor* is a member of such a body. *Counsel* usually means "advice" and can also mean "lawyer"; a *counselor* is one who gives advice or guidance. *The councilors met to draft the council's position paper. The pastor offered wise counsel to the troubled teenager.*

criteria *Criteria* is the plural of *criterion*, which means "a standard, rule, or test on which a judgment or decision can be based." *The only criterion for the scholarship is ability.*

data *Data* is a plural noun meaning "facts or results." *The new data suggest that our theory is correct.* Except in scientific writing, *data* is increasingly being accepted as a singular noun.

different from, different than Ordinarily, write *different from*. *Your sense of style is different from Jim's.* However, *different than* is acceptable to avoid an awkward construction. *Please let me know if your plans are different than* (to avoid *from what*) *they were six weeks ago.*

disinterested, uninterested *Disinterested* means "impartial, objective"; *uninterested* means "not interested." *We sought the advice of a disinterested counselor to help us solve our problem. Mark was uninterested in anyone's opinion but his own.*

each See sections 10d and 12a.

effect See *affect, effect.*

either See sections 10d and 12a.

elicit, illicit *Elicit* is a verb meaning "to bring out" or "to evoke." *Illicit* is an adjective meaning "unlawful." *The reporter was unable to elicit any information from the police about illicit drug traffic.*

emigrate from, immigrate to *Emigrate* means "to leave one place to settle in another." *My great-grandfather emigrated from Russia to escape the religious pogroms. Immigrate* means "to enter another place and reside there." *Thousands of Bosnians immigrated to the United States in the 1990s.*

etc. Avoid ending a list with *etc.* It is more emphatic to end with an example, and usually readers will understand that the list is not exhaustive. When you don't wish to end with an example, *and so on* is more graceful than *etc.*

everybody, everyone See sections 10d and 12a.

everyone, every one *Everyone* is an indefinite pronoun. *Everyone wanted to go. Every one*, the pronoun *one* preceded by the adjective *every*, means "each individual or thing in a particular group." *Every one* is usually followed by *of*. *Every one of the missing books was found.*

except See *accept, except*.

farther, further *Farther* describes distances. *Further* suggests quantity or degree. *Detroit is farther from Miami than I thought. You extended the curfew further than necessary.*

fewer, less *Fewer* refers to items that can be counted; *less* refers to items that cannot be counted. *Fewer people are living in the city. Please put less sugar in my tea.*

firstly *Firstly* is nonstandard, and it leads to the ungainly series *firstly, secondly, thirdly, fourthly,* and so on. Write *first, second, third* instead.

further See *farther, further*.

good, well See sections 13a and 13b.

hanged, hung *Hanged* is the past-tense and past-participle form of the verb *hang*, meaning "to execute." *The prisoner was hanged at dawn. Hung* is the past-tense and past-participle form of the verb *hang*, meaning "to fasten or suspend." *The stockings were hung by the chimney with care.*

hardly Avoid expressions such as *can't hardly* and *not hardly*, which are considered double negatives. *I can* (not *can't*) *hardly describe my elation at getting the job.*

hopefully *Hopefully* means "in a hopeful manner." *We looked hopefully to the future.* Some usage experts object to the use of *hopefully* as a sentence adverb, apparently on grounds of clarity. To be safe, avoid using *hopefully* in sentences such as the following: *Hopefully, your son will recover soon.* Instead, indicate who is doing the hoping: *I hope that your son will recover soon.*

however Some writers object to *however* at the beginning of a sentence, but experts advise placing the word according to the meaning and emphasis intended. Any of the following sentences is correct, depending on the intended contrast: *Pam decided, however, to attend the lecture. However, Pam decided to attend the lecture.* (She had been considering other activities.) *Pam, however, decided to attend the lecture.* (Unlike someone else, Pam opted for the lecture.)

hung See *hanged, hung*.

illusion See *allusion, illusion*.

immigrate See *emigrate from, immigrate to*.

immoral See *amoral, immoral*.

imply, infer *Imply* means "to suggest or state indirectly"; *infer* means "to draw a conclusion." *John implied that he* *knew all about computers, but the interviewer inferred that John was inexperienced.*

in, into   *In* indicates location or condition; *into* indicates movement or a change in condition. *They found the lost letters in a box after moving into the house.*

irregardless   *Irregardless* is nonstandard. Use *regardless.*

is when, is where   See section 6c.

its, it's   *Its* is a possessive pronoun; *it's* is a contraction for *it is. It's always fun to watch a dog chase its tail.*

kind of, sort of   Avoid using *kind of* or *sort of* to mean "somewhat." *The movie was a little* (not *kind of*) *boring.* Do not put *a* after either phrase. *That kind of* (not *kind of a*) *salesclerk annoys me.*

lay, lie   See page 24.

lead, led   *Lead* is a metallic element; it is a noun. *Led* is the past tense of the verb *lead. He led me to the treasure.*

less   See *fewer, less.*

liable   *Liable* means "obligated" or "responsible." Do not use it to mean "likely." *You're likely* (not *liable*) *to trip if you don't tie your shoelaces.*

lie, lay   See page 24.

like, as   *Like* is a preposition, not a subordinating conjunction. It should be followed only by a noun or a noun phrase. *As* is a subordinating conjunction that introduces a subordinate clause. In casual speech, you may say *She looks like she has not slept.* But in formal writing, use *as. She looks as if she has not slept.*

loose, lose   *Loose* is an adjective meaning "not securely fastened." *Lose* is a verb meaning "to misplace" or "to not win." *Did you lose all your loose change?*

may   See *can, may.*

maybe, may be   *Maybe* is an adverb meaning "possibly"; *may be* is a verb phrase. *Maybe the sun will shine tomorrow. Tomorrow may be a brighter day.*

may of, might of   *May of* and *might of* are nonstandard for *may have* and *might have.*

media, medium   *Media* is the plural of *medium. Of all the media that cover the Olympics, television is the medium that best captures the spectacle of the events.*

must of   *Must of* is nonstandard for *must have.*

myself   *Myself* is a reflexive or intensive pronoun. Reflexive: *I cut myself.* Intensive: *I will drive you myself.* Do not use *myself* in place of *I* or *me: He gave the plants to Melinda and me* (not *myself*).

neither   See sections 10d and 12a.

none   See section 10d.

nowheres   *Nowheres* is nonstandard for *nowhere.*

number   See *amount, number.*

off of   *Off* is sufficient. Omit *of.*

passed, past   *Passed* is the past tense of the verb *pass. Emily passed me a slice of cake. Past* usually means "belonging to a former time" or "beyond a time or place." *Our past president spoke until past 10:00. The hotel is just past the station.*

plus   *Plus* should not be used to join independent clauses. *This raincoat is dirty; moreover* (not *plus*), *it has a hole in it.*

precede, proceed   *Precede* means "to come before." *Proceed* means "to go forward." *As we proceeded up the mountain, we saw evidence that some hikers had preceded us.*

principal, principle   *Principal* is a noun meaning "the head of a school or an organization" or "a sum of money." It is also an adjective meaning "most important." *Principle* is a noun meaning "a basic truth or law." *The principal expelled her for three principal reasons. We believe in the principle of equal justice for all.*

proceed, precede   See *precede, proceed.*

quote, quotation   *Quote* is a verb; *quotation* is a noun. Avoid using *quote* as a shortened form of *quotation. Her quotations* (not *quotes*) *from Shakespeare intrigued us.*

real, really   *Real* is an adjective; *really* is an adverb. *Real* is sometimes used informally as an adverb, but avoid this use in formal writing. *She was really* (not *real*) *angry.* See also section 13.

reason . . . is because   See section 6c.

reason why   The expression *reason why* is redundant. *The reason* (not *The reason why*) *Jones lost the election is clear.*

respectfully, respectively   *Respectfully* means "showing or marked by respect." *He respectfully submitted his opinion. Respectively* means "each in the order given." *John, Tom, and Larry were a butcher, a baker, and a lawyer, respectively.*

sensual, sensuous   *Sensual* means "gratifying the physical senses," especially those associated with sexual pleasure. *Sensuous* means "pleasing to the senses," especially involving art, music, and nature. *The sensuous music and balmy air led the dancers to more sensual movements.*

set, sit   *Set* means "to put" or "to place"; *sit* means "to be seated." *She set the dough in a warm corner of the kitchen. The cat sits in the warmest part of the room.*

should of   *Should of* is nonstandard for *should have*.

since   Do not use *since* to mean "because" if there is any chance of ambiguity. *Because* (not *Since*) *we won the game, we have been celebrating. Since* here could mean "because" or "from the time that."

sit   See *set, sit*.

site, cite   See *cite, site*.

somebody, someone, something   See sections 10d and 12a.

suppose to   Write *supposed to*.

sure and   *Sure and* is nonstandard for *sure to*. *Be sure to* (not *sure and*) *bring a gift for the host*.

take   See *bring, take*.

than, then   *Than* is a conjunction used in comparisons; *then* is an adverb denoting time. *That pizza is more than I can eat. Tom laughed, and then we recognized him.*

that   See *who, which, that*.

that, which   Many writers reserve *that* for restrictive clauses, *which* for nonrestrictive clauses. (See p. 57.)

then   See *than, then*.

there, their, they're   *There* is an adverb specifying place; it is also an expletive (placeholder). Adverb: *Sylvia is sitting there patiently.* Expletive: *There are two plums left.* (See also p. 323.) *Their* is a possessive pronoun. *Fred and Jane finally washed their car. They're* is a contraction of *they are. They're late today.*

to, too, two   *To* is a preposition; *too* is an adverb; *two* is a number. *Too many of your shots slice to the left, but the last two were right on the mark.*

toward, towards   *Toward* and *towards* are generally interchangeable, although *toward* is preferred in American English.

try and   *Try and* is nonstandard for *try to. I will try to* (not *try and*) *be better about writing to you.*

uninterested   See *disinterested, uninterested*.

unique   See page 39.

use to   Write *used to. We used to live in an apartment.*

utilize   *Utilize* is often a pretentious substitute for *use*; in most cases, *use* is sufficient. *I used* (not *utilized*) *the printer.*

wait for, wait on   *Wait for* means "to be in readiness for" or "to await." *Wait on* means "to serve." *We're waiting for* (not *waiting on*) *Ruth before we can leave.*

ways   *Ways* is colloquial when used in place of *way* to mean "distance." *The city is a long way* (not *ways*) *from here.*

weather, whether The noun *weather* refers to the state of the atmosphere. *Whether* is a conjunction indicating a choice between alternatives. *We wondered whether the weather would clear up in time for our picnic.*

well, good See sections 13a and 13b.

which See *that, which* and *who, which, that.*

while Avoid using *while* to mean "although" or "whereas" if there is any chance of ambiguity. *Although* (not *While*) *Gloria lost money in the slot machine, Tom won it at roulette.* Here *While* could mean either "although" or "at the same time that."

who, which, that Use *who*, not *which*, to refer to persons. Generally, use *that* to refer to things or, occasionally, to a group or class of people. *The player who* (not *that* or *which*) *made the basket at the buzzer was named MVP. The team that scores the most points in this game will win the tournament.*

who, whom See section 12d.

who's, whose *Who's* is a contraction of *who is; whose* is a possessive pronoun. *Who's ready for more popcorn? Whose coat is this?*

would of *Would of* is nonstandard for *would have.*

you See page 32.

your, you're *Your* is a possessive pronoun; *you're* is a contraction of *you are. Is that your bike? You're in the finals.*

Glossary of grammatical terms

This glossary gives definitions for parts of speech, such as nouns; parts of sentences, such as subjects; and types of sentences, clauses, and phrases.

If you are looking up the name of an error (sentence fragment, for example), consult the index or the table of contents instead.

absolute phrase A word group that modifies a whole clause or sentence, usually consisting of a noun followed by a participle or participial phrase: *Her words echoing in the large arena,* the senator mesmerized the crowd.

active vs. passive voice When a verb is in the active voice, the subject of the sentence does the action: *Hernando caught* the ball. In the passive voice, the subject receives the action: *The ball was caught* by Hernando. Often the actor does not appear in a passive-voice sentence: *The ball was caught.* See also section 2.

adjective   A word used to modify (describe) a noun or pronoun: the *frisky* horse, *rare old* stamps, *sixteen* candles, the *blue* one. Adjectives usually answer one of these questions: Which one? What kind of? How many or how much? See also section 13a.

adjective clause   A subordinate clause that modifies a noun or pronoun. An adjective clause begins with a relative pronoun (*who, whom, whose, which, that*) or with a relative adverb (*when, where*) and usually appears right after the word it modifies: The book *that goes unread* is a writer's worst nightmare. See also *subordinate clause.*

adverb   A word used to modify a verb, an adjective, or another adverb: rides *smoothly, unusually* attractive, *very* slowly. An adverb usually answers one of these questions: When? Where? How? Why? Under what conditions? How often? To what degree? See also section 13b.

adverb clause   A subordinate clause that modifies a verb (or occasionally an adjective or adverb). An adverb clause begins with a subordinating conjunction such as *although, because, if, unless,* or *when* and usually appears at the beginning or the end of a sentence: *When the sun went down,* the hikers prepared their camp. See also *subordinate clause; subordinating conjunction.*

agreement   See sections 10 and 12a.

antecedent   A noun or pronoun to which a pronoun refers: When the *battery* wears down, we recharge *it.* The noun *battery* is the antecedent of the pronoun *it.*

appositive   A noun or noun phrase that renames a nearby noun or pronoun: Bloggers, *conversationalists at heart,* are the online equivalent of talk show hosts.

article   The word *a, an,* or *the,* used to mark a noun. See also section 16b.

case   See sections 12c and 12d.

clause   A word group containing a subject, a verb, and any objects, complements, or modifiers. See *independent clause; subordinate clause.*

collective noun   See sections 10e and 12a.

common noun   See section 22a.

complement   See *object complement; subject complement.*

complex sentence   A sentence consisting of one independent clause and one or more subordinate clauses. In the following example, the subordinate clause is italicized: We walked along the river *until we came to the bridge.*

compound-complex sentence   A sentence consisting of at least two independent clauses and at least one subordinate clause: Jan dictated a story, and the children wrote whatever he said. In the preceding sentence, the subordinate clause is *whatever he said*. The two independent clauses are *Jan dictated a story* and *the children wrote whatever he said*.

compound sentence   A sentence consisting of two or more independent clauses, with no subordinate clauses. The clauses are usually joined with a comma and a coordinating conjunction (*and, but, or, nor, for, so, yet*) or with a semicolon: The car broke down, *but* a rescue van arrived within minutes. A shark was spotted near shore; people left the water immediately.

conjunction   A joining word. See *conjunctive adverb; coordinating conjunction; correlative conjunction; subordinating conjunction*.

conjunctive adverb   An adverb used with a semicolon to connect independent clauses: The bus was stuck in traffic; *therefore*, the team was late for the game. The most commonly used conjunctive adverbs are *consequently, furthermore, however, moreover, nevertheless, then, therefore,* and *thus*. See page 62 for a longer list.

coordinating conjunction   One of the following words, used to join elements of equal grammatical rank: *and, but, or, nor, for, so, yet*.

correlative conjunction   A pair of conjunctions connecting grammatically equal elements: *either . . . or, neither . . . nor, whether . . . or, not only . . . but also, both . . . and*. See also section 3b.

count noun   See page 47.

demonstrative pronoun   A pronoun used to identify or point to a noun: *this, that, these, those*. *This* is my favorite chair.

direct object   A word or word group that receives the action of the verb: The hungry cat clawed *the bag of dry food*. The complete direct object is *the bag of dry food*. The simple direct object is always a noun or a pronoun, in this case *bag*.

expletive   The word *there* or *it* when used at the beginning of a sentence to delay the subject: *There* are eight planes waiting to take off. *It* is healthy to eat breakfast every day. The delayed subjects are the noun *planes* and the infinitive phrase *to eat breakfast every day*.

gerund   A verb form ending in *-ing* used as a noun: *Reading* aloud helps children appreciate language. The gerund *reading* is used as the subject of the verb *helps*.

gerund phrase   A gerund and its objects, complements, or modifiers. A gerund phrase always functions as a noun, usually as a subject, a subject complement, a direct object, or the object of a preposition. In the following example, the phrase functions as a direct object: We tried *planting tulips.*

helping verb   One of the following words, when used with a main verb: *be, am, is, are, was, were, being, been; has, have, had; do, does, did; can, will, shall, should, could, would, may, might, must.* Helping verbs always precede main verbs: *will work, is working, had worked.* See also *modal verb.*

indefinite pronoun   A pronoun that refers to a non-specific person or thing: *Something* is burning. The most common indefinite pronouns are *all, another, any, anybody, anyone, anything, both, each, either, everybody, everyone, everything, few, many, neither, nobody, none, no one, nothing, one, some, somebody, someone,* and *something.* See also sections 10d and 12a.

independent clause   A word group containing a subject and a verb that could or does stand alone as a sentence. In addition to at least one independent clause, many sentences contain subordinate clauses that function as adjectives, adverbs, or nouns. See also *clause; subordinate clause.*

indirect object   A noun or pronoun that names to whom or for whom the action of a sentence is done: We gave *her* some leftover yarn. An indirect object always precedes a direct object, in this case *some leftover yarn.*

infinitive   The word *to* followed by the base form of a verb: *to think, to dream.*

infinitive phrase   An infinitive and its objects, comple-ments, or modifiers. An infinitive phrase can function as a noun, an adjective, or an adverb. Noun: *To live without health insurance* is risky. Adjective: The Nineteenth Amendment gave women the right *to vote.* Adverb: Volunteers knocked on doors *to rescue people from the flood.*

intensive or reflexive pronoun   A pronoun ending in *-self* (or *-selves*): *myself, yourself, himself, herself, itself, ourselves, yourselves, themselves.* An intensive pronoun emphasizes a noun or another pronoun: I *myself* don't have a job. A reflexive pronoun names a receiver of an action identical with the doer of the action: Did Paula cut *herself*?

interjection   A word expressing surprise or emotion: *Oh! Wow! Hey! Hooray!*

interrogative pronoun   A pronoun used to introduce a question: *who, whom, whose, which, what. What* does history teach us?

intransitive verb   See *transitive and intransitive verbs*.

irregular verb   See *regular and irregular verbs*. See also section 11a.

linking verb   A verb that links a subject to a subject complement, a word or word group that renames or describes the subject: The winner *was* a teacher. The cherries *taste* sour. The most common linking verbs are forms of *be*: *be, am, is, are, was, were, being, been*. The following sometimes function as linking verbs: *appear, become, feel, grow, look, make, seem, smell, sound, taste*. See also *subject complement*.

modal verb   A helping verb that cannot be used as a main verb. There are nine modals: *can, could, may, might, must, shall, should, will*, and *would*. We *must* shut the windows before the storm. The verb phrase *ought to* is often classified as a modal as well. See also *helping verb*.

modifier   A word, phrase, or clause that describes or qualifies the meaning of a word. Modifiers include adjectives, adverbs, prepositional phrases, participial phrases, some infinitive phrases, and adjective and adverb clauses.

mood   See section 11c.

noncount noun   See pages 48–49.

noun   The name of a person, place, thing, or concept (*freedom*, for example): The *lion* in the *cage* growled at the *zookeeper*.

noun clause   A subordinate clause that functions like a noun, usually as a subject, a subject complement, a direct object, or the object of a preposition. In the following sentence, the italicized noun clause functions as the subject: *Whoever leaves the house last* must lock the door. Noun clauses usually begin with *how, who, whom, whoever, that, what, whatever, whether*, or *why*.

noun equivalent   A word or word group that functions like a noun: a pronoun, a noun and its modifiers, a gerund phrase, some infinitive phrases, or a noun clause.

object   See *direct object*; *indirect object*.

object complement   A word or word group that renames or describes a direct object. It always appears after the direct object: The kiln makes clay *firm and strong*.

object of a preposition   See *prepositional phrase*.

participial phrase   A present or past participle and its objects, complements, or modifiers. A participial phrase always functions as an adjective describing a noun or pronoun. Usually it appears immediately before or after the word it modifies: *Being a weight-bearing joint*, the knee is often injured. Plants *kept in moist soil* will thrive.

participle, past   A verb form usually ending in *-d, -ed, -n, -en,* or *-t : asked, stolen, fought.* Past participles are used with helping verbs to form perfect tenses (had *spoken*) and the passive voice (were *required*). They are also used as adjectives (the *stolen* car).

participle, present   A verb form ending in *-ing.* Present participles are used with helping verbs in progressive forms (is *rising,* has been *walking*). They are also used as adjectives (the *rising* tide).

parts of speech   A system for classifying words. Many words can function as more than one part of speech. See *adjective, adverb, conjunction, interjection, noun, preposition, pronoun, verb.*

passive voice   See *active vs. passive voice.*

personal pronoun   One of the following pronouns, used to refer to a specific person or thing: *I, me, you, she, her, he, him, it, we, us, they, them. After Julia won the award, she gave half of the prize money to a literacy program.* See also *antecedent.*

phrase   A word group that lacks a subject, a verb, or both. Most phrases function within sentences as adjectives, as adverbs, or as nouns. See *absolute phrase; appositive; gerund phrase; infinitive phrase; participial phrase; prepositional phrase.*

possessive case   See section 19a.

possessive pronoun   A pronoun used to indicate ownership: *my, mine, your, yours, her, hers, his, its, our, ours, your, yours, their, theirs. The guest made his own breakfast.*

predicate   A verb and any objects, complements, and modifiers that go with it: The horses *exercise in the corral every day.*

preposition   A word placed before a noun or noun equivalent to form a phrase modifying another word in the sentence. The preposition indicates the relation between the noun (or noun equivalent) and the word the phrase modifies. The most common prepositions are *about, above, across, after, against, along, among, around, at, before, behind, below, beside, besides, between, beyond, by, down, during, except, for, from, in, inside, into, like, near, of, off, on, onto, out, outside, over, past, since, than, through, to, toward, under, unlike, until, up, with, within,* and *without.*

prepositional phrase   A phrase beginning with a preposition and ending with a noun or noun equivalent (called the *object of the preposition*). Most prepositional phrases function as adjectives or adverbs. Adjective phrases usually come right after the noun or pronoun they modify: The road *to the summit* was treacherous. Adverb phrases usually appear at the beginning or the end of the sentence: *To the hikers*, the brief shower was a welcome relief. The brief shower was a welcome relief *to the hikers*.

progressive verb forms See pages 27 and 45–46.

pronoun A word used in place of a noun. Usually the pronoun substitutes for a specific noun, known as the pronoun's *antecedent*. In the following example, *alarm* is the antecedent of the pronoun *it*: When the *alarm* rang, I reached over and turned *it* off. See also *demonstrative pronoun; indefinite pronoun; intensive or reflexive pronoun; interrogative pronoun; personal pronoun; possessive pronoun; relative pronoun.*

proper noun See section 22a.

regular and irregular verbs When a verb is regular, both the past tense and the past participle are formed by adding *-ed* or *-d* to the base form of the verb: *walk, walked, walked*. The past tense and past participle of irregular verbs are formed in a variety of other ways: *ride, rode, ridden; begin, began, begun; go, went, gone;* and so on. See also section 11a.

relative adverb The word *when* or *where*, when used to introduce an adjective clause: The park *where* we had our picnic closes on October 1. See also *adjective clause.*

relative pronoun One of the following words, when used to introduce an adjective clause: *who, whom, whose, which, that*. The writer *who* won the award refused to accept it.

sentence A word group consisting of at least one independent clause. See also *complex sentence; compound sentence; compound-complex sentence; simple sentence.*

simple sentence A sentence consisting of one independent clause and no subordinate clauses: Without a passport, Eva could not visit her parents in Poland.

subject A word or word group that names who or what the sentence is about. In the following example, the complete subject (the simple subject and all of its modifiers) is italicized: *The devastating effects of famine* can last for many years. The simple subject is *effects*. See also *subject after verb; understood subject.*

subject after verb Although the subject normally precedes the verb, sentences are sometimes inverted. In the following example, the subject *the sleepy child* comes after the verb *sat*: Under the table *sat the sleepy child*. When a sentence begins with the expletive *there* or *it*, the subject always follows the verb. See also *expletive.*

subject complement A word or word group that follows a linking verb and either renames or describes the subject of the sentence. If the subject complement renames the subject, it is a noun or a noun equivalent: That signature may be *a forgery.* If it describes the subject, it is an adjective: Love is *blind.*

subjunctive mood   See section 11c.

subordinate clause   A word group containing a subject and a verb that cannot stand alone as a sentence. Subordinate clauses function within sentences as adjectives, adverbs, or nouns. They begin with subordinating conjunctions such as *although, because, if,* and *until* or with relative pronouns such as *who, which,* and *that.* See *adjective clause; adverb clause; independent clause; noun clause.*

subordinating conjunction   A word that introduces a subordinate clause and indicates the relation of the clause to the rest of the sentence. The most common subordinating conjunctions are *after, although, as, as if, because, before, even though, if, since, so that, than, that, though, unless, until, when, where, whether,* and *while.* Note: The relative pronouns *who, whom, whose, which,* and *that* also introduce subordinate clauses.

tenses   See section 11b.

transitive and intransitive verbs   Transitive verbs take direct objects, nouns or noun equivalents that receive the action. In the following example, the transitive verb *wrote* takes the direct object *a story*: Each student *wrote* a story. Intransitive verbs do not take direct objects: The audience *laughed.* If any words follow an intransitive verb, they are adverbs or word groups functioning as adverbs: The audience *laughed* at the talking parrot.

understood subject   The subject *you* when it is understood but not actually present in the sentence. Understood subjects occur in sentences that issue commands or give advice: [*You*] Put your clothes in the hamper.

verb   A word that expresses action (*jump, think*) or being (*is, was*). A sentence's verb is composed of a main verb possibly preceded by one or more helping verbs: The band *practiced* every day. The report *was* not *completed* on schedule. Verbs have five forms: the base form, or dictionary form (*walk, ride*); the past-tense form (*walked, rode*); the past participle (*walked, ridden*); the present participle (*walking, riding*); and the *-s* form (*walks, rides*). See also *predicate.*

verbal phrase   See *gerund phrase; infinitive phrase; participial phrase.*

Index

327

Exercises

Answers to sentence-style exercises begin on page 369.

Answers to sentence-style exercises begin on page 369.

Clarity

1 Wordy sentences

Exercise 1-1 Edit the following sentences to reduce wordiness.

> The Wilsons moved into the house ~~in spite of the fact~~ *even though* ~~that~~ the back door was only ten yards from the train tracks.

a. Martin Luther King Jr. was a man who set a high standard for future leaders to meet.
b. Alice has been deeply in love with cooking since she was little and could first peek over the edge of a big kitchen tabletop.
c. In my opinion, Bloom's race for the governorship is a futile exercise.
d. It is pretty important in being a successful graphic designer to have technical knowledge and at the same time an eye for color and balance.
e. Your task will be the delivery of mailed correspondence to all employees in the company.

Exercise 1-2 Revise the following business memo to reduce wordiness.

To: District managers
From: Margaret Davenport, Vice President
Subject: Customer database

It has recently been brought to my attention that a percentage of our sales representatives have been failing to log reports of their client calls in our customer database each and every day. I have also learned that some representatives are not checking the database on a routine basis.

Our clients sometimes receive a multiple number of sales calls from us when a sales representative is not cognizant of the fact that the client has been contacted at a previous time. Repeated telephone calls from our representatives annoy our customers. These repeated telephone calls also portray our company as one that is lacking in organization.

Effective as of immediately, direct your representatives to do the following:

• Record each and every customer contact in the customer database at the end of each day, without fail.

- Check the database at the very beginning of each day to ensure that telephone communications will not be initiated with clients who have already been called.
  Let me extend my appreciation to you for cooperating in this important matter.

2   Active verbs

Exercise 2-1   Revise any weak, unemphatic sentences by replacing passive verbs or *be* verbs with active alternatives. You may need to name in the subject the person or thing doing the action. If a sentence is emphatic, do not change it.

The ranger doused the campfire before giving us
~~The campfire was doused by the ranger before we~~
^
~~were given~~ a ticket for unauthorized use of a campsite.

a. The Prussians were victorious over the Saxons in 1745.
b. The entire operation is managed by Ahmed, the producer.
c. The sea kayaks were expertly paddled by the tour guides.
d. I jumped from the top bunk and landed on my buddy below, who was crawling on the floor looking for his boots.
e. The congresswoman heard shouts from the protestors as she walked up the steps of the Capitol.

Exercise 2-2   For each writing situation below, decide whether it is more appropriate to use the active voice or the passive voice.

a. You are writing a research paper explaining the effects of a deadly bacterial outbreak in a remote Chilean village. (active / passive)
b. You are writing a letter to the editor, praising an emergency medical technician whose quick action saved an injured motorist. (active / passive)
c. You are writing a summary of the procedure you used in an experiment for your biology class. (active / passive)
d. To accompany your résumé, you must write a cover letter explaining your recent accomplishments as a manager. (active / passive)
e. You must fill out an incident report, explaining in detail how your actions led to a collision between the forklift you were operating and a wall of fully stocked shelves. (active / passive)

3   Parallelism

Exercise 3-1   Edit the following sentences to correct faulty parallelism.

Rowena began her workday by pouring a cup
checking
of coffee and ~~checked~~ her email.
^

a. Police dogs are used for finding lost children, tracking criminals, and the detection of bombs and illegal drugs.
b. Hannah told her rock-climbing partner that she bought a new harness and of her desire to climb Otter Cliffs.

Continued ➔

c. It is more difficult to sustain an exercise program than starting one.
d. During basic training, I was not only told what to do but also what to think.
e. Jan wanted to drive either to San Francisco or Sausalito.

Exercise 3-2 Revise the following paragraph to balance parallel ideas.

   Community service can provide tremendous benefits not only for the organization receiving the help but the volunteer providing the help, too. This dual benefit idea is behind a recent move to make community service hours a graduation requirement in high schools across the country. For many nonprofit organizations, seeking volunteers is often smarter financially than to hire additional employees. For many young people, community service positions can help develop empathy, being committed, and leadership. Opponents of the trend argue that volunteerism should not be mandatory, but research shows that community service requirements are keeping students engaged in school and lower dropout rates dramatically. Parents, school administrators, and people who are leaders in the community all seem to favor the new initiatives.

4   Needed words

Exercise 4-1 Add any words needed for grammatical or logical completeness in the following sentences.

                        that
   The officer feared the prisoner would escape.
                      ^

a. Oranges provide more vitamin C.
b. The women entering the military academy can expect haircuts as short as the male cadets.
c. Looking out the family room window, Sarah saw her favorite tree, which she had climbed as a child, was gone.
d. The graphic designers are interested and knowledgeable about producing posters for the balloon race.
e. My town's high school is much larger than the neighboring town.

5   Shifts

Exercise 5-1 Revise the following paragraph to eliminate distracting shifts in point of view (person and number). Create two versions. First, imagine that this is an introductory paragraph designed to engage the reader with a personal story; write it in the first person (using *I* and *we*). Can you think of other contexts in which the first-person point of view would be the best choice? Then write the paragraph in the third person (using *people* and *they*). In what contexts would this version be the best choice?

   When online dating first became available, many people thought that it would simplify romance. We believed that you could type in a list of criteria—sense of humor, college education, green eyes, good job—and a database would select the perfect mate. Thousands of people signed up for services and filled out their profiles, confident that true love was only a few clicks away. As it turns out, however, virtual dating is no easier than traditional dating. I still have to contact the people I find, exchange messages and phone calls, and meet him in the real world. Although a database might produce a list of possibilities and screen out obviously undesirable people, you can't predict chemistry. More often than not, people who seem perfect online just don't click in person. Electronic services do help a single person expand their pool of potential dates, but it's no substitute for the hard work of romance.

Exercise 5-2   Revise the following paragraph to eliminate distracting shifts in tense.

The English colonists who settled in Massachusetts received assistance at first from the local native tribes, but by 1675 there had been friction between the two groups for many years. In that year, Metacomet, whom the colonists called Philip, leads the Wampanoag tribe in the first of a series of attacks on the colonial settlements. The war, known as King Philip's War, rages on for more than a year and leaves three thousand American Indians and six hundred colonists dead. Metacomet's attempt to retain his power failed. He too is killed, and the colonists sell his wife and children into slavery. One of the few accounts of this period to survive was written by Mary Rowlandson. She is a minister's wife who is held captive by the Wampanoags in 1676. Her history, *A Narrative of the Captivity and Restoration of Mrs. Mary Rowlandson*, tells the story of her experiences with the Wampanoag tribe. Although it did not paint a balanced picture, Rowlandson's story, which is still considered a classic early American text, showed its author to be a keen observer of life in an Indian camp.

6   Mixed constructions

Exercise 6-1   Edit the following sentences to untangle mixed constructions.

Taking
~~By taking~~ the oath of allegiance made Ling a US
     ^

citizen.

a. Using surgical gloves is a precaution now worn by dentists to prevent contact with patients' blood and saliva.
b. A physician, the career my brother is pursuing, requires at least ten years of challenging work.
c. The reason the pharaohs had bad teeth was because tiny particles of sand found their way into Egyptian bread.
d. Recurring bouts of flu among team members set a record for number of games forfeited.
e. In this box contains the key to your future.

7 Misplaced and dangling modifiers

Exercise 7-1 Edit the following sentences to correct misplaced or awkwardly placed modifiers.

> in a phone survey
> Answering questions can be annoying. ~~in a phone~~
> ^
> ~~survey.~~
> ^

a. The manager asked her employees to if they had time submit their reports today.
b. Many students graduate with debt from college totaling more than fifty thousand dollars.
c. It is a myth that humans only use 10 percent of their brains.
d. Daria found the old nightgown she used to wear to sleep in the closet.
e. All geese do not fly beyond Narragansett for the winter.

Exercise 7-2 Edit the following sentences to correct dangling modifiers. Most sentences can be revised more than one way.

> a student must complete
> To acquire a degree in almost any field, two science
> ^
> courses. ~~must be completed.~~
> ^

a. To complete an online purchase with a credit card, the expiration date and the security code must be entered.
b. Though only sixteen, UCLA accepted Martha's application.
c. Settled in the cockpit, the pounding of the engine was muffled only slightly by my helmet.
d. After studying polymer chemistry, computer games seemed less complex to Phuong.
e. When a young man, my mother enrolled me in tap dance classes.

8 Sentence variety

Exercise 8-1 Combine each set of sentences by subordinating minor ideas or by coordinating ideas of equal importance. You must decide which ideas are minor because the sentences are given out of context.

> Agnes, ~~was~~ a girl I worked with/. ~~She~~ was a hyperactive
> ^   ^
> child.

a. The X-Men comic books and Japanese woodcuts of kabuki dancers were part of Marlena's research project on popular culture. They covered the tabletop and the chairs.
b. Our waitress was costumed in a kimono. She had painted her face white. She had arranged her hair in a lacquered beehive.

c. Students can apply for a spot in the leadership program. The program teaches thinking and communication skills.

d. Ice cream typically contains 10 percent milk fat. Premium ice cream may contain up to 16 percent milk fat. There is considerably less air in the product.

e. Laura Thackray was an engineer at Volvo Car Corporation. She addressed women's safety needs. She designed a pregnant crash-test dummy.

Exercise 8-2 Improve sentence variety in each of the following sentences by varying the openings.

> To protect endangered marine turtles, fishing
> ~~Fishing~~ crews place turtle excluder devices in fishing
> ^
>
> nets. ~~to protect endangered marine turtles.~~
> ^

a. The exhibits for insects and spiders are across the hall from the fossils exhibit.

b. Sayuri became a successful geisha after growing up desperately poor in Japan.

c. The veterinarian, surprised by the rest results, decided to run a few more tests to be certain of her diagnosis.

d. The Grammy Awards ceremony often includes extensive tributes to legendary songwriters or performers.

e. The economy may recover more quickly than expected if home values climb.

9 Appropriate voice

Exercise 9-1 Revise the following email message to eliminate jargon.

Dear Ms. Jackson:

We members of the Nakamura Reyes team value our external partnering arrangements with Creative Software, and we look forward to seeing you next week at the trade show in Fresno. Per Mr. Reyes, please let us know when you'll have some downtime there so that he and I can conduct a strategizing session with you concerning our production schedule. It's crucial that we all be on the same page re: our product release dates.

Before we have some face time, however, I have some findings to share. Our customer-centric approach to the new products will necessitate that user testing periods trend upward. The enclosed data should help you effectuate any adjustments to your timeline; let me know ASAP if you require any additional information to facilitate the above.

Before we convene in Fresno, Mr. Reyes and I will agendize any further talking points.

Sincerely,

Sylvia Nakamura

Exercise 9-2 Edit the following sentences to eliminate sexist language or sexist assumptions.

> Scholarship athletes
> A̶ ̶s̶c̶h̶o̶l̶a̶r̶s̶h̶i̶p̶ ̶a̶t̶h̶l̶e̶t̶e̶ must be as concerned about
> ^
> their   they are   their
> h̶i̶s̶ academic performance as h̶e̶ ̶i̶s̶ about h̶i̶s̶ athletic
> ^   ^   ^
>
> performance.

a. Mrs. Geralyn Farmer, who is the mayor's wife, is the chief surgeon at University Hospital. Dr. Paul Green is her assistant.
b. Every applicant wants to know how much he will earn.
c. An elementary school teacher should understand the concept of nurturing if she intends to be effective.
d. An obstetrician needs to be available to his patients at all hours.
e. If man does not stop polluting his environment, mankind will perish.

Grammar

10   Subject-verb agreement

Exercise 10-1 Edit the following sentences to eliminate problems with subject-verb agreement. If a sentence is correct, write "correct" after it.

> were
> Jack's first days in the military w̶a̶s̶ grueling.
> ^

a. One of the main reasons for elephant poaching are the profits received from selling the ivory tusks.
b. Not until my interview with Dr. Hwang were other possibilities opened to me.
c. A number of students in the seminar was aware of the importance of joining the discussion.
d. Batik cloth from Bali, blue and white ceramics from Delft, and a bocce ball from Turin has made Angelie's room the talk of the dorm.
e. The board of directors, ignoring the wishes of the neighborhood, has voted to allow further development.

Exercise 10-2 For each sentence in the following passage, underline the subject (or compound subject) and then select the verb that agrees with it.

Loggerhead sea turtles (migrate / migrates) thousands of miles before returning to their nesting location every two to three years. The nesting season for loggerhead turtles (span / spans) the hottest months of the summer. Although the habitat of Atlantic loggerheads (range / ranges) from Newfoundland to Argentina, nesting for these turtles (take / takes) place primarily along the southeastern coast of the United States. Female turtles that have reached sexual maturity (crawl / crawls) ashore at night to lay their eggs. The cavity that serves as a nest for the eggs (is / are) dug out with the female's strong flippers. Deposited into each nest (is / are) anywhere from fifty to two hundred spherical eggs, also known as a clutch. After a two-month incubation period, all eggs in the clutch (begin / begins) to hatch, and within a few days the young turtles attempt to make their way into the ocean. A major cause of the loggerhead's decreasing numbers (is / are) natural predators such as raccoons, birds, and crabs. Beach erosion and coastal development also (threaten / threatens) the turtles' survival. For example, a crowd of curious humans or lights from beachfront residences (is / are) enough to make the female abandon her nesting plans and return to the ocean. Since only one in one thousand loggerheads survives to adulthood, special care should be taken to protect this threatened species.

Exercise 10-3 Edit the following sentences to eliminate problems with subject-verb agreement. If a sentence is correct, write "correct" after it.

> The 1962 song "Little Boxes" ~~satirize~~ ^{satirizes} the development
>
> of the suburbs in the 1950s and 1960s.

a. My uncle and my cousin mows the lawn for their elderly neighbor.
b. Particularly tricky are the triple axel and the quad lutz, two figure skating moves that require a high skill level.
c. No one on any of the committees plan to vote "yes" on the proposal.
d. The mayor or the superintendent gives a speech at the school fundraiser every year.
e. The last two chocolate chip cookies in the jar on the counter has gotten stale.

11 Other problems with verbs

Exercise 11-1 Edit the following sentences to eliminate problems with irregular verbs. If a sentence is correct, write "correct" after it.

> The ranger ~~seen~~ ^{saw} the forest fire ten miles away.

a. When I get the urge to exercise, I lay down until it passes.
b. Grandmother had drove our new hybrid to the sunrise church service, so we were left with the station wagon.
c. A pile of dirty rags was laying at the bottom of the stairs.
d. How did the game know that the player had went from the room with the blue ogre to the hall where the gold was heaped?
e. Abraham Lincoln took good care of his legal clients; the contracts he drew for the Illinois Central Railroad could never be broke.

Exercise 11-2   Edit the following sentences to eliminate errors in verb tense and mood. If a sentence is correct, write "correct" after it.

> had been
> After the path ~~was~~ plowed, we were able to walk
> ⌃
> in the park.

a. The palace of Knossos in Crete is believed to have been destroyed by fire around 1375 BCE.
b. Watson and Crick discovered the mechanism that controlled inheritance in all life: the workings of the DNA molecule.
c. When city planners proposed rezoning the waterfront, did they know that the mayor promised to curb development in that neighborhood?
d. Tonight's concert begins at 9:30. If it was earlier, I'd consider going.
e. The math position was filled by the instructor who had been running the tutoring center.

Exercise 11-3   Edit the following sentences to eliminate errors with irregular verbs, verb tense, and verb mood. If a sentence is correct, write "correct" after it.

> taught
> Julio ~~teached~~ a seminar on public speaking at the
> ⌃
> community center.

a. The glass sculptures of the Swan Boats was prominent in the brightly lit lobby.
b. Visitors to the glass museum were not supposed to touch the exhibits.
c. Our administrative assistant keeped a record of all of last year's events and meetings.
d. Most focus group participants agreed that the second advertisement would be more effective than the first.
e. Every year, my son wishes that he has a pet dinosaur before he blows out his birthday cake candles.

12   Pronouns

Exercise 12-1   Edit the following sentences to eliminate problems with pronoun-antecedent agreement. Most of the sentences can be revised in more than one way, so experiment before choosing a solution. If a sentence is correct, write "correct" after it.

> Recruiters may tell the truth, but there is much that
> they choose
> ~~he chooses~~ not to tell.
> ⌃

a. Every presidential candidate must appeal to a wide variety of ethnic and social groups if he wants to win the election.

b. If anyone wants to ride David's motorcycle, he/she has to wear a helmet.

c. The dance instructor motioned for everyone to move his or her arms in wide, slow circles.

d. The parade committee was unanimous in its decision to allow all groups and organizations to join the festivities.

e. The applicant should be bilingual if she wants to qualify for this position.

Exercise 12-2 Edit the following sentences to correct errors in pronoun reference. In some cases, you will need to decide on an antecedent to which the pronoun might logically refer.

Although Apple makes the most widely recognized

tablet device, other companies have gained a share of
the market. ~~This~~ _∧The competition has kept prices from skyrocketing.

a. They say that engineering students should have hands-on experience with dismantling and reassembling machines.

b. She had decorated her living room with posters from chamber music festivals. This led her date to believe that she was interested in classical music. Actually she preferred rock.

c. The high school principal congratulated the seniors that were graduating that day.

d. Marianne told Jenny that she was worried about her mother's illness.

e. Though Lewis cried for several minutes after scraping his knee, eventually it subsided.

Exercise 12-3 Edit the following sentences to eliminate errors in pronoun case. If a sentence is correct, write "correct" after it.

Grandfather cuts down trees for neighbors much
younger than ~~him.~~ _∧he.

a. Rick applied for the job even though he heard that other candidates were more experienced than he.

b. The volleyball team could not believe that the coach was she.

c. She appreciated him telling the truth in such a difficult situation.

d. The director has asked you and I to draft a proposal for a new recycling plan.

e. Five close friends and myself rented a station wagon, packed it with food, and drove two hundred miles to Mardi Gras.

Exercise 12-4 Revise the following sentences to eliminate errors in the use of *who* and *whom* (or *whoever* and *whomever*). If a sentence is correct, write "correct" after it.

> **What is the address of the artist ~~who~~ Antonio hired?**
> _whom_ (inserted above, caret below *who*)

a. Arriving late for rehearsal, we had no idea who was supposed to dance with whom.

b. The environmental policy conference featured scholars who I had never heard of.

c. Whom did you support in last month's election for student government president?

d. Daniel always gives a holiday donation to whomever needs it.

e. The singers who Natalia selected for the choir attended their first rehearsal last night.

13   Adjectives and adverbs

Exercise 13-1 Edit the following sentences to eliminate errors in the use of adjectives and adverbs. If a sentence is correct, write "correct" after it.

> **We weren't surprised by how ~~good~~ the sidecar racing**
> _well_ (inserted above, caret below *good*)
>
> **team flowed through the tricky course.**

a. Do you expect to perform good on the nursing board exam next week?

b. With the budget deadline approaching, our office has been handling routine correspondence more slow than we usually do.

c. When I worked in a flower shop, I learned that some flowers smell surprisingly bad.

d. The customer complained that he hadn't been treated nice by the agent on the phone.

e. Of all the smart people in my family, Uncle Roberto is the most cleverest.

Exercise 13-2 Revise the following passage to eliminate errors in the use of adjectives and adverbs.

Doctors recommend that to give skin the most fullest protection from ultraviolet rays, people should use plenty of sunscreen, limit sun exposure, and wear protective clothing. The commonest sunscreens today are known as "broad spectrum" because they block out both UVA and UVB rays. These lotions don't feel any differently on the skin from the old UVA-only types, but they work best at preventing premature aging and skin cancer. Many sunscreens claim to be waterproof, but they won't hardly provide adequate coverage after extended periods of swimming or perspiring. To protect good, even waterproof sunscreens should be reapplied liberal and often. All areas of exposed skin, including ears, backs of hands, and tops of feet, need to be coated good to avoid burning or damage. Some people's skin reacts bad to PABA, or para-aminobenzoic acid, so PABA-free (hypoallergenic) sunscreens are widely available. In addition to recommending sunscreen, doctors almost unanimously agree that people should stay out of the sun when rays are the most strongest — between 10:00 a.m. and 3:00 p.m. — and should limit time in the sun.

14   Sentence fragments

Exercise 14-1   Repair any fragment by attaching it to a nearby sentence or by rewriting it as a complete sentence.

> One Greek island that should not be missed is
>
> Mykonos/. A vacation spot for Europeans and a
>
> playground for the rich and famous.

a. Listening to the CD her sister had sent, Mia was overcome with a mix of emotions. Happiness, homesickness, and nostalgia.
b. Cortés and his soldiers were astonished when they looked down from the mountains and saw Tenochtitlán. The magnificent capital of the Aztecs.
c. Although my spoken Spanish is not very good. I can read the language with ease.
d. There are several reasons for not eating meat. One reason being that dangerous chemicals are used throughout the various stages of meat production.
e. To learn how to sculpt beauty from everyday life. This is my intention in studying art and archaeology.

Exercise 14-2   Repair each fragment in the following passage by attaching it to a sentence nearby or by rewriting it as a complete sentence.

Digital technology has revolutionized information delivery. Forever blurring the lines between information and entertainment. Yesterday's readers of books and newspapers are today's readers of e-books and blogs. Countless readers have moved on from print information entirely. Choosing instead to point, click, and scroll their way through a text online or on an e-reader. Once a nation of people spoon-fed television commercials and the six o'clock evening news. We are now seemingly addicted to YouTube and social media. Remember the family trip when Dad or Mom wrestled with a road map? On the way to St. Louis or Seattle? No wrestling is required with a GPS device. Unless it's Mom and Dad wrestling over who gets to program the address. Accessing information now seems to be America's favorite pastime. John Horrigan, associate director for research at the Pew Internet and American Life Project, reports that nearly half of American adults are "elite" users of technology. Who are "highly engaged" with digital content. As a country, we embrace information and communication technologies.

Continued ➜

Which now include smartphones, smartwatches, tablets, and AI home assistants. Among children and adolescents, social media and other technology use are well established. For activities like socializing, gaming, and information gathering.

Exercise 14-3 Repair any fragment by attaching it to a nearby sentence or by rewriting it as a complete sentence. If a word group is correct, write "correct" after it.

> **Asking for forgiveness afterward/ ~~This~~ is often considered easier than asking for permission beforehand.**

a. Jamal agreed to drive his younger brother to school. Even though he would have to get out of bed earlier.
b. You don't need to tell me again. I know.
c. Despite the quotation's popularity. Marie Antoinette probably did not actually say, "Let them eat cake!"
d. After they had been digging for hours. The pirates finally found the buried gold.
e. Reading was the only way to pass the time in the waiting room. There was no television, Wi-Fi, or cell phone reception.

15 Run-on sentences

Exercise 15-1 Revise the following run-on sentences using the method of revision suggested in brackets.

a. The city had one public swimming pool, it stayed packed with children all summer long. [Restructure the sentence.]
b. The building is being renovated, therefore at times we have no heat, water, or electricity. [Use a comma and a coordinating conjunction.]
c. The view was not what the travel agent had described, where were the rolling hills and the shimmering rivers? [Make two sentences.]
d. Walker's coming-of-age novel is set against a gloomy scientific backdrop, the Earth's rotation has begun to slow down. [Use a semicolon.]
e. City officials had good reason to fear a major earthquake, most of the business district was built on landfill. [Use a colon.]

Exercise 15-2 Revise any run-on sentences using a technique that you find effective. If a sentence is correct, write "correct" after it.

> **Crossing so many time zones on an eight-hour flight, I knew I would be tired when I arrived, ~~however,~~ _{but} I was too excited to sleep on the plane.**

a. Wind power for the home is a supplementary source of energy, it can be combined with electricity, gas, or solar energy.

b. Aidan viewed Sofia Coppola's *Lost in Translation* three times and then wrote a paper describing the film as the work of a mysterious modern painter.

c. In the Middle Ages, the streets of London were dangerous places, it was safer to travel by boat along the Thames.

d. "He's not drunk," I said, "he's in a state of diabetic shock."

e. Are you able to endure extreme angle turns, high speeds, frequent jumps, and occasional crashes, then supermoto racing may be a sport for you.

Exercise 15-3   In the following rough draft, revise any run-on sentences.

Some parents and educators argue that requiring uniforms in public schools would improve student behavior and performance. They think that uniforms give students a more professional attitude toward school, moreover, they believe that uniforms help create a sense of community among students from diverse backgrounds. But parents and educators should consider the drawbacks to requiring uniforms in public schools.

Uniforms do create a sense of community, they do this, however, by stamping out individuality. Youth is a time to express originality, it is a time to develop a sense of self. One important way young people express their identities is through the clothes they wear. The self-patrolled dress code of high school students may be stricter than any school-imposed code, nevertheless, trying to control dress habits from above will only lead to resentment or to mindless conformity.

If children are going to act like adults, they need to be treated like adults, they need to be allowed to make their own choices. Telling young people what to wear to school merely prolongs their childhood. Requiring uniforms undermines the educational purpose of public schools, it is not just to teach facts and figures but also to help young people grow into adults who are responsible for making their own choices.

16   Grammar topics for multilingual writers

Exercise 16-1   Revise the following sentences to correct errors in verb forms and tenses in the active and the passive voice. You may need to look in section 11a for the correct form of some irregular verbs or in section 11b for help with tenses.

> begins
> The meeting ~~begin~~ tonight at 7:30.
>   ^

a. In the past, tobacco companies deny any connection between smoking and health problems.

b. The volunteer's compassion has touch many lives.

c. I am wanting to register for a summer tutoring session.

d. By the end of the year, the state will have test 139 birds for avian flu.

e. The golfers were prepare for all weather conditions.

Exercise 16-2 Edit the following sentences to correct errors in the use of verb forms with modals. If a sentence is correct, write "correct" after it.

We should ~~to~~ order pizza for dinner.

a. A major league pitcher can to throw a baseball faster than ninety-five miles per hour.
b. The writing center tutor will helps you revise your essay.
c. A reptile must adjusted its body temperature to its environment.
d. In some states, individuals may renew a driver's license online.
e. My uncle, a cartoonist, could sketched a face in less than a minute.

Exercise 16-3 Edit the following sentences for proper use of articles and nouns. If a sentence is correct, write "correct" after it.

~~The~~ Josefina's dance routine was flawless.

a. Doing volunteer work often brings a satisfaction.
b. As I looked out the window of the plane, I could see the Cape Cod.
c. Melina likes to drink her coffee with lots of cream.
d. Recovering from abdominal surgery requires patience.
e. I completed the my homework assignment quickly.

Exercise 16-4 Articles have been omitted from the following description of winter weather. Insert the articles *a*, *an*, and *the* where English requires them and be prepared to explain the reasons for your choices.

Many people confuse terms *hail*, *sleet*, and *freezing rain*. Hail normally occurs in thunderstorm and is caused by strong updrafts that lift growing chunks of ice into clouds. When chunks of ice, called hailstones, become too heavy to be carried by updrafts, they fall to ground. Hailstones can cause damage to crops, windshields, and people. Sleet occurs during winter storms and is caused by snowflakes falling from layer of cold air into warm layer, where they become raindrops, and then into another cold layer. As they fall through last layer of cold air, raindrops freeze and become small ice pellets, forming sleet. When it hits car windshield or windows of house, sleet can make annoying racket. Driving and walking can be hazardous when sleet accumulates on roads and sidewalks. Freezing rain is basically rain that falls onto ground and then freezes after it hits ground. It causes icy glaze on trees and any surface that is below freezing.

Exercise 16-5 In the following sentences, add needed subjects or expletives and delete any repeated subjects, objects, or adverbs.

> The new geology professor is the one whom we saw ~~him~~ on TV.

a. Are some cartons of ice cream in the freezer.
b. I don't use the subway because am afraid.
c. The prime minister she is the most popular leader in my country.
d. We tried to get in touch with the same manager whom we spoke to him earlier.
e. Recently have been a number of earthquakes in Turkey.

Exercise 16-6 In the following sentences, replace prepositions that are not used correctly. You may need to refer to the chart in section 16d. If a sentence is correct, write "correct" after it.

>   *at*
> The play begins ~~on~~ 7:20 p.m.
>   ^

a. Whenever we eat at the Centerville Café, we sit at a small table on the back of the room.
b. In the 1990s, entrepreneurs created new online businesses in record numbers.
c. In Thursday, Nancy will attend her first home repair class at the community center.
d. Alex began looking for her lost mitten in another location.
e. We decided to go to a restaurant because there was no fresh food on the refrigerator.

Punctuation

17 The comma

Exercise 17-1 Add or delete commas where necessary in the following sentences. If a sentence is correct, write "correct" after it.

> Because we had been saving molding for a few weeks‚ we
>   ^
>
> had enough wood to frame all thirty paintings.

a. Alisa brought the injured bird home, and fashioned a splint out of Popsicle sticks for its wing.
b. Considered a classic of early animation *The Adventures of Prince Achmed* used hand-cut silhouettes against colored backgrounds.
c. If you complete the evaluation form and return it within two weeks you will receive a free breakfast during your next stay.

Continued ➔

d. After retiring from the New York City Ballet in 1965, legendary dancer Maria Tallchief went on to found the Chicago City Ballet.

e. Roger had always wanted a handmade violin but he couldn't afford one.

Exercise 17-2 Add or delete commas where necessary in the following sentences. If a sentence is correct, write "correct" after it.

> We gathered our essentials, took off for the great
>
> outdoors, and ignored the fact that it was Friday the 13th.
>   ^

a. The cold impersonal atmosphere of the university was unbearable.

b. An ambulance threaded its way through police cars, fire trucks and irate citizens.

c. The *1812 Overture* is a stirring, magnificent piece of music.

d. After two broken arms, three cracked ribs and one concussion, Ken quit the varsity football team.

e. My cat's pupils had constricted to small black shining slits.

Exercise 17-3 Edit the following paragraph to correct any comma errors.

Hope for Paws, a nonprofit rescue organization in Los Angeles tells many sad stories of animal abuse and neglect. Most of the stories, however have happy endings. One such story involves Woody, a dog left behind, after his master died. For a long lonely year, Woody took refuge under a neighbor's shed, waiting in vain, for his master's return. He survived on occasional scraps from his neighbors who eventually contacted Hope for Paws. When rescuers reached Woody, they found a malnourished, and frightened dog who had one blind eye and dirty, matted, fur. Gently, Woody was pulled from beneath the shed, and taken to the home of a volunteer, who fosters orphaned pets. There, Woody was fed, shaved, bathed and loved. Woody's story had the happiest of endings, when a family adopted him. Now Woody has a new forever home and he is once again a happy, well-loved dog.

Exercise 17-4 Add or delete commas where necessary in the following sentences. If a sentence is correct, write "correct" after it.

> "Yes, dear, you can have dessert," my mother said.
>   ^

a. On January 15, 2012 our office moved to 29 Commonwealth Avenue, Mechanicsville VA 23111.

b. The coach having resigned after the big game, we left the locker room in shock.

c. Ms. Carlson you are a valued customer whose satisfaction is very important to us.

d. Some modern musicians, (trumpeter John Hassell is an example) blend several cultural traditions into a unique sound.

e. On the display screen, was a soothing pattern of light and shadow.

18   The semicolon and the colon

Exercise 18-1   Edit the following sentences to correct errors in the use of the comma and the semicolon. If a sentence is correct, write "correct" after it.

> Love is blind; envy has its eyes wide open.
> ^

a. Strong black coffee will not sober you up, the truth is that time is the only way to get alcohol out of your system.

b. Margaret was not surprised to see hail and vivid lightning, conditions had been right for violent weather all day.

c. There is often a fine line between right and wrong; good and bad; truth and deception.

d. My mother always says that you can't learn common sense; either you're born with it or you're not.

e. Severe, unremitting pain is a ravaging force; especially when the patient tries to hide it from others.

Exercise 18-2   Edit the following sentences to correct errors in the use of the comma, the semicolon, or the colon. If a sentence is correct, write "correct" after it.

> Lifting the cover gently, Luca found the source of
>
> the odd sound/: a marble in the gears.
>   ^

a. We always looked forward to Thanksgiving in Vermont: It was our only chance to see our Grady cousins.

b. If we have come to fight, we are far too few, if we have come to die, we are far too many.

c. The travel package includes: a round-trip ticket to Athens, a cruise through the Cyclades, and all hotel accommodations.

d. The news article portrays the land use proposal as reckless; although 62 percent of the town's residents support it.

e. Psychologists Kindlon and Thompson (2000) offer parents a simple starting point for raising male children, "Teach boys that there are many ways to be a man" (p. 256).

19   The apostrophe

Exercise 19-1   Edit the following sentences to correct errors in the use of the apostrophe. If a sentence is correct, write "correct" after it.

> Richard's
> Our favorite barbecue restaurant is Poor ~~Richards~~ Ribs.
>   ^

a. This diet will improve almost anyone's health.

b. The innovative shoe fastener was inspired by the designers young son.

Continued ➜

c. Each days menu features a different European country's dish.

d. Sue worked overtime to increase her families earnings.

e. Ms. Jacobs is unwilling to listen to students complaints about computer failures.

Exercise 19-2 Edit the following passage to correct errors in the use of the apostrophe.

Its never too soon to start holiday shopping. In fact, some people choose to start shopping as early as January, when last seasons leftover's are priced at their lowest. Many stores try to lure customers in with promise's of savings up to 90 percent. Their main objective, of course, is to make way for next years inventory. The big problem with postholiday shopping, though, is that there isn't much left to choose from. Store's shelves have been picked over by last-minute shoppers desperately searching for gifts. The other problem is that its hard to know what to buy so far in advance. Next year's hot items are anyones guess. But proper timing, mixed with lot's of luck and determination, can lead to good purchases at great price's.

20 Quotation marks

Exercise 20-1 Add or delete quotation marks as needed and make any other necessary changes in punctuation in the following sentences. If a sentence is correct, write "correct" after it.

Gandhi once said, "An eye for an eye only ends up
making the whole world blind."

a. As for the advertisement "Sailors have more fun", if you consider chipping paint and swabbing decks fun, then you will have plenty of it.

b. Even after forty minutes of discussion, our class could not agree on an interpretation of Robert Frost's poem "The Road Not Taken."

c. After winning the lottery, Juanita said that "she would give half the money to charity."

d. After the film, Vicki said, "The reviewer called this movie "trash of the first order." I guess you can't believe everything you read."

e. "Cleaning your house while your kids are still growing," said Phyllis Diller, "is like shoveling the walk before it stops snowing."

Exercise 20-2 Add or delete quotation marks as needed and make any other necessary changes in punctuation in the following passage. Citations should conform to MLA style (see 33a).

In his article The Moment of Truth, former vice president Al Gore argues that global warming is a genuine threat to life on Earth and that we must act now to avoid catastrophe. Gore calls our situation a "true planetary emergency" and cites scientific evidence of the greenhouse effect and its consequences (170-71). "What is at stake, Gore insists, is the survival of our civilization and the habitability of the Earth (197)." With such a grim predicament at hand, Gore questions why so many political and economic leaders are reluctant to act. "Is it simply more convenient to ignore the warnings," he asks (171)?

The crisis, of course, will not go away if we just pretend it isn't there. Gore points out that in Chinese two symbols form the character for the word crisis. The first of those symbols means "danger", and the second means "opportunity;" the danger we face, he claims, is accompanied by "unprecedented opportunity." (172) Gore contends that throughout history we have won battles against seemingly unbeatable evils such as slavery and fascism and that we did so by facing the truth and choosing the moral high ground. Gore's final appeal is to our humanity:

> "Ultimately, [the fight to end global warming] is not about any scientific discussion or political dialogue; it is about who we are as human beings. It is about our capacity to transcend our limitations, to rise to this new occasion. To see with our hearts, as well as our heads, the response that is now called for." (244)

Gore feels that the fate of our world rests in our own hands, and his hope is that we will make the choice to save the planet.

Source of quotations: Al Gore, "The Moment of Truth," *Vanity Fair*, May 2006, pp. 170+.

21 Other punctuation marks

Exercise 21-1   Add appropriate end punctuation in the following paragraph.

Although I am generally rational, I am superstitious I never walk under ladders or put shoes on the table If I spill the salt, I go into frenzied calisthenics picking up the grains and tossing them over my left shoulder As a result of these curious activities, I've always wondered whether knowing the roots of superstitions would quell my irrational responses Superstition has it, for example, that one should never place a hat on the bed This superstition arises from a time when head lice were common and placing a guest's hat on the bed stood a good chance of spreading lice through the host's bed Doesn't this make good sense And doesn't it stand to reason that, if I know that my guests don't have lice, I shouldn't care where their hats go Of course it does It is fair to ask, then, whether I have changed my ways and place hats on beds Are you kidding I wouldn't put a hat on a bed if my life depended on it

Exercise 21-2 Edit the following sentences to correct errors in punctuation, focusing especially on appropriate use of the dash, parentheses, brackets, the ellipsis, and the slash. If a sentence is correct, write "correct" after it.

Social insects/—bees, for example/—are able to

communicate complicated messages to one another.

a. A client left his/her cell phone in our conference room after the meeting.

b. The films we made of Kilauea—on our trip to Hawaii Volcanoes National Park—illustrate a typical spatter cone eruption.

c. Although he was confident in his course selections, Greg chose the pass/fail option for Chemistry 101.

d. Of three engineering fields, chemical, mechanical, and materials, Keegan chose materials engineering for its application to toy manufacturing.

e. The writer Chitra Divakaruni explained her work with other Indian American immigrants: "Many women who came to Maitri [a women's support group in San Francisco] needed to know simple things like opening a bank account or getting citizenship. . . . Many women in Maitri spoke English, but their English was functional rather than emotional. They needed someone who understands their problems and speaks their language."

Mechanics

22 Capitalization

Exercise 22-1 Edit the following sentences to correct errors in capitalization. If a sentence is correct, write "correct" after it.

On our trip to the West, we visited the grand canyon
                                        G   C

and the great salt desert.
          G   S   D

a. Assistant dean Shirin Ahmadi recommended offering more world language courses.

b. We went to the Mark Taper Forum to see a production of *Angels in America*.

c. Kalindi has an ambitious semester, studying differential calculus, classical hebrew, brochure design, and greek literature.

d. Lydia's Aunt and Uncle make modular houses as beautiful as modernist works of art.

e. We amused ourselves on the long flight by discussing how Spring in Kyoto stacks up against Summer in London.

23 Abbreviations, numbers, and italics

Exercise 23-1   Edit the following sentences to correct errors in the use of abbreviations. If a sentence is correct, write "correct" after it.

> This year ~~Xmas~~ <u>Christmas</u> will fall on a ~~Tues.~~ <u>Tuesday.</u>

a. Since its inception, the BBC has maintained a consistently high standard of radio and television broadcasting.
b. Some combat soldiers are trained by govt. diplomats to be sensitive to issues of culture, history, and religion.
c. Mahatma Gandhi has inspired many modern leaders, including Martin Luther King Jr.
d. How many lb have you lost since you began running four miles a day?
e. Denzil spent all night studying for his psych. exam.

Exercise 23-2   Edit the following sentences to correct errors in the use of numbers. If a sentence is correct, write "correct" after it.

> By the end of the evening, Ashanti had only ~~three dollars and six cents~~ <u>$3.06</u> left.

a. The carpenters located 3 maple timbers, 21 sheets of cherry, and 10 oblongs of polished ebony for the theater set.
b. The program's cost is well over one billion dollars.
c. The score was tied at 5–5 when the momentum shifted and carried the Standards to a decisive 12–5 win.
d. 8 students in the class had to retake the exam.
e. The Vietnam Veterans Memorial in Washington, DC, had fifty-eight thousand one hundred thirty-two names inscribed on it when it was dedicated in 1982.

Exercise 23-3   Edit the following sentences to correct errors in the use of italics. If a sentence is correct, write "correct" after it.

> We had a lively discussion about Gini Alhadeff's memoir, *The Sun at Midday.* <u>Correct</u>

a. Howard Hughes commissioned the Spruce Goose, a beautifully built but thoroughly impractical wooden aircraft.
b. The old man *screamed* his anger, *shouting* to all of us, "I will not leave my money to you worthless layabouts!"
c. I learned the Latin term ad infinitum from an old nursery rhyme about fleas: "Great fleas have little fleas upon their back to bite 'em, / Little fleas have lesser fleas and so on ad infinitum."
d. Cinema audiences once gasped at hearing the word *damn* in *Gone with the Wind*.
e. Neve Campbell's lifelong interest in ballet inspired her involvement in the film "The Company," which portrays a season with the Joffrey Ballet.

24 Hyphenation

Exercise 24-1 Edit the following sentences to correct errors in hyphenation. If a sentence is correct, write "correct" after it.

> Émile Zola's first readers were scandalized by his slice-
>
> of-life novels.
> ⌃

a. Gold is the seventy-ninth element in the periodic table.
b. The swiftly-moving tugboat pulled alongside the barge and directed it away from the oil spill in the harbor.
c. The ice-encrusted fossil was a major find.
d. Your dog is well-known in our neighborhood.
e. Road-blocks were set up along all the major highways leading out of the city.

Answers to Exercises

Exercise 1-1, page 346   *Possible revisions:*

a. Martin Luther King Jr. set a high standard for future leaders.
b. Alice has loved cooking since she could first peek over a kitchen tabletop.
c. Bloom's race for the governorship is futile.
d. A successful graphic designer must have technical knowledge and an eye for color and balance.
e. You will deliver mail to all employees.

Exercise 2-1, page 347   *Possible revisions:*

a. The Prussians defeated the Saxons in 1745.
b. Ahmed, the producer, manages the entire operation.
c. The tour guides expertly paddled the sea kayaks.
d. Emphatic and active; no change
e. The congresswoman heard the protestors' shouts as she walked up the Capitol steps.

Exercise 2-2, page 347

a. passive; b. active; c. passive; d. active; e. active

Exercise 3-1, page 347   *Possible revisions:*

a. Police dogs are used for finding lost children, tracking criminals, and detecting bombs and illegal drugs.
b. Hannah told her rock-climbing partner that she bought a new harness and that she wanted to climb Otter Cliffs.
c. It is more difficult to sustain an exercise program than to start one.
d. During basic training, I was told not only what to do but also what to think.
e. Jan wanted to drive either to San Francisco or to Sausalito.

Exercise 4-1, page 348   *Possible revisions:*

a. Oranges provide more vitamin C than any other fruit.
b. The women entering the military academy can expect haircuts as short as those of the male cadets.
c. Looking out the family room window, Sarah saw that her favorite tree, which she had climbed as a child, was gone.
d. The graphic designers are interested in and knowledgeable about producing posters for the balloon race.
e. My town's high school is much larger than the neighboring town's high school.

Exercise 6-1, page 349   *Possible revisions:*

a. Using surgical gloves is a precaution now taken by dentists to prevent contact with patients' blood and saliva.
b. A career in medicine, which my brother is pursuing, requires at least ten years of challenging work.
c. The pharaohs had bad teeth because tiny particles of sand found their way into Egyptian bread.
d. Recurring bouts of flu caused the team to forfeit a record number of games.

e. This box contains the key to your future.
f. 7 Misplaced and dangling modifiers

Exercise 7-1, page 350 *Possible revisions:*

a. The manager asked her employees to submit their reports today if they had time.
b. Many students graduate from college with debt totaling more than fifty thousand dollars.
c. It is a myth that humans use only 10 percent of their brains.
d. When Daria looked in the closet, she found the old nightgown she used to wear to sleep.
e. Not all geese fly beyond Narragansett for the winter.

Exercise 7-2, page 350 *Possible revisions:*

a. To complete an online purchase with a credit card, you must enter the expiration date and the security code.
b. Though Martha was only sixteen, UCLA accepted her application.
c. As I settled in the cockpit, the pounding of the engine was muffled only slightly by my helmet.
d. After studying polymer chemistry, Phuong found computer games less complex.
e. When I was a young man, my mother enrolled me in tap dance classes.

Exercise 8-1, page 350 *Possible revisions:*

a. The X-Men comic books and Japanese woodcuts of kabuki dancers, all part of Marlena's research project on popular culture, covered the tabletop and the chairs.
b. Our waitress, costumed in a kimono, had painted her face white and arranged her hair in a lacquered beehive.
c. Students can apply for a spot in the leadership program, which teaches thinking and communication skills.
d. Although ice cream typically contains 10 percent milk fat, premium ice cream may contain up to 16 percent milk fat and has considerably less air in it.
e. Laura Thackray, an engineer at Volvo Car Corporation, addressed women's safety needs by designing a pregnant crash-test dummy.

Exercise 8-2, page 351 *Possible revisions:*

a. Across the hall from the fossils exhibit are the exhibits for insects and spiders.
b. After growing up desperately poor in Japan, Sayuri became a successful geisha.
c. Surprised by the test results, the veterinarian decided to run a few more tests to be certain of her diagnosis.
d. Often the Grammy Awards ceremony includes extensive tributes to legendary songwriters or performers.
e. If home values climb, the economy may recover more quickly than expected.

Exercise 9-2, page 352 *Possible revisions:*

a. Dr. Geralyn Farmer is the chief surgeon at University Hospital. Dr. Paul Green is her assistant.
b. All applicants want to know how much they will earn.

c. An elementary school teacher should understand the concept of nurturing to be effective.
d. Obstetricians need to be available to their patients at all hours.
e. If we do not stop polluting our environment, we will perish.

Exercise 10-1, page 352

a. One of the main reasons for elephant poaching is the profits received from selling the ivory tusks.
b. Correct
c. A number of students in the seminar were aware of the importance of joining the discussion.
d. Batik cloth from Bali, blue and white ceramics from Delft, and a bocce ball from Turin have made Angelie's room the talk of the dorm.
e. Correct.

Exercise 10-3, page 353

a. My uncle and my cousin mow the lawn for their elderly neighbor.
b. Correct
c. No one on any of the committees plans to vote "yes" on the proposal.
d. Correct
e. The last two chocolate chip cookies in the jar on the counter have gotten stale.

Exercise 11-1, page 353

a. When I get the urge to exercise, I lie down until it passes.
b. Grandmother had driven our new hybrid to the sunrise church service, so we were left with the station wagon.
c. A pile of dirty rags was lying at the bottom of the stairs.
d. How did the game know that the player had gone from the room with the blue ogre to the hall where the gold was heaped?
e. Abraham Lincoln took good care of his legal clients; the contracts he drew for the Illinois Central Railroad could never be broken.

Exercise 11-2, page 354

a. Correct
b. Watson and Crick discovered the mechanism that controls inheritance in all life: the workings of the DNA molecule.
c. When city planners proposed rezoning the waterfront, did they know that the mayor had promised to curb development in that neighborhood?
d. Tonight's concert begins at 9:30. If it were earlier, I'd consider going.
e. Correct

Exercise 11-3, page 354

a. The glass sculptures of the Swan Boats were prominent in the brightly lit lobby.
b. Correct
c. Our administrative assistant kept a record of all of last year's events and meetings.

d. Correct
e. Every year, my son wishes that he had a pet dinosaur before he blows out his birthday cake candles.

Exercise 12-1, page 354   *Possible revisions:*

a. Every presidential candidate must appeal to a wide variety of ethnic and social groups to win the election.
b. Anyone who wants to ride David's motorcycle has to wear a helmet.
c. The trainer motioned for all of the students to move their arms in wide, slow circles.
d. Correct
e. Applicants should be bilingual if they want to qualify for this position.

Exercise 12-2, page 355   *Possible revisions:*

a. Some professors say that engineering students should have hands-on experience with dismantling and reassembling machines.
b. Because she had decorated her living room with posters from chamber music festivals, her date believed that she was interested in classical music. Actually she preferred rock.
c. The high school principal congratulated the seniors who were graduating that day.
d. Marianne told Jenny, "I am worried about your mother's illness." [*or* ". . . about my mother's illness."]
e. Though Lewis cried for several minutes after scraping his knee, eventually his crying subsided.

Exercise 12-3, page 355

a. Correct [But the writer could change the end of the sentence: . . . than he was.]
b. Correct [But the writer could change the end of the sentence: . . . that she was the coach.]
c. She appreciated his telling the truth in such a difficult situation.
d. The director has asked you and me to draft a proposal for a new recycling plan.
e. Five close friends and I rented a station wagon, packed it with food, and drove two hundred miles to Mardi Gras.

Exercise 12-4, page 356

a. Correct
b. The environmental policy conference featured scholars whom I had never heard of. [*or* . . . scholars I had never heard of.]
c. Correct
d. Daniel always gives a holiday donation to whoever needs it.
e. The singers whom Natalia selected for the choir attended their first rehearsal last night. [*or* The singers Natalia selected ...]

Exercise 13-1, page 356

a. Do you expect to perform well on the nursing board exam next week?
b. With the budget deadline approaching, our office has been handling routine correspondence more slowly than we usually do.

c. Correct
d. The customer complained that he hadn't been treated nicely by the agent on the phone.
e. Of all the smart people in my family, Uncle Roberto is the cleverest. [or . . . most clever.]

Exercise 14-1, page 357 *Possible revisions:*

a. Listening to the CD her sister had sent, Mia was overcome with a mix of emotions: happiness, homesickness, and nostalgia.
b. Cortés and his soldiers were astonished when they looked down from the mountains and saw Tenochtitlán, the magnificent capital of the Aztecs.
c. Although my spoken Spanish is not very good, I can read the language with ease.
d. There are several reasons for not eating meat. One reason is that dangerous chemicals are used throughout the various stages of meat production.
e. To learn how to sculpt beauty from everyday life is my intention in studying art and archaeology.

Exercise 14-3, page 358 *Possible revisions:*

a. Jamal agreed to drive his younger brother to school even though he would have to get out of bed earlier.
b. Correct
c. Despite the quotation's popularity, Marie Antoinette probably did not actually say, "Let them eat cake!"
d. After they had been digging for hours, the pirates finally found the buried gold.
e. Correct

Exercise 15-1, page 358 *Possible revisions:*

a. The city had one public swimming pool that stayed packed with children all summer long.
b. The building is being renovated, so at times we have no heat, water, or electricity.
c. The view was not what the travel agent had described. Where were the rolling hills and the shimmering rivers?
d. Walker's coming-of-age novel is set against a gloomy scientific backdrop; the Earth's rotation has begun to slow down.
e. City officials had good reason to fear a major earthquake: Most [or most] of the business district was built on landfill.

Exercise 15-2, page 358 *Possible revisions:*

a. Wind power for the home is a supplementary source of energy that can be combined with electricity, gas, or solar energy.
b. Correct
c. In the Middle Ages, when the streets of London were dangerous places, it was safer to travel by boat along the Thames.
d. "He's not drunk," I said. "He's in a state of diabetic shock."
e. Are you able to endure extreme angle turns, high speeds, frequent jumps, and occasional crashes? Then supermoto racing may be a sport for you.

Exercise 16-1, page 359

a. In the past, tobacco companies denied any connection between smoking and health problems.
b. The volunteer's compassion has touched many lives.
c. I want to register for a summer tutoring session.
d. By the end of the year, the state will have tested 139 birds for avian flu.
e. The golfers were prepared for all weather conditions.

Exercise 16-2, page 360

a. A major league pitcher can throw a baseball faster than ninety-five miles per hour.
b. The writing center tutor will help you revise your essay.
c. A reptile must adjust its body temperature to its environment.
d. Correct
e. My uncle, a cartoonist, could sketch a face in less than a minute.

Exercise 16-3, page 360

a. Doing volunteer work often brings satisfaction.
b. As I looked out the window of the plane, I could see Cape Cod.
c. Correct
d. Correct
e. I completed my homework assignment quickly.
   [*or* I completed the homework ...]

Exercise 16-5, page 361

a. There are some cartons of ice cream in the freezer.
b. I don't use the subway because I am afraid.
c. The prime minister is the most popular leader in my country.
d. We tried to get in touch with the same manager whom we spoke to earlier.
e. Recently there have been a number of earthquakes in Turkey.

Exercise 16-6, page 361

a. Whenever we eat at the Centerville Café, we sit at a small table in the back of the room.
b. Correct
c. On Thursday, Nancy will attend her first home repair class at the community center.
d. Correct
e. We decided to go to a restaurant because there was no fresh food in the refrigerator.

Exercise 17-1, page 361

a. Alisa brought the injured bird home and fashioned a splint out of Popsicle sticks for its wing.
b. Considered a classic of early animation, *The Adventures of Prince Achmed* used hand-cut silhouettes against colored backgrounds.
c. If you complete the evaluation form and return it within two weeks, you will receive a free breakfast during your next stay.

d. Correct
e. Roger had always wanted a handmade violin, but he couldn't afford one.

Exercise 17-2, page 362

a. The cold, impersonal atmosphere of the university was unbearable.
b. An ambulance threaded its way through police cars, fire trucks, and irate citizens.
c. Correct
d. After two broken arms, three cracked ribs, and one concussion, Ken quit the varsity football team.
e. Correct

Exercise 17-4, page 362

a. On January 15, 2012, our office moved to 29 Commonwealth Avenue, Mechanicsville, VA 23111.
b. Correct
c. Ms. Carlson, you are a valued customer whose satisfaction is very important to us.
d. Some modern musicians (trumpeter John Hassell is an example) blend several cultural traditions into a unique sound.
e. On the display screen was a soothing pattern of light and shadow.

Exercise 18-1, page 363

a. Strong black coffee will not sober you up; the truth is that time is the only way to get alcohol out of your system.
b. Margaret was not surprised to see hail and vivid lightning; conditions had been right for violent weather all day.
c. There is often a fine line between right and wrong, good and bad, truth and deception.
d. Correct
e. Severe, unremitting pain is a ravaging force, especially when the patient tries to hide it from others.

Exercise 18-2, page 363

a. Correct [Either *It* or *it* is correct.]
b. If we have come to fight, we are far too few; if we have come to die, we are far too many.
c. The travel package includes a round-trip ticket to Athens, a cruise through the Cyclades, and all hotel accommodations.
d. The news article portrays the land use proposal as reckless, although 62 percent of the town's residents support it.
e. Psychologists Kindlon and Thompson (2000) offer parents a simple starting point for raising male children: "Teach boys that there are many ways to be a man" (p. 256).

Exercise 19-1, page 363

a. Correct
b. The innovative shoe fastener was inspired by the designer's young son.
c. Each day's menu features a different European country's dish.
d. Sue worked overtime to increase her family's earnings.
e. Ms. Jacobs is unwilling to listen to students' complaints about computer failures.

Exercise 20-1, page 364

a. As for the advertisement "Sailors have more fun," if you consider chipping paint and swabbing decks fun, then you will have plenty of it.
b. Correct
c. After winning the lottery, Juanita said that she would give half the money to charity.
d. After the film, Vicki said, "The reviewer called this movie 'trash of the first order.' I guess you can't believe everything you read."
e. Correct

Exercise 21-2, page 366

a. A client left a [or their] cell phone in our conference room after the meeting.
b. The films we made of Kilauea on our trip to Hawaii Volcanoes National Park illustrate a typical spatter cone eruption.
c. Correct
d. Of three engineering fields—chemical, mechanical, and materials—Keegan chose materials engineering for its application to toy manufacturing.
e. Correct

Exercise 22-1, page 366

a. Assistant Dean Shirin Ahmadi recommended offering more world language courses.
b. Correct
c. Kalindi has an ambitious semester, studying differential calculus, classical Hebrew, brochure design, and Greek literature.
d. Lydia's aunt and uncle make modular houses as beautiful as modernist works of art.
e. We amused ourselves on the long flight by discussing how spring in Kyoto stacks up against summer in London.

Exercise 23-1, page 367

a. Correct
b. Some combat soldiers are trained by government diplomats to be sensitive to issues of culture, history, and religion.
c. Correct
d. How many pounds have you lost since you began running four miles a day?
e. Denzil spent all night studying for his psychology exam.

Exercise 23-2, page 367

a. *MLA style*: The carpenters located three maple timbers, twenty-one sheets of cherry, and ten oblongs of polished ebony for the theater set. *APA style*: The carpenters located three maple timbers, 21 sheets of cherry, and 10 oblongs of polished ebony for the theater set.
b. Correct
c. Correct
d. Eight students in the class had to retake the exam.
e. The Vietnam Veterans Memorial in Washington, DC, had 58,132 names inscribed on it when it was dedicated in 1982.

Exercise 23-3, page 367

a. Howard Hughes commissioned the *Spruce Goose,* a beautifully built but thoroughly impractical wooden aircraft.

b. The old man screamed his anger, shouting to all of us, "I will not leave my money to you worthless layabouts!"

c. I learned the Latin term *ad infinitum* from an old nursery rhyme about fleas: "Great fleas have little fleas upon their back to bite 'em, / Little fleas have lesser fleas and so on *ad infinitum.*"

d. *MLA style*: Correct. *APA style*: Cinema audiences once gasped at hearing the word "damn" in *Gone with the Wind.*

e. Neve Campbell's lifelong interest in ballet inspired her involvement in the film *The Company,* which portrays a season with the Joffrey Ballet.

Exercise 24-1, page 368

a. Correct

b. The swiftly moving tugboat pulled alongside the barge and directed it away from the oil spill in the harbor.

c. Correct

d. Your dog is well known in our neighborhood.

e. Roadblocks were set up along all the major highways leading out of the city.

Editing Marks

abbr	abbreviation **23a**	" "	quotation marks **20**
add	add needed word **4**	.	period **21a**
adj/ adv	adjective or adverb **13**	?	question mark **21b**
agr	agreement **10, 12a**	!	exclamation point **21c**
appr	inappropriate language **9**	—	dash **21d**
art	article **16b**	( )	parentheses **21e**
awk	awkward **1–8**	[ ]	brackets **21f**
cap	capital letter **22**	...	ellipsis mark **21g**
case	case **12c, 12d**	/	slash **21h**
cliché	cliché **9b**	pass	ineffective passive **2b**
cs	comma splice **15**	pn agr	pronoun agreement **12a**
dm	dangling modifier **7c**	ref	pronoun reference **12b**
-ed	-ed ending **11a**	run-on	run-on sentence **15**
ESL	English as a second language/ multilingual writers **16**	-s	-s ending on verb **10, 16a**
frag	sentence fragment **14**	sexist	sexist language **9d, 12a**
fs	fused sentence **15**	shift	distracting shift **5**
hyph	hyphen **24**	sl	slang **9c**
irreg	irregular verb **11a**	sp	misspelled word
ital	italics **23c**	sv agr	subject-verb agreement **10**
jarg	jargon **9a**	t	verb tense **11b**
lc	use lowercase letter **22**	usage	see glossary of usage
mix	mixed construction **6**	v	voice **2**
mm	misplaced modifier **7a–b, 7d**	var	sentence variety **8**
mood	mood **11c**	vb	problem with verb **11, 16a**
num	numbers **23b**	w	wordy **1**
om	omitted word **4, 16c**	//	faulty parallelism **3**
p	punctuation	∧	insert
⌃,	comma **17a–i**	x	obvious error
no ,	no comma **17j**	#	insert space
;	semicolon **18a**	⌒	close up space
:	colon **18b**		
⌄,	apostrophe **19**		

Detailed Menu